EVERYONE'S MONEY BOOK

ON REAL ESTATE

JORDAN E. GOODMAN

Dearborn™
Trade Publishing
A **Kaplan Professional** Company

This publication is designed to provide accurate and authoritative information in regard to the subject matter covered. It is sold with the understanding that the publisher is not engaged in rendering legal, accounting, or other professional service. If legal advice or other expert assistance is required, the services of a competent professional should be sought.

Vice President and Publisher: Cynthia A. Zigmund
Editorial Director: Donald J. Hull
Senior Project Editor: Trey Thoelcke
Interior Design: Lucy Jenkins
Cover Design: Design Alliance, Inc.
Typesetting: the dotted i

Published by Dearborn Trade Publishing
A Kaplan Professional Company

Printed in the United States of America

01 02 03 10 9 8 7 6 5 4 3 2 1

Library of Congress Cataloging-in-Publication Data

Goodman, Jordan Elliot.
    Everyone's money book on real estate / Jordan Goodman.
       p.   cm.
    Includes bibliographical references and index.
    ISBN 0-7931-5380-8
    1. House buying—United States. 2. House selling—United States 3. Mortgage
loans—United States. 4. Real estate investment—United States. I. Title: Real estate.
II. Title.
    HD259 .G66 2002
    333.33′8—dc21

                        2002009048

Contents

List of Figures

Introduction

The ultimate dream for most Americans, despite some of the hurdles it poses, is owning a home. Indeed, the prospect of finding, financing, and maintaining a home can be fraught with complexities. But in the end, home ownership can provide several major benefits, including tax breaks, appreciation potential, and the pride of controlling the place you call home. The idea of paying off a mortgage by retirement age, forever eliminating monthly mortgage payments, is a goal for many Americans. In contrast, renters often feel as if they throw their money away each month because they are unable to build any equity in the place they live. Once they retire, their rent continues unabated. Perhaps, for that and many other reasons, two-thirds of Americans now own their own homes.

However, making the decision to buy real estate for personal shelter or investment can have a dark side: a home can become a huge liability, sapping your finances and burdening you with debt and obligations that ruin your lifestyle. That is why it's so important to understand how different real estate investments work. With a better understanding of the different types of real estate investments, you can determine what is best for you. This book will guide you through two processes: choosing and financing your own home, and investing in real estate for financial security and gain.

Throughout the 1970s and early 1980s, real estate was the sure-fire way to accumulate wealth. The combination of a housing shortage, a surging number of baby boomers entering the real estate market, generous tax advantages, and high inflation expectations resulted in startling gains in home prices. The bubble burst in the mid-1980s and continued into the 1990s, however, as most housing markets became overbuilt, fewer boomers could afford homes, tax breaks were curtailed, and inflation plunged. By the end of the 1990s and into 2000, real estate prices again shot up, only to soften with the economic slowdown of the early 2000s. Despite low interest rates and nearly nonexistent inflation, this watershed event sent most segments of the economy into an even more pronounced tailspin. The real estate landscape is, therefore, much more treacherous now, particularly if you purchase a home as an investment rather than a comfortable place in which to live.

Many people who bought homes at inflated prices now feel burdened by huge mortgage payments on property that has fallen sharply in value. These homeowners often rationalize their purchase by saying, "We couldn't stand not earning any mortgage interest deductions to lower our taxes" or "We had to buy before prices got out of reach." In retrospect, these buyers' financial situations might have been improved if they had rented for less than their current monthly mortgage payment, owed a bit more in taxes, and invested the difference between their rent and their mortgage payment in the surging stock and bond markets. The economic boom of the late 1990s and early 2000s brought some relief to these homeowners in areas of the country where housing prices recovered substantially, encouraging real estate investors to jump on and take a ride on another real estate boom bandwagon.

The makeup of American households has changed substantially over the past few decades. According to Rutgers University's National Marriage Project, the majority of Americans don't have a child at home. Today, only about one-third of U.S. households contain children. In addition to this, fewer couples are marrying, and more than half of those who do wed for the first time are living together before tying the knot. Single motherhood is also a growing segment that was once considered an exception to the rule a generation ago. Because of demographic changes such as these, housing needs are changing as well, with far more singles and single parents buying homes than ever before.

Baby boomers, the postwar generation that makes up a huge segment of the population, is now another force changing the landscape and buying habits of America. As the leading edge of this generation gets used to the proverbial empty nest and begins to think about what is now called *active retirement,* housing options become even more diverse.

Whichever demographic niche you occupy, it's important to understand where your investment dollar may stretch farthest. This book will guide you through the two important processes of choosing and financing your own home, and investing in real estate.

Everyone's Money Book on Real Estate would not have been possible without the extreme hard work of real estate writer Dena Amoruso, who expertly pulled together the threads of this book into a wonderful and comprehensive resource on everything you need to know about real estate. I also want to thank Gerald J. Robinson, a New York-based real estate tax attorney and author of *Federal Income Taxation of Real Estate,* who gave generously of his time and ideas to make this book as complete and accurate as possible.

CHAPTER 1

Buying versus Renting

The first question you must ask yourself when deciding where to live is whether to buy or rent. Although you may be bombarded with well-meaning friends and relatives who encourage you either to be a footloose mortgage-free renter or take the plunge and invest in a homestead, no one can analyze your own needs better than you.

The following factors will help you make your decision.

ADVANTAGES OF BUYING

- You'll build up *equity,* or ownership, in your home over time as you pay off your mortgage, as long as your home is appreciating in value. Having to make mortgage payments becomes a form of forced savings. In addition, maintaining an excellent track record of on-time mortgage payments can positively affect your overall financial worth and credit profile. Currently, the median home price nationally is five times what the same house cost in 1970.
- If you buy the right home in a good *location* and maintain it well, you'll increase the chance of substantial capital appreciation over time. A home provides one of the best hedges against inflation.
- You'll be able to *remodel* or add on to your home to suit your needs, tastes, and changing personal circumstances. Generally, you are not allowed to do so to a rental home, or you may be unwilling to spend money to improve someone else's property.

- Owning your own home will give you a deeper sense of commitment to your community. Homeowners, in an effort to maintain property values, tend to take better care of their homes than renters because they have a vested interest in doing so. They also tend to be more involved in civic issues, such as local schools and neighborhood improvement, and take personal interest in activities and new construction that is in close proximity to their homes.
- As a homeowner, you'll qualify for several significant tax advantages. First, all mortgage interest you pay up to $1 million qualifies as a tax deduction, reducing both your federal and state income tax burdens. In addition, you can deduct any interest charged on *home equity loans* of up to $100,000 taken out against the value of your home. Local property taxes are also deductible from your federal income tax. If you sell your home, you will not have to pay any capital gains if you have lived in the home as your principal residence for two of the previous five years and your profit does not exceed $500,000 for married couples filing taxes jointly, or $250,000 for an individual filing taxes as a single. Rent is a nondeductible personal expense.
- Your home can be used as a source of cash in the future. Whether you borrow against it with a home equity loan or you pull out the cash slowly through a *reverse mortgage* (explained in more detail in Chapter 7), you can put your equity to work for you when you need it most. As long as you continue to build equity, you'll have a type of nest-egg to use as a source of funds for financial or medical emergencies, home improvements, or college tuition for your children. Home ownership can also be part of a retirement program because your equity, enhanced by your home's appreciation, can become the source of an annuity-like reverse mortgage after retirement.
- *Property taxes* are deductible. The value of your home and location of your residence will dictate the amount of tax you pay.
- When you buy a house, you may put as little as 5 percent down (even less in some loan programs). When you buy stocks or mutual funds, you usually are paying full price up front (unless you buy on margin), and in some cases increasing your investment risk.

ADVANTAGES OF RENTING

- The costs of home ownership, from the *down payment* to the monthly mortgage payment and *maintenance* costs, may take a larger bite out of your household budget than you can afford. Many people sacrifice their entire lifestyle by sinking 50 percent or more of their income into home ownership costs. If you can rent for a substantially smaller percentage of your income, you may suffer far less financial stress.

- Prices of homes may fall in your neighborhood. By renting, you will not be hurt by eroding real estate prices. Once you think a market has bottomed out, you can get a better deal on a house. The fact that you will not have to sell property in order to take advantage of a *buyer's market* such as this is an added bonus.
- By renting, you can invest the money you save into stocks, bonds, and mutual funds, which may rise in value faster than home prices. This is particularly true if you are lucky enough to pay below-market rent or live in a rent-controlled area. If you have the discipline to follow through with this strategy, you may be able to build up much more equity over time by funneling the money you would be paying in mortgage payments and maintenance costs into a diversified portfolio of securities. Stocks, bonds, and mutual funds are much more liquid than real estate, allowing you to buy and sell easily to take advantage of the latest trends. Also, securities, unlike a home, generate regular income which you can reinvest.
- Homeowners with *adjustable-rate mortgages* risk higher mortgage payments if interest rates rise. Depending on the strength of your local rental market, you may be able to avoid rent increases or even pay below market rent.
- If you already know that you will relocate several times during your career, it may make more sense to rent than to buy and sell a home each time you move. Unless your local real estate market is extremely active, you probably cannot expect enough appreciation in a year or two to compensate for the significant costs of buying and selling a home.
- If you possess less-than-perfect credit, there may be fewer options open to you in terms of qualifying for *fixed-rate financing* which is considered the most desirable type of loan when you are in the home buying market.
- You may be at a life stage that sees many changes in a relatively short period of time, meaning your housing needs may be different several years from now. For example, if you are young and single, it might make more sense to rent a small apartment if you anticipate getting married and having children in a few years. Those going through a divorce may be too unsettled to purchase a home. By the same token, if you are within sight of your retirement years, you may want the carefree lifestyle renting can offer, using your retirement income for investments, spur-of-the-moment trips and vacations, or family visits.

• When you own a home, you own its repairs as well. When you rent, your landlord becomes the responsible party when a pipe breaks or a roof leaks. If you don't have a lot of spare time on your hands and don't picture yourself being able to afford a gardener or professional repair people, it may be wiser to rent than to own.

All of this means that the buy-versus-rent decision should be based not only on finances but also on expectations of your future lifestyle. However, to calculate the financial trade-offs, you might try to use one of the real estate software packages on the market such as *Buying Your Home* or *Buy or Rent*. Other handy tools also are available such as the rent calculator located online at Quicken.com (see Figure 1.1, Renting versus Buying). These resources will help you sort through the true value of housing tax benefits, the realistic costs of buying and maintaining a home, the alternative returns on your money if you rent, the number of years you must stay in a house for it to pay off, and other complex factors you should consider. Figure 1.2 presents a sample comparison of buying versus renting.

RESOURCES

These resources will help you further explore the concepts discussed in this chapter.

Dictionary of Real Estate Terms, by Jack Friedman (Barron's Educational Series, 250 Wireless Boulevard, Hauppauge, NY 11788; 631-434-3311; 800-645-3476). A complete guide to the many terms used in the real estate market.

Handbook of Real Estate Terms Revised, by Dennis Tosh (Prentice Hall Press, One Lake Street, Upper Saddle River, NJ 07458; 201-236-7156; 800-382-3419; www.prenticehall.com). Defines more than 2,900 real estate terms. Also includes standardized forms for trusts, deeds, appraisals, and other real estate transactions.

Home Buying for Dummies, by Eric Tyson and Ray Brown (IDG Books, 919 E. Hillsdale Boulevard, Suite 400, Foster City, CA 94404; 650-653-7000; 800-434-3422; www.idg.com, www.dummies.com). Shows readers how buying a home fits into their financial picture, from saving for the down payment to selecting the best loan and figuring the after-tax cost of ownership.

Language of Real Estate, by John W. Reilly (Dearborn Trade, Chicago, IL; 312-836-4400; 800-245-2665; www.dearborntrade.com). Virtually an encyclopedia of real estate with more than 2,800 detailed definitions on appraising, mortgaging, listing, selling, or exchanging your property. The ultimate technical reference for real estate owners, practitioners, attorneys, or students.

Semenow's Questions and Answers on Real Estate, by Robert Williams Semenow (Prentice Hall Press, One Lake Street, Upper Saddle River, NJ 07458; 201-

Figure 1.1 Renting versus Buying

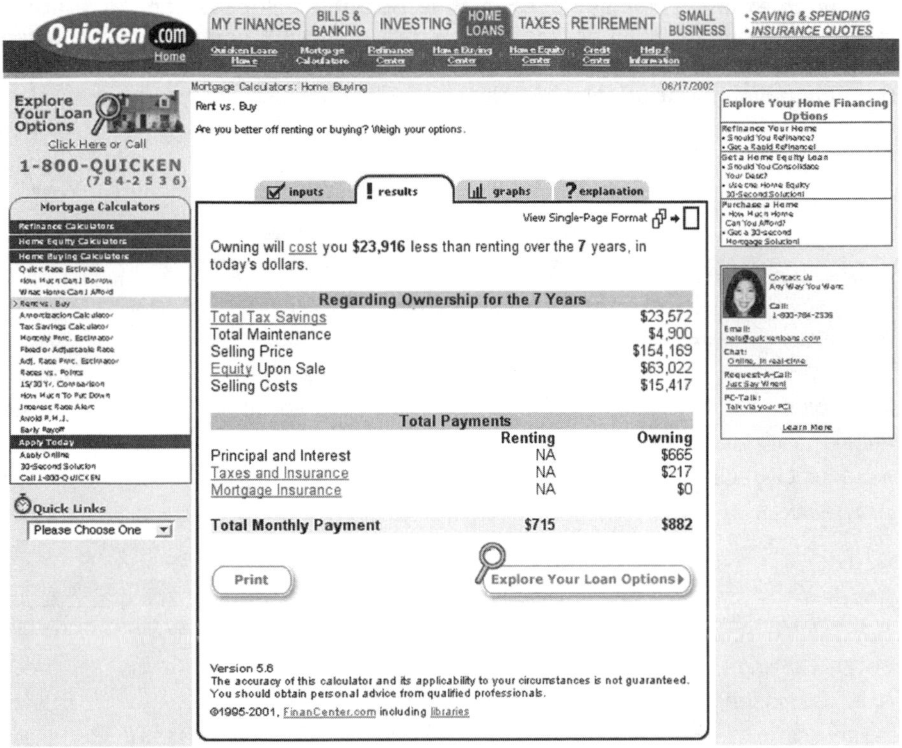

Screen capture from http://quickenloans.quicken.com/lpcontent/CnUtPage/ql/conte.../mtc_hbc_rent_v_buy.en.htm

236-7156; 800-382-3419; www.prenticehall.com). A reference book covering the gamut of real estate issues. Includes a fill-in-the-blank, true/false, and multiple choice test on real estate math. Discusses land use, financing techniques, tax laws, and real estate buyers' and sellers' rights. Features a glossary of more than 400 commonly used real estate terms.

Figure 1.2   Buy versus Rent Example

This is an example calculation estimating possible values of renting a 3 bedroom apartment for $650 per month versus owning a 3 bedroom home based on a $100,000 purchase price, 10% down payment, 8% interest rate, and a $661 monthly payment for principal & interest.

	First Year		Fifth Year	
	Rent	**Own**	**Rent**	**Own**
HOUSING COSTS				
RENT	$7,800	$0	$39,000	$0
PRINCIPAL	$0	$727	$0	$4,266
INTEREST	$0	$7,200	$0	$35,370
INSURANCE	$80	$300	$400	$1,500
PROPERTY TAXES	$0	$600	$0	$3,000
ASSOCIATION FEES	$0	$0	$0	$0
MAINTENANCE	$0	$500	$0	$2,500
SERVICE COSTS				
GAS HEAT	$0	$420	$0	$2,100
ELECTRICITY	$480	$480	$2,400	$2,400
WATER & SEWAGE	$0	$192	$0	$960
GARBAGE PICKUP	$0	$95	$0	$475
TELEPHONE	$300	$300	$1,500	$1,500
CABLE TV	$300	$300	$1,500	$1,500
COSTS SUB-TOTALS	$8,960	$11,114	$44,800	$55,571
INCREASED VALUES OR SAVINGS				
MORTGAGE EQUITY ACCUMULATION	$0	$727	$0	$4,266
MARKET VALUE GROWTH (3% per year growth)	$0	$2,187	$0	$11,611
TAX SAVINGS (28% tax bracket)	$0	$2,200	$0	$10,700
TOTAL INCREASED VALUES OR SAVINGS	$0	$5,114	$0	$26,577
TOTAL FINAL EFFECTIVE COSTS	$8,960	$6,000	$44,800	$28,994
ACCRUED VALUE OF OWNERSHIP (Cost of Renting minus Effective Cost of Owning)		**$2,960 for 1 Year**		**$15,806 for 5 Years**

Screen capture from http://www.homebuyerconsultants.com/buyer/buyer_buy_vs_rent.htm

CHAPTER 2

If You Decide to Rent

When you've completed the buy-versus-rent analysis, you may conclude that it makes more sense to rent your housing and invest your money in securities that may grow faster than property values over time. There are a number of useful Web sites to aid you in your search, the best of which are listed in the Resources sections throughout this book. If you plan to rent, the following tips can help you get the most for your money.

- Before beginning your search for an apartment or a home to rent, refer to the *Cash Flow Worksheet* in Figure 2.1 to determine how much rent you can afford. You should be able to comfortably meet your rent plus all your other expenses—which include saving and investing. Remember that one of the main advantages of renting is that it should leave you with enough cash to invest about 10 percent of your gross income. Clearly, that can't happen if you saddle yourself with an exorbitant rent. Ideally, your rent (including utilities) should absorb no more than 30 percent of your gross income or 25 percent of your net income.
- Hone in on a good *location.* The best is usually a location close to your job or one that provides convenient transportation options for you to get to work. The neighborhood you choose should also offer quality stores, schools, parks, and other recreational facilities. Above all, it should feel safe. If your plan is not to rent a single-family house, you may find many desirable apartment or townhouse complexes nestled within single-family home communities, giving you a more secure

Figure 2.1   Cash Flow Worksheet

Annual Income	$ Amount	$ Total

1. Earned Income
Salary after Deductions $ _____
Bonuses   _____
Commissions   _____
Deferred Compensation   _____
Overtime   _____
Stock Options   _____
Tips   _____
Other   _____

TOTAL EARNED INCOME $ _____

2. Self-Employment Income
Freelance Income $ _____
Income from Partnerships   _____
Income from Running a Small
   Business   _____
Rental Income from Real Estate _____
Royalties   _____
Other   _____

TOTAL SELF-EMPLOYMENT INCOME $ _____

3. Family Income
Alimony Income $ _____
Child Support Income   _____
Family Trust Income   _____
Gifts from Family Members   _____
Inheritance Income   _____
Other   _____

TOTAL FAMILY INCOME $ _____

4. Government Income
Aid to Families with Dependent
   Children Income $ _____
Disability Insurance Income _____
Unemployment Insurance Income _____
Veterans Benefits   _____
Welfare Income   _____
Workers' Compensation Income _____
Other   _____

TOTAL GOVERNMENT INCOME $ _____

Figure 2.1   (continued)

	$ Amount	$ Total
5. Retirement Income		
Annuity Payments	$ _____	
Social Security Income	_____	
Pension Income	_____	
Income from IRAs	_____	
Income from Keogh Accounts	_____	
Income from Profit-Sharing Accounts	_____	
Income from Salary Reduction Plans		
(401(k), 403(b), 457 plans)	_____	
Other	_____	
TOTAL RETIREMENT INCOME		$ _____
6. Investment Income		
Bank Account Interest		
CDs	$ _____	
Money-Market Accounts	_____	
NOW Accounts	_____	
Saving Accounts	_____	
Bonds and Bond Funds		
Capital Gains	_____	
Dividends	_____	
Interest	_____	
Other	_____	
Limited Partnerships (real estate, oil, gas)	_____	
Money Funds and T-Bills		
Taxable Funds	_____	
Tax-Exempt Funds	_____	
T-Bills	_____	
Stock and Stock Funds		
Capital Gains	_____	
Dividends	_____	
Interest	_____	
Other	_____	
Other	_____	
TOTAL INVESTMENT INCOME		$ _____
7. Other Income (specify)		
_____	$ _____	
TOTAL OTHER INCOME		$ _____
TOTAL ANNUAL INCOME		$ _____

Figure 2.1   Cash Flow Worksheet (continued)

Annual Expenses	$ Amount	$ Total

1. Fixed Expenses

Automobile-Related
   Car Payment (loan or lease) $ _____
   Gasoline or Oil   _____
   Other   _____
   Total $ _____

Family
   Alimony   _____
   Child Support Payments   _____
   Food and Beverage   _____
   School Tuition   _____
   Other   _____
   Total   _____

Home-Related
   Cable Television Fees   _____
   Mortgage Payments Home #1   _____
   Mortgage Payments Home #2   _____
   Rent   _____
   Total   _____

Insurance
   Auto   _____
   Disability   _____
   Dental   _____
   Health   _____
   Homeowners   _____
   Life   _____
   Other   _____
   Total   _____

Savings and Investments
   Bank Loan Repayment   _____
   Emergency Fund Contributions   _____
   Salary Reduction Plans   _____
   Contributions (401(k), 403(b),
      457 plans)   _____
   Other   _____
   Total   _____

Taxes
   Federal   _____
   Local   _____
   Property   _____
   Social Security (self-employed)   _____

Figure 2.1 (continued)

	$ Amount	$ Total
State	$ _____	
Other	_____	
Total		$ _____
Utilities		
Electricity	_____	
Gas	_____	
Telephone	_____	
Water and Sewage	_____	
Other	_____	
Total		
Other (specify)		
_____	_____	
Total		_____
TOTAL FIXED EXPENSES		$ _____

2. Flexible Expenses

Children		
Allowances	$ _____	
Babysitting	_____	
Books		
Camp Fees	_____	
Day Care	_____	
Events (parties, class trips, etc.)	_____	
Toys	_____	
Other	_____	
Total		$ _____
Clothing		
New Purchases	_____	
Shoes	_____	
Upkeep (cleaning, tailoring, dry cleaning, etc.)	_____	
Total		_____
Contributions and Dues		
Charitable Donations	_____	
Gifts (Christmas, birthdays, etc.)	_____	
Political Contributions	_____	
Religious Contributions	_____	
Union Dues	_____	
Other	_____	
Total		_____
Education		
Room and Board	_____	

Figure 2.1   Cash Flow Worksheet (continued)

	$ Amount	$ Total
Books and Supplies (parents and/or children)	$	
Tuition (parents and/or children)		
Other		
Total		$
Equipment and Vehicles		
Appliance Purchases and Maintenance		
Car, Boat, and Other Vehicle Purchases and Maintenance		
Computer Purchases, etc.		
Consumer Electronics Purchases		
Licenses and Registration of Cars, Boats, etc.		
Parking		
Other		
Total		
Financial and Professional Services		
Banking Fees		
Brokerage Commissions and Fees		
Financial Advice		
Legal Advice		
Tax Preparation Fees		
Other		
Total		
Food		
Alcohol		
Foods and Snacks away from Home		
Restaurant Meals		
Tobacco		
Other		
Total		
Home Maintenance		
Garbage Removal		
Garden Supplies and Maintenance		
Home Office Supplies		
Home Furnishings		
Home or Apartment Repairs and Renovations		
Home Cleaning Services		
Home Supplies		
Lawn Care and Snow Removal		
Linens		

Figure 2.1   (continued)

	$ Amount	$ Total
Uninsured Casualty or Theft Loss	$ _____	
Other	_____	
Total		$ _____
Medical Care		
Dentist Bills	_____	
Drugs (over the counter)	_____	
Drugs (prescriptions)	_____	
Eyecare and Eyeglasses	_____	
Hospital (uninsured portion)	_____	
Medical Devices (wheelchairs, canes, etc.)	_____	
Medical Expenses (parents, etc.)	_____	
Nursing Home Fees (parents, etc.)	_____	
Personal Beauty Care (hair stylist, manicurist, etc.)	_____	
Personal Care (cosmetics, toiletries, etc.)	_____	
Physician Bills	_____	
Unreimbursed Medical Expenses	_____	
Other	_____	
Total		_____
Miscellaneous		
Mystery Cash	_____	
Postage and Stamps	_____	
Recurring Nonrecurring Expenses	_____	
Unreimbursed Business Expenses	_____	
Other	_____	
Total		_____
Recreation and Entertainment		
Animal Care	_____	
Books	_____	
Club Dues	_____	
Cultural Events	_____	
Health Club Memberships	_____	
Hobbies	_____	
Lottery Tickets	_____	
Magazine and Newspaper Subscriptions	_____	
Movie Admissions	_____	
Music Admissions	_____	
Photography (cameras, developing, film, etc.)	_____	
Play Admissions	_____	

Figure 2.1   Cash Flow Worksheet (continued)

	$ Amount	$ Total
Recreational Equipment (games, sports, etc.)	$	
Sporting Events Admission		
Videotape Rentals		
Other		
Total		$
Savings and Investments		
Bank Savings Contributions		
Stock, Bond, and Mutual Fund Contributions		
IRA Contributions		
Keogh Account Contributions		
Other		
Total		
Travel and Vacations		
Bus Fares		
Subway Costs		
Tolls		
Train Fares		
Travel Expenses (other than vacations)		
Unreimbursed Business Travel Expenses		
Vacations (airfare)		
Vacations (car rental)		
Vacations (food)		
Vacations (hotel)		
Vacations (other)		
Other		
Total		
Other (specify)		
Total		
TOTAL FLEXIBLE EXPENSES		$
TOTAL ANNUAL EXPENSES		$
TOTAL ANNUAL INCOME (MINUS)		$
TOTAL ANNUAL EXPENSES EQUALS		( )
TOTAL NET ANNUAL POSITIVE (OR NEGATIVE) CASH FLOW		$

feeling, in addition to a sense of neighborhood. Before you settle on a neighborhood, tour it extensively during both the day and evening, on weekdays and weekends, to get a feel for it.

- Once you've decided on a location, look for rental homes or apartments advertised in the newspaper, at real estate brokers' offices, on office bulletin boards, on billboards, and in rental publications available in many supermarkets and bank lobbies. Depending on the strength of the market, you or the landlord will have to pay a fee if you find your rental home through a real estate agent. If there are few rentals in the local market, renters usually pay the fee; if there are many apartments for rent, landlords tend to pay the fee. However, you can avoid that cost if you deal directly with a landlord or with a renter who offers a *sublease.*

- Don't rent the first home or apartment you see. The more time you take, the better deal you will find. Patience is a key to finding the right rental.

- When looking at apartments or rental homes, check everything carefully. Run all appliances, and mechanical and electrical systems, including the dishwasher, washing machine, toilets, showers, sinks, stove, waste disposal system, and intercom. Also, make sure the refrigerator is in good condition and that heating and air conditioning systems work well. Inquire about parking facilities, guest parking, security procedures, pest control, grounds maintenance, and recreational facilities, if applicable. Determine which utility costs are included in and excluded from your rent. Finally, visit the property to see—and even chat with—your potential neighbors, and to determine the property and neighborhood noise level. An important question to ask neighbors, especially in an apartment or townhouse community, is whether they have any knowledge of the complex being for sale or set to be converted to condominiums, a situation that may eventually force you to find another place to live.

- Once you've found a place that meets your needs, lock in as low a rent as possible. You will have much more leverage if a surplus of rentals exists in the area, of course. Your landlord will ask for references from your employer or past landlords. Have them ready, in writing, in advance. If you want to be meticulously prepared to show your qualifications, obtain a copy of your credit report. You can do this by contacting any of the three major credit bureaus—Experian, Equifax, or Trans Union—or by going online to freecreditreports.com or guardmycredit .com (Privista). Landlords will also require at least one month's security deposit and possibly two months' rent. In many states, landlords are required to put that money into an escrow bank account and credit you with any interest it earns.

- If you plan on staying in the apartment or rental home at least a year, insist on getting a yearlong lease. Otherwise, you will rent under a *tenant-at-will agreement,* which means that you can leave whenever you want, but the landlord can evict you at will. If you plan to stay a while, you should sign a *renewable lease.* In addition to allowing you to extend your rental, this lease gives you the right to have the landlord maintain the basic facilities in your apartment at an acceptable level. Ask the landlord whether your lease grants you the right to *sublease* to another renter and under what conditions you can get out of your lease before it officially terminates (see Figure 2.2, Residential Lease or Month-to-Month Rental Agreement).
- If you like your apartment or rental home so much that you may want to own it some day, ask the landlord whether he or she would apply your rent toward a down payment on the purchase of the property. *Rent-to-own agreements* are gaining popularity and may work to your advantage if you can lock in a price now that may become a bargain if real estate prices rise later. Plus, most rent-to-own agreements do not obligate you to buy, so you can walk away from the purchase if your situation changes or real estate values fall. Be careful of these agreements (also called *lease-options*) when an up-front fee is required. That fee may be considered nonrefundable if you choose not to exercise your option to purchase (see Figure 2.3, Option Agreement).

Once the lease has been signed, you'll want to prepare for your move. Besides the perfunctory flurry of phone calls arranging for telephone, cable, or other services not included in your rent, you may consider the physical move itself. The Internet is a useful tool for getting moving advice (see Figure 2.4, Movingcompanies.com, and Figure 2.5, Relocation Trip Kit from fatform.net).

IF YOU USE A REAL ESTATE AGENT IN YOUR SEARCH

Don't dismiss the services of a real estate agent who may be familiar with many areas you may not have time to tour, and who may be able to arrange favorable terms if they are experts at finding rentals. Brokers don't charge for their services when they take you on as a client (if they do, you should look elsewhere). Instead, they are paid by the landlord. Before you meet with a real estate broker or agent in your quest for a rental, make a list of your priorities. Specify locations, the range you are willing to pay for both rent and up-front deposits, whether you are interested in or open to a lease-option, and your

Figure 2.2　Residential Lease

CALIFORNIA ASSOCIATION OF REALTORS®

RESIDENTIAL LEASE OR MONTH-TO-MONTH RENTAL AGREEMENT
(C.A.R. Form LR, Revised 10/01)

_____ ("Landlord") and
_____ ("Tenant") agree as follows:

1. **PROPERTY:**
   A. Landlord rents to Tenant and Tenant rents from Landlord, the real property and improvements described as: _____
   _____ ("Premises").
   B. The following personal property is included: _____

2. **TERM:** The term begins on (date) _____ ("Commencement Date"), **(Check A or B):**
   ☐ **A. Month-to-month:** and continues as a month-to-month tenancy. Either party may terminate the tenancy by giving written notice to the other at least 30 days prior to the intended termination date, subject to any applicable local laws. Such notice may be given on any date.
   ☐ **B. Lease:** and shall terminate on (date) _____ at _____ AM/PM.
   Any holding over after the term of this Agreement expires, with Landlord's consent, shall create a month-to-month tenancy which either party may terminate as specified in paragraph 2A. Rent shall be at a rate equal to the rent for the immediately preceding month, unless otherwise notified by Landlord, payable in advance. All other terms and conditions of this Agreement shall remain in full force and effect.

3. **RENT:**
   A. Tenant agrees to pay rent at the rate of $ _____ per month for the term of the Agreement.
   B. Rent is payable in advance on the **1st** (or ☐ _____) day of each calendar month, and is delinquent on the next day.
   C. If Commencement Date falls on any day other than the first day of the month, rent shall be prorated based on a 30-day period. If Tenant has paid one full month's rent in advance of Commencement Date, rent for the second calendar month shall be prorated based on a 30-day period.
   D. PAYMENT: The rent shall be paid by ☐ cash, ☐ personal check, ☐ money order, ☐ cashier check, ☐ other_____, to
   (name) _____ (phone) _____ at
   (address) _____
   (or at any other location specified by Landlord in writing to Tenant) between the hours of _____ and _____
   on the following days_____

4. **SECURITY DEPOSIT:**
   A. Tenant agrees to pay $ _____ as a security deposit. Security deposit will be ☐ transferred to and held by the Owner of the Premises; or ☐ held in Owner's Broker's trust account.
   B. All or any portion of the security deposit may be used, as reasonably necessary, to: (1) cure Tenant's default in payment of rent, Late Charges, non-sufficient funds ("NSF") fees, or other sums due; (2) repair damage, excluding ordinary wear and tear, caused by Tenant or by a guest or licensee of Tenant; (3) clean Premises, if necessary, upon termination of tenancy; and (4) replace or return personal property or appurtenances. **SECURITY DEPOSIT SHALL NOT BE USED BY TENANT IN LIEU OF PAYMENT OF LAST MONTH'S RENT.** If all or any portion of the security deposit is used during tenancy, Tenant agrees to reinstate the total security deposit within five days after written notice is delivered to Tenant. Within three weeks after Tenant vacates the Premises, Landlord shall: (1) furnish Tenant an itemized statement indicating the amount of any security deposit received and the basis for its disposition; and (2) return any remaining portion of security deposit to Tenant.
   C. No interest will be paid on security deposit unless required by local ordinance.
   D. If security deposit is held by Owner, Tenant agrees not to hold Broker responsible for its return. If security deposit is held in Owner's Broker's trust account, and Broker's authority is terminated before expiration of this Agreement, and security deposits are released to someone other than Tenant, then Broker shall notify Tenant, in writing, where and to whom security deposit has been released. Once Tenant has been provided such notice, Tenant agrees not to hold Broker responsible for security deposit.

5. **MOVE-IN COSTS RECEIVED/DUE:**

Category	Total Due	Payment Received	Balance Due	Date Due
Rent from _____ to _____ (date)				
*Security Deposit				
Other _____				
Other _____				
Total				

   *The maximum amount that Landlord may receive as security deposit, however designated, cannot exceed two month's rent for an unfurnished Premises, or three month's rent for a furnished premises.

6. **PARKING: (Check A or B)**
   ☐ **A.** Parking is permitted as follows:
   The right to parking ☐ is, ☐ is not, included in the rent charged pursuant to paragraph 3. If not included in the rent, the parking rental fee shall be an additional $ _____ per month. Parking space(s) are to be used for parking operable motor vehicles, except for trailers, boats, campers, buses or trucks (other than pick-up trucks). Tenant shall park in assigned space(s) only. Parking space(s) are to be kept clean. Vehicles leaking oil, gas or other vehicle fluids shall not be parked on the Premises. Mechanical work or storage of inoperable vehicles is not allowed in parking space(s) or elsewhere on the Premises.
   OR ☐ **B.** Parking is not permitted on the Premises.

LR-11 REVISED DATE 10/01 (PAGE 1 OF 4)　**Print Date**

Landlord and Tenant acknowledge receipt of copy of this page.
Landlord's Initials (_____)(_____)
Tenant's Initials (_____)(_____)

EQUAL HOUSING OPPORTUNITY

Reviewed by
Broker or Designee _____ Date _____

RESIDENTIAL LEASE OR MONTH-TO-MONTH RENTAL AGREEMENT (LR-11 PAGE 1 OF 4)

Source: California Association of REALTORS®

Figure 2.2   Residential Lease (continued)

Premises: _____   Date: _____

7. STORAGE: (Check A or B) _____
 ☐ **A.** Storage is permitted as follows: _____
  The right to storage space ☐ is, ☐ is not, included in the rent charged pursuant to paragraph 3. If not included in rent, storage space shall be an additional $ _____ per month. Tenant shall store only personal property that Tenant owns, and shall not store property that is claimed by another or in which another has any right, title, or interest. Tenant shall not store any improperly packaged food or perishable goods, flammable materials, explosives, or other inherently dangerous material.
 OR ☐ **B.** Storage is not permitted on the Premises.

8. LATE CHARGE/NSF CHECKS: Tenant acknowledges that either late payment of rent or issuance of a NSF check may cause Landlord to incur costs and expenses, the exact amount of which are extremely difficult and impractical to determine. These costs may include, but are not limited to, processing, enforcement and accounting expenses, and late charges imposed on Landlord. If any installment of rent due from Tenant is not received by Landlord within 5 (or ☐ _____) **calendar days** after date due, or if a check is returned NSF, Tenant shall pay to Landlord, respectively, an additional sum of $ _____ as Late Charge and $25.00 as a NSF fee, either or both of which shall be deemed additional rent. Landlord and Tenant agree that these charges represent a fair and reasonable estimate of the costs Landlord may incur by reason of Tenant's late or NSF payment. Any Late Charge or NSF fee due shall be paid with the current installment of rent. Landlord's acceptance of any Late Charge or NSF fee shall not constitute a waiver as to any default of Tenant. Landlord's right to collect a Late Charge or NSF fee shall not be deemed an extension of the date rent is due under paragraph 3, or prevent Landlord from exercising any other rights and remedies under this Agreement, and as provided by law.

9. CONDITION OF PREMISES: Tenant has examined Premises, all furniture, furnishings, appliances, landscaping, if any, and fixtures, including smoke detector(s).
 (Check one:)
 ☐ **A.** Tenant acknowledges that these items are clean and in operative condition, with the following exceptions _____
 OR ☐ **B.** Tenant's acknowledgment of the condition of these items is contained in an attached statement of condition (such as C.A.R.'s MIMO-11).
 OR ☐ **C.** Tenant will provide Landlord a list of items that are damaged or not in operable condition within 3 (or ☐ _____) **days** after Commencement Date, not as a contingency of this Agreement but rather as an acknowledgment of the condition of the Premises.
 OR ☐ **D.** Other: _____

10. NEIGHBORHOOD CONDITIONS: Tenant is advised to satisfy him or herself as to neighborhood or area conditions, including schools, proximity and adequacy of law enforcement, crime statistics, registered felons or offenders, fire protection, other governmental services, proximity to commercial, industrial or agricultural activities, existing and proposed transportation, construction and development that may affect noise, view, or traffic, airport noise, noise or odor from any source, wild and domestic animals, other nuisances, hazards, or circumstances, facilities and condition of common areas, conditions and influences of significance to certain cultures and/or religions, and personal needs, requirements and preferences of Tenant.

11. UTILITIES: Tenant agrees to pay for all utilities and services, and the following charges: _____
except _____, which shall be paid for by Landlord. If any utilities are not separately metered, Tenant shall pay Tenant's proportional share, as reasonably determined by Landlord.

12. OCCUPANTS: The Premises are for the sole use as a personal residence by the following named persons only: _____

13. PETS: No animal or pet shall be kept on or about the Premises without Landlord's prior written consent, except _____

14. RULES/REGULATIONS: Tenant agrees to comply with all rules and regulations of Landlord, which are at any time posted on the Premises or delivered to Tenant. Tenant shall not, and shall ensure that guests and licensees of Tenant shall not, disturb, annoy, endanger, or interfere with other tenants of the building or neighbors, or use the Premises for any unlawful purposes, including, but not limited to, using, manufacturing, selling, storing, or transporting illicit drugs or other contraband, or violate any law or ordinance, or commit a waste or nuisance on or about the Premises.

15. CONDOMINIUM/PLANNED UNIT DEVELOPMENT: ☐ (If checked) The Premises is a unit in a condominium, planned unit, or other development governed by a homeowners' association ("HOA"). The name of the HOA is _____.
Tenant agrees to comply with all covenants, conditions and restrictions, bylaws, rules and regulations and decisions of HOA. Landlord shall provide Tenant copies of rules and regulations, if any. Tenant shall reimburse Landlord for any fines or charges imposed by HOA or other authorities, due to any violation by Tenant, or the guests or licensees of Tenant.

16. MAINTENANCE:
 A. Tenant shall properly use, operate and safeguard Premises, including if applicable, any landscaping, furniture, furnishings, and appliances, and all mechanical, electrical, gas and plumbing fixtures, and keep them clean and sanitary. Tenant shall immediately notify Landlord, in writing, of any problem, malfunction or damage. Tenant shall pay for all repairs or replacements caused by Tenant, or guests of Tenant, excluding ordinary wear and tear. Tenant shall pay for all damage to Premises as a result of failure to report a problem in a timely manner. Tenant shall pay for repair of drain blockages or stoppages, unless caused by defective plumbing parts or tree roots invading sewer lines.
 B. ☐ Landlord ☐ Tenant shall water the garden, landscaping, trees and shrubs, except _____
 C. ☐ Landlord ☐ Tenant shall maintain the garden, landscaping, trees and shrubs, except _____

17. ALTERATIONS: Tenant shall not make any alterations in or about the Premises without Landlord's prior written consent, including: painting, wallpapering, adding or changing locks, installing antenna or satellite dish(es), placing signs, displays or exhibits, or using screws, fastening devices, large nails or adhesive materials.

18. KEYS/LOCKS:
 A. Tenant acknowledges receipt of (or Tenant will receive ☐ prior to the Commencement Date, or ☐ _____):
  ☐ _____ key(s) to Premises,   ☐ _____ remote control device(s) for garage door/gate opener(s),
  ☐ _____ key(s) to mailbox,   ☐ _____
  ☐ _____ key(s) to common area(s),   ☐ _____
 B. Tenant acknowledges that locks to the Premises ☐ have, ☐ have not, been rekeyed.
 C. If Tenant rekeys existing locks or opening devices, Tenant shall immediately deliver copies of all keys to Landlord. Tenant shall pay all costs and charges related to loss of any keys or opening devices. Tenant may not remove locks, even if installed by Tenant.

The copyright laws of the United States (Title 17 U.S. Code) forbid the unauthorized reproduction of this form, or any portion thereof, by photocopy machine or any other means, including facsimile or computerized formats. Copyright © 1994-2001, CALIFORNIA ASSOCIATION OF REALTORS®, INC. ALL RIGHTS RESERVED.

LR-11 REVISED DATE 10/01 (PAGE 2 OF 4)   Print Date

Landlord and Tenant acknowledge receipt of copy of this page.

Landlord's Initials (_____)(_____)
Tenant's Initials (_____)(_____)

Reviewed by _____
Broker or Designee _____   Date _____

RESIDENTIAL LEASE OR MONTH-TO-MONTH RENTAL AGREEMENT   (LR-11 PAGE 2 OF 4)

Figure 2.2   (continued)

Premises: _____ Date: _____

19. **ENTRY:** Tenant shall make Premises available to Landlord or representative for the purpose of entering to make necessary or agreed repairs, decorations, alterations, or improvements, or to supply necessary or agreed services, or to show Premises to prospective or actual purchasers, tenants, mortgagees, lenders, appraisers, or contractors. Landlord and Tenant agree that twenty-four (24) hours notice (oral or written) shall be reasonable and sufficient notice. In an emergency, Landlord or representative may enter Premises at any time without prior notice.
20. **SIGNS:** Tenant authorizes Landlord to place For Sale/Lease signs on the Premises.
21. **ASSIGNMENT/SUBLETTING:** Tenant shall not sublet all or any part of Premises, or assign or transfer this Agreement or any interest in it, without prior written consent of Landlord. Unless such consent is obtained, any assignment, transfer or subletting of Premises or this Agreement or tenancy, by voluntary act of Tenant, operation of law, or otherwise, shall be null and void, and at the option of Landlord, terminate this Agreement. Any proposed assignee, transferee or sublessee shall submit to Landlord an application and credit information for Landlord's approval, and if approved, sign a separate written agreement with Landlord and Tenant. Landlord's consent to any one assignment, transfer or sublease, shall not be construed as consent to any subsequent assignment, transfer or sublease and does not release Tenant of Tenant's obligation under this Agreement.
22. ☐ **LEAD PAINT (CHECK IF APPLICABLE):** Premises was constructed prior to 1978. In accordance with federal law, Landlord gives and Tenant acknowledges receipt of the disclosures on the attached form (such as C.A.R. Form FLD-11) and a federally approved lead pamphlet.
23. **POSSESSION:** If Landlord is unable to deliver possession of Premises on Commencement Date, such Date shall be extended to date on which possession is made available to Tenant. If Landlord is unable to deliver possession within 5 (or ☐ _____) calendar days after agreed Commencement Date, Tenant may terminate this Agreement by giving written notice to Landlord, and shall be refunded all rent and security deposit paid.
24. **TENANT'S OBLIGATIONS UPON VACATING PREMISES:** Upon termination of Agreement, Tenant shall: (a) give Landlord all copies of all keys or opening devices to Premises, including any common areas; (b) vacate Premises and surrender it to Landlord empty of all persons; (c) vacate any/all parking and/or storage space; (d) deliver Premises to Landlord in the same condition as referenced in paragraph 9; (e) clean Premises, including professional cleaning of carpet and drapes; (f) give written notice to Landlord of Tenant's forwarding address; and (g) _____.

    All improvements installed by Tenant, with or without Landlord's consent, become the property of Landlord upon termination.
25. **BREACH OF CONTRACT/EARLY TERMINATION:** In addition to any obligations established by paragraph 24, in event of termination by Tenant prior to completion of the original term of Agreement, Tenant shall also be responsible for lost rent, rental commissions, advertising expenses and painting costs necessary to ready Premises for rerental.
26. **TEMPORARY RELOCATION:** Tenant agrees, upon demand of Landlord, to temporarily vacate Premises for a reasonable period, to allow for fumigation, or other methods, to control wood destroying pests or organisms, or other repairs to Premises. Tenant agrees to comply with all instructions and requirements necessary to prepare Premises to accommodate pest control, fumigation or other work, including bagging or storage of food and medicine, and removal of perishables and valuables. Tenant shall only be entitled to a credit of rent equal to the per diem rent for the period of time Tenant is required to vacate Premises.
27. **DAMAGE TO PREMISES:** If, by no fault of Tenant, Premises are totally or partially damaged or destroyed by fire, earthquake, accident or other casualty, which render Premises uninhabitable, either Landlord or Tenant may terminate Agreement by giving the other written notice. Rent shall be abated as of date of damage. The abated amount shall be the current monthly rent prorated on a 30-day basis. If Agreement is not terminated, Landlord shall promptly repair the damage, and rent shall be reduced based on the extent to which the damage interferes with Tenant's reasonable use of Premises. If damage occurs as a result of an act of Tenant or Tenant's guests, only Landlord shall have the right of termination, and no reduction in rent shall be made.
28. **INSURANCE:** Tenant's or guest's personal property and vehicles are not insured by Landlord or, if applicable, HOA, against loss or damage due to fire, theft, vandalism, rain, water, criminal or negligent acts of others, or any other cause. Tenant is, to carry Tenant's own insurance (renter's insurance) to protect Tenant from any such loss.
29. **WATERBEDS:** Tenant shall not use or have waterbeds on the Premises unless: (a) Tenant obtains a valid waterbed insurance policy; (b) Tenant increases the security deposit in an amount equal to one-half of one month's rent; and (c) the bed conforms to the floor load capacity of Premises.
30. **WAIVER:** The waiver of any breach shall not be construed as a continuing waiver of the same or any subsequent breach.
31. **NOTICE:** Notices may be served at the following address, or at any other location subsequently designated:
    Landlord: _____   Tenant: _____

32. **TENANT ESTOPPEL CERTIFICATE:** Tenant shall execute and return a tenant estoppel certificate delivered to Tenant by Landlord or Landlord's agent within 3 days after its receipt. The tenant estoppel certificate acknowledges that this Agreement is unmodified and in full force, or in full force as modified, and states the modifications. Failure to comply with this requirement shall be deemed Tenant's acknowledgment that the tenant estoppel certificate is true and correct, and may be relied upon by a lender or purchaser.
33. **JOINT AND INDIVIDUAL OBLIGATIONS:** If there is more than one Tenant, each one shall be individually and completely responsible for the performance of all obligations of Tenant under this Agreement, jointly with every other Tenant, and individually, whether or not in possession.
34. ☐ **MILITARY ORDNANCE DISCLOSURE:** (If applicable and known to Landlord) Premises is located within one mile of an area once used for military training, and may contain potentially explosive munitions.
35. **TENANT REPRESENTATIONS; CREDIT:** Tenant warrants that all statements in Tenant's rental application are accurate. Tenant authorizes Landlord and Broker(s) to obtain Tenant's credit report at time of application and periodically during tenancy in connection with approval, modification, or enforcement of this Agreement. Landlord may cancel this Agreement: (a) before occupancy begins; (b) upon disapproval of the credit report(s); or (c) at any time, upon discovering that information in Tenant's application is false. A negative credit report reflecting on Tenant's record may be submitted to a credit reporting agency if Tenant fails to fulfill the terms of payment and other obligations under this Agreement.
36. If Landlord has entered into a contract for periodic pest control treatment of the Premises, Landlord shall give tenant a copy of the notice originally given to Landlord by the pest control company.

Landlord and Tenant acknowledge receipt of copy of this page.
Landlord's Initials (_____)(_____)
Tenant's Initials (_____)(_____)

LR-11 REVISED DATE 10/01 (PAGE 3 OF 4)   Print Date

Reviewed by
Broker or Designee _____ Date _____

RESIDENTIAL LEASE OR MONTH-TO-MONTH RENTAL AGREEMENT   (LR-11 PAGE 3 OF 4)

Figure 2.2 Residential Lease (continued)

Premises: _____ Date: _____

37. **DATA BASE DISCLOSURE:** NOTICE: The California Department of Justice, sheriff's departments, police departments serving jurisdictions of 200,000 or more, and many other local law enforcement authorities maintain for public access a data base of the locations of persons required to register pursuant to paragraph (1) of subdivision (a) of Section 290.4 of the Penal Code. The data base is updated on a quarterly basis and a source of information about the presence of these individuals in any neighborhood. The Department of Justice also maintains a Sex Offender Identification Line through which inquiries about individuals may be made. This is a "900" telephone service. Callers must have specific information about individuals they are checking. Information regarding neighborhoods is not available through the "900" telephone service.

38. **OTHER TERMS AND CONDITIONS/SUPPLEMENTS:** _____
_____
_____

The following ATTACHED supplements are incorporated in this Agreement: _____

39. **ATTORNEY FEES:** In any action or proceeding arising out of this Agreement, the prevailing party between Landlord and Tenant shall be entitled to reasonable attorney fees and costs.

40. **ENTIRE CONTRACT:** Time is of the essence. All prior agreements between Landlord and Tenant are incorporated in this Agreement, which constitutes the entire contract. It is intended as a final expression of the parties' agreement, and may not be contradicted by evidence of any prior agreement or contemporaneous oral agreement. The parties further intend that this Agreement constitutes the complete and exclusive statement of its terms, and that no extrinsic evidence whatsoever may be introduced in any judicial or other proceeding, if any, involving this Agreement. Any provision of this Agreement that is held to be invalid shall not affect the validity or enforceability of any other provision in this Agreement.

41. **AGENCY:**
   A. Confirmation: The following agency relationship(s) are hereby confirmed for this transaction:
   Listing Agent: (Print firm name) _____ is the agent of
   (check one): ☐ the Landlord exclusively; or ☐ both the Landlord and Tenant.
   Leasing Agent: (Print firm name) _____ (if not same as Listing Agent) is the agent of
   (check one): ☐ the Tenant exclusively; or ☐ the Landlord exclusively; or ☐ both the Tenant and Landlord.
   B. Disclosure: ☐ (If checked): The term of this lease exceeds one year. A disclosure regarding real estate agency relationships (such as C.A.R. form AD-11), has been provided to Landlord and Tenant, who each acknowledge its receipt.

42. ☐ **INTERPRETER/TRANSLATOR:** The terms of this Agreement have been interpreted/translated for Tenant into the following language: _____ Interpretation/translation service has been provided by (print name) _____
_____, who has the following Driver's License or other identification number: _____.
Tenant has been advised to rely on, and has in fact solely relied on the interpretation/translation services of the above-named individual, and not on the Landlord or other person involved in negotiating the Agreement. If the Agreement has been negotiated primarily in Spanish, Tenant has been provided a Spanish language translation of this Agreement pursuant to the California Civil Code. (C.A.R. form LR-14-S fulfills this requirement.)

Signature of interpreter/translator _____ Date _____

Landlord and Tenant acknowledge and agree that Brokers: (a) do not guarantee the condition of the Premises; (b) cannot verify representations made by others; (c) cannot provide legal or tax advice; (d) will not provide other advice or information that exceeds the knowledge, education or experience required to obtain a real estate license. Furthermore, if Brokers are not also acting as Landlord in this Agreement, Brokers: (e) do not decide what rental rate a Tenant should pay or Landlord should accept; and (f) do not decide upon the length or other terms of tenancy. Landlord and Tenant agree that they will seek legal, tax, insurance and other desired assistance from appropriate professionals.

Tenant _____ Date _____
Tenant _____ Date _____
Landlord _____ Date _____
(Owner or Agent with authority to enter into this lease)
Landlord _____ Date _____
(Owner or Agent with authority to enter into this lease)

Landlord Address _____ Telephone _____

Agency relationships are confirmed as above. Real estate brokers who are not also Landlord in this Agreement are not a party to the Agreement between Landlord and Tenant.

Real Estate Broker _____ By _____ Date _____
(Leasing Firm Name)
Address _____ Telephone _____ Fax _____
Real Estate Broker _____ By _____ Date _____
(Listing Firm Name)
Address _____ Telephone _____ Fax _____

THIS FORM HAS BEEN APPROVED BY THE CALIFORNIA ASSOCIATION OF REALTORS® (C.A.R.). NO REPRESENTATION IS MADE AS TO THE LEGAL VALIDITY OR ADEQUACY OF ANY PROVISION IN ANY SPECIFIC TRANSACTION. A REAL ESTATE BROKER IS THE PERSON QUALIFIED TO ADVISE ON REAL ESTATE TRANSACTIONS. IF YOU DESIRE LEGAL OR TAX ADVICE, CONSULT AN APPROPRIATE PROFESSIONAL.

This form is available for use by the entire real estate industry. It is not intended to identify the user as a REALTOR®. REALTOR® is a registered collective membership mark which may be used only by members of the NATIONAL ASSOCIATION OF REALTORS® who subscribe to its Code of Ethics.

Published and Distributed by:
REAL ESTATE BUSINESS SERVICES, INC.
a subsidiary of the CALIFORNIA ASSOCIATION OF REALTORS®
525 South Virgil Avenue, Los Angeles, California 90020

Reviewed by
Broker or Designee _____ Date _____

EQUAL HOUSING OPPORTUNITY

LR-11 REVISED DATE 10/01 (PAGE 4 OF 4) Print Date

RESIDENTIAL LEASE OR MONTH-TO-MONTH RENTAL AGREEMENT (LR-11 PAGE 4 OF 4)

Figure 2.3 Option Agreement

CALIFORNIA
ASSOCIATION
OF REALTORS®

OPTION AGREEMENT

To be used with a purchase agreement. May also be used with a lease.

Date_____, at _____, California
_____, ("Optionor"), grants to
_____, ("Optionee"),
an option ("Agreement") to purchase the real property and improvements situated in (city) _____,
_____, County of _____,
California, described as _____ ("Property") as specified in the
attached: ☐ Real Estate Purchase Agreement ☐ Other_____, which is incorporated
by this reference as a part of this Agreement, on the following terms and conditions.

1. **OPTION CONSIDERATION:**
   A. _____ Dollars $_____,
   ☐ (If checked) and/or (circle one), the amount specified in paragraph 6B.
   B. By ☐ cash, ☐ cashier's check, ☐ personal check, or ☐ _____
   made payable to_____.
   C. ☐ Payable upon execution of this Agreement,
   OR ☐ Payable within _____ days after acceptance of this Agreement, by which time Optionee shall have completed a
   due diligence investigation and accepted the condition of the Property. At least 5 (or _____) days before expiration of this time
   period, Optionor shall provide to Optionee (i) any mandatory disclosures (such as those required by paragraph 7), (ii) a
   preliminary title report, and (iii) _____.
   OR ☐ _____
   D. If payment is not made by the time specified in paragraph 1C above, this Agreement shall become immediately null and void.
   E. If this Option is exercised, ☐ all, or ☐ $_____ of the Option Consideration shall be applied toward
   Optionee's down payment obligations under the terms of the attached purchase agreement, upon close of escrow of that
   agreement. Optionee is advised that the full amount of the option consideration applied toward any down payment may not be
   counted by a lender for financing purposes.
2. **OPTION PERIOD:** The Option shall begin on (date) _____, and shall end at 11:59 p.m.
   (or at ☐ _____), on (date) _____.
3. **MANNER OF EXERCISE:** Optionee may exercise the Option **only** by delivering a written unconditional notice of exercise, signed
   by Optionee, to Optionor, or _____, who is authorized to receive it, no earlier than
   _____ and no later than _____.
   A copy of the unconditional notice of exercise shall be delivered to the Brokers identified in this Agreement.
4. **EFFECT OF DEFAULT ON OPTION:** Optionee shall have no right to exercise this Option if Optionee has not performed any
   obligation imposed by, or is in default of, any obligation of this Agreement, any addenda, or any document incorporated by reference.
5. **NON-EXERCISE:** If the Option is not exercised in the manner specified, within the option period or any written extension thereof,
   or if it is terminated under any provision of this Agreement, then:
   A. The Option and all rights of Optionee to purchase the Property shall immediately terminate without notice; and
   B. All Option Consideration paid, rent paid, services rendered to Optionor, and improvements made to the Property, if any, by
   Optionee, shall be retained by Optionor in consideration of the granting of the Option; and.
   C. Optionee shall execute, acknowledge, and deliver to Optionor, within 5 (or ☐ _____) calendar days of Optionor's request, a
   release, quitclaim deed, or any other document reasonably required by Optionor or a title insurance company to verify the
   termination of the Option.

Optionee and Optionor acknowledge receipt of copy of this page, which constitutes Page 1 of _____ Pages.
Optionee's Initials (_____) (_____)   Optionor's Initials (_____) (_____)

Published and Distributed by:
REAL ESTATE BUSINESS SERVICES, INC.
a subsidiary of the CALIFORNIA ASSOCIATION OF REALTORS®
525 South Virgil Avenue, Los Angeles, California 90020
PRINT DATE

REVISED 10/98

┌─ OFFICE USE ONLY ─┐
Reviewed by Broker
or Designee _____
Date _____

EQUAL HOUSING
OPPORTUNITY

OPTION AGREEMENT (OA-11 PAGE 1 OF 3)

Source: California Association of REALTORS®

Figure 2.3   Option Agreement (continued)

Property Address: _____   Date: _____

6. ☐ **LEASE (If checked):**
   A. The attached lease agreement, dated _____, between Optionee as Tenant and Optionor as Landlord, is incorporated by reference as part of this Agreement.
   B. $_____ per month of rent actually paid by Optionee shall be treated as Option Consideration pursuant to paragraph 1.
   C. The lease obligations shall continue until termination of the lease. If the Option is exercised, the lease shall continue until the earliest of (i) the date scheduled for close of escrow under the purchase agreement, or as extended in writing, (ii) the close of escrow of the purchase agreement, or (iii) mutual cancellation of the purchase agreement.
   D. In addition to the reason stated in paragraph 4, Optionee shall have no right to exercise this Option if Optionor, as landlord, has given to Optionee, as tenant, two or more notices to cure any default or non-performance under the terms of the lease.
7. **DISCLOSURE STATEMENTS:** Unless exempt, if the Property contains one-to-four residential dwelling units, Optionor must comply with Civil Code §1102 et seq., by providing Optionee with a Real Estate Transfer Disclosure Statement and Natural Hazard Disclosure Statement.
8. **RECORDING:** Optionor or Optionee shall, upon request, execute, acknowledge, and deliver to the other a memorandum of this Agreement for recording purposes. All resulting fees and taxes shall be paid by the party requesting recordation.
9. **DAMAGE OR DESTRUCTION:** If, prior to exercise of this Option, by no fault of Optionee, the Property is totally or partially damaged or destroyed by fire, earthquake, accident or other casualty, Optionee may cancel this Agreement by giving written notice to Optionor, and is entitled to the return of all Option Consideration paid. However, if, prior to Optionee giving notice of cancellation to Optionor, the Property has been repaired or replaced so that it is in substantially the same condition as of the date of acceptance of this Agreement, Optionee shall not have the right to cancel this Agreement.
10. **PURCHASE AGREEMENT:** All of the time limits contained in the attached purchase agreement, which begin on the date of Acceptance of the purchase agreement, shall instead begin to run on the date the Option is exercised. After exercise of this Option, if any contingency in the attached purchase agreement, including but not limited to any right of inspection or financing provision, is not satisfied or is disapproved by Optionee at any time, all option consideration paid, rent paid, services rendered to Optionor, and improvements to the Property, if any, by Optionee, shall be retained by Optionor in consideration of the granting of the Option.
11. **NOTICES:** Unless otherwise provided in this Agreement, any notice, tender, or delivery to be given by either party to the other may be performed by personal delivery or by registered or certified mail, postage prepaid, return receipt requested, and shall be deemed delivered when mailed (except for acceptance of the offer to enter into this Agreement, which must be done in the manner specified in paragraph 16). Mailed notices shall be addressed as shown below, but each party may designate a new address by giving written notice to the other.
12. **DISPUTE RESOLUTION:** Optionee and Optionor agree that any dispute or claim arising between them out of this Agreement shall be decided by the same method agreed to for resolving disputes in the attached purchase agreement.
13. **OTHER TERMS AND CONDITIONS,** including attached supplements: _____
   _____
   _____
   _____
   _____
   _____
   _____
   _____
   _____
   _____
   _____
   _____
   _____
   _____
   _____

14. **ATTORNEY'S FEES:** In any action, proceeding, or arbitration between Optionee and Optionor arising out of this Agreement, the prevailing Optionee or Optionor shall be entitled to reasonable attorney's fees and costs from the non-prevailing Optionee or Optionor.

Optionee and Optionor acknowledge receipt of copy of this page, which constitutes Page 2 of _____ Pages.
   Optionee's Initials (_____) (_____)   Optionor's Initials (_____) (_____)

┌─ OFFICE USE ONLY ─┐
Reviewed by Broker
or Designee _____
Date _____
└───────────────────┘
EQUAL HOUSING OPPORTUNITY

REVISED 10/98

PRINT DATE

OPTION AGREEMENT (OA-11 PAGE 2 OF 3)

Figure 2.3   (continued)

Property Address: _____   Date: _____

15. **TIME OF ESSENCE; ENTIRE CONTRACT; CHANGES:** Time is of the essence. All understandings between the parties are incorporated in this Agreement. Its terms are intended by the parties as a final, complete, and exclusive expression of their agreement with respect to its subject matter, and may not be contradicted by evidence of any prior agreement or contemporaneous oral agreement. **This Agreement may not be extended, amended, modified, altered, or changed, except in writing signed by Optionee and Optionor.**

16. **OFFER:** This is an offer for an Option to purchase Property on the above terms and conditions. Unless Acceptance of Offer is signed by Optionor, and a signed copy delivered in person, by mail, or facsimile, and personally received by Optionee, or by _____, who is authorized to receive it, by (date) _____, at _____ AM/PM, the offer shall be deemed revoked. Optionee has read and acknowledges receipt of a copy of the offer. This Agreement and any supplement, addendum, or modification, including any photocopy or facsimile, may be signed in two or more counterparts, all of which shall constitute one and the same writing.

OPTIONEE _____

OPTIONEE _____
Address _____
_____
Telephone _____   Fax _____

17. **BROKER COMPENSATION:** Optionor agrees to pay compensation for services as follows:
_____, to _____, Broker, and
_____, to _____, Broker,
payable upon execution of this Agreement.

18. **ACCEPTANCE OF OPTION:** Optionor warrants that Optionor is the owner of the Property or has the authority to execute this Agreement. Optionor accepts and agrees to grant an Option to purchase the Property on the above terms and conditions.

If checked: ☐ **SUBJECT TO ATTACHED COUNTER OFFER, DATED** _____.

OPTIONOR _____

OPTIONOR _____
Address _____
_____
Telephone _____   Fax _____

Real Estate Brokers are not parties to the Agreement between Optionee and Optionor.

Broker _____ By _____ Date _____
Address _____
_____
Telephone _____   Fax _____

Broker _____ By _____ Date _____
Address _____
_____
Telephone _____   Fax _____

Page 3 of _____ Pages.

REVISED 10/98

OFFICE USE ONLY
Reviewed by Broker
or Designee _____
Date _____

OPTION AGREEMENT (OA-11 PAGE 3 OF 3)

Figure 2.4   Movingcompanies.com

Screen capture from http://movingcompanies.com/

needs for square footage, parking or garage arrangements, a security system, a washer and dryer, pet possibilities, and any other luxury or amenity you know you can't live without (such as an exercise room or pool area).

Use more than one agent in your search for just the right rental situation. See how many possibilities each one provides you and how seriously they are considering your criteria; then filter out the ones you know are not listening. Be careful not to let an agent pressure you by telling you that there are ten other potential tenants ready to make a decision on the same apartment. Don't permit them to talk you into something you know you can't afford, or make you feel guilty if you don't rent any of the properties you have seen. A good agent

Figure 2.5   Relocation Trip Kit

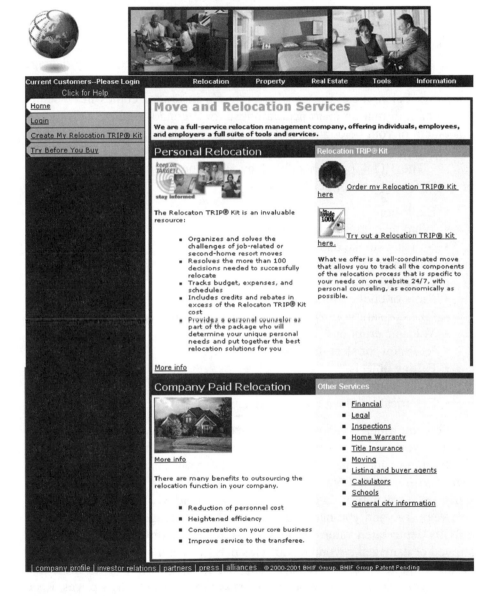

or broker will be patient, using perseverance and common sense to find just the right place for you. Some agents feel that if they are of great assistance now, you may remember them when you are in the market to buy a home.

A WORD ON RENTER'S INSURANCE

If a disaster strikes, your landlord's insurance should cover any damage to the structure you occupy, but you would be left high and dry in regard to your own belongings. This is where renter's insurance comes in. Whether you decide to rent an apartment, a house, or a condo, dealing with the replacement of your belongings and protecting yourself against a liability lawsuit could take a horrible toll on your finances.

The HO-4 policies offered by insurance companies protect your property from a host of perils, such as:

- Explosions
- Wind, hail, and lightning damage
- Fire and smoke damage
- Theft and vandalism
- Car and aircraft accidents
- Riots or civil commotion
- Glass or safety-glazing materials that are a part of the structure
- Volcanic eruptions
- Ice, snow, or sleet damage
- Falling objects
- Water damage from broken utilities
- Electrical overload (surge) damage

Separate rider policies can be added for earthquakes, hurricanes, and floods if you are in areas prone to those natural disaster risks.

It's important to pay attention to whether your insurance company uses *actual cash value* (ACV) or *replacement cost coverage.* The descriptions are fairly self-explanatory. In other words, if you paid $1,000 for a leather sofa five years ago and you had arranged for ACV coverage, you would receive only its depreciated value, minus your policy deductible if the sofa was destroyed or damaged beyond repair. This may well end up being only pennies on the dollar. Conversely, replacement cost coverage will pay for the actual cost for you to replace the sofa with a comparable one at today's prices. Keep in mind that you may have to go ahead and buy the replacement sofa and then submit a claim for reimbursement through an adjuster, but the alternative ACV coverage would pay you next to nothing. Replacement cost coverage is more expensive than the ACV type, but you get what you pay for.

If you collect valuable antiques, artwork, jewelry, electronic equipment, or sophisticated computer components, these items may exceed the maximum dollar amounts allowed in your basic policy. Talk to your agent about getting extra coverage, known as a *rider.*

If your rental home or unit becomes uninhabitable due to a disaster, your renter's insurance will cover your living expenses up to a point, with some limits on dollar amounts and imposed time frames.

There are several other advantages to having this coverage. For instance, if something you own causes damage within your rental or to those units around you (such as a leaking waterbed), renter's insurance steps in. If someone slips and falls in your apartment and chooses to litigate, you have some coverage for legal expenses and the court judgement.

The cost of a renter's policy is generally lower than a homeowner's policy, but the dollar amounts and deductibles imposed will dictate the final premium cost. Discounts for fire detectors, security devices, fire extinguishers, and nonsmokers may also apply. Your insurance company may "bundle" coverage of car and rental insurance to offer you even lower premiums.

FURNISHING YOUR RENTAL HOME

It's important to pay special attention to what items may or may not "fit" into the spaces provided within your apartment *before* you load them onto the moving van. A second-story apartment's elevator may not easily accommodate extremely large or heavy items, such as pianos or other large furniture items that cannot be broken down into smaller pieces. Waterbeds or heavy exercise equipment may also be prohibited, so get a clear picture from your new landlord as to the limitations that exist for your unit. It may be wise to store these items with friends or family for a time, or consider selling them.

When purchasing furniture for your new digs, try to stay with neutral colors and practical furniture design. The same lime green contemporary sofa with angled features that looked great in a loft apartment may seem hopelessly out of place in a home you may decide to buy some day. Give some thought to its staying power in the larger scheme of things. Although most apartments and rentals are painted in rather drab, neutral tones, you can add color with the less costly accessories such as rugs, drapes, pictures, and knick-knacks. Of course, if you never plan to reuse your rental furnishings anywhere else, you can go crazy decorating, as long as your landlord doesn't object.

You may be able to exercise your creative juices by renting furniture instead of purchasing it. The furniture rental industry is booming, and renters have many more options to furnish their homes elegantly and change their surroundings frequently if they wish to. (See Figure 2.6, CORT Furniture Rental.)

Figure 2.6   CORT Furniture Rental

Residential Furniture

CORT's Online Catalog
Take a look at our Online Catalog featuring color pictures and specifications of our residential furniture styles.

Why Rent Furniture?
We deliver comfort with style. In just 48 hours, our brand name rental furniture can bring new life to any home. From traditional to contemporary, you'll find unlimited possibilities and flexible lease terms to match...all backed by the industry's only written Personal Service Guarantee®.

Need to Buy?
CORT Clearance Centers offers a wide variety of new and previously-leased brand name furniture at savings of 30-70%.

One Call Does it All
Our National Accounts program conveniently offers your company a single contact and other special programs for all of your furniture and temporary housing needs coast to coast.

Discount Coupons
To be able to receive additional savings on CORT furniture, click here for discount coupons.

Still
Need more information, brochures, etc.? Want to speak to someone in person? Request Info here.

Suddenly, we've made your place a Home.™

Home | Residential Furniture | Office Furniture | Relocation Assistance | Other Businesses | Trade Shows

Powered by LivePerson™

Contact us at:
1-888-669-CORT
1-888-669-2678
sales@cort.net

Click for CORT Locations

Online Catalog
Rental
Clearance Ctr.
Nat'l. Accounts
FAQs
Request Info
Trade Shows
Testimonials
Credit Applications
About CORT
Employment
Contact Us
Search
Site Map

CORT Coupons | FAQ | Request Info | Testimonials | Credit Applications | About CORT | Employment | Contact Us | Search | Site Map

Screen capture from http://www.cort1.com/resident/resident.htm

KEEPING A PET

If you have a pet, you will, of course be concerned with whether you will be able to keep man's best friend, his feline counterpart, or your pet iguana before deciding on where to rent. If your landlord permits pets on the premises, he or she will more than likely ask for a heftier security or "pet" deposit. Find out under what circumstances this extra deposit money is refundable, and what guidelines must be observed in order to keep pets in your rental home. There may be size and weight limitations, a ceiling on how many pets are permitted, and fines you can incur if your pets create damage to your unit or are a disturbance to your neighbors.

For more information on moving with a pet, visit SpringStreet.com, the rental advice site within HomeStore.com. There you'll find a checklist for pet owners and information about your rights as a pet owner.

A word to the wise: Don't rent an apartment or home on the hopes that your pet will behave properly or that you can clandestinely exceed the landlord's parameters for keeping a pet. Most rental agreements specify strong language allowing the landlord to evict you if the rules are violated.

RESOURCES

Books

Every Tenant's Legal Guide, by Janet Portman, Marcia Stewart, and Mary Randolph (Nolo Press, 950 Parker Street, Berkeley, CA 94710; 800-992-6656; www .nolo.com). Walks readers through each step of renting, from finding an apartment to giving notice. Credit reports, rent control, grace periods for late rent, privacy rights, and eviction are all covered.

Landlord and Tenant, by Steven D. Strauss (W.W. Norton, 500 Fifth Avenue, New York, NY 10110; 212-354-5500; www.wwnorton.com). Covers the rights, responsibilities, and duties of landlords and tenants, some ways of dealing with your landlord or tenant, and reasonable solutions to problems. The book includes sample scenarios of cases to illustrate the methods that can be used to deal with a variety of situations.

Renter's Rights (Quick & Legal Series), by Janet Portman and Marcia Stewart (Nolo Press, 950 Parker Street, Berkeley, CA 94710; 800-992-6656; www.nolo .com). Covers tenants' rights in all 50 states, providing information in such key areas as rent, privacy, discrimination, roommates, and security deposits.

The Savvy Renter's Kit, by Ed Sacks (Dearborn Trade, Chicago, IL; 312-836-4400; 800-245-2665; www.dearborntrade.com). Discusses where to find good rentals, how to inspect the property, how to negotiate a fair lease, how to manage the details of the move, and how to resolve disputes with your landlord.

Web Site

Monstermoving.com. Offers comprehensive help for those relocating. Offers lists of moving companies, storage companies, and mortgage companies, most with links to their sites. Helps with moving automobiles, and pets, truck rentals, and buying storage boxes. <www.monstermoving.com>

CHAPTER 3

If You Decide to Buy

If you conclude from the buy-versus-rent analysis that you should buy a home, you have a much more complex task ahead of you than if you decide to rent. You must now determine how much house you can afford, what kind of house to buy, where you want to live, how to find the best deal, how to make an offer that is accepted, and how to finance your home with a mortgage. After you have done all of this, you must maintain the home and possibly remodel it to fit your needs. All these tasks, however, center on owning your own piece of the pie, something tangible that is now a reality for nearly two-thirds of Americans. For that reason, a large segment of the population feels the rewards are undoubtedly worth the effort they put into buying a home. (See Figure 3.1.)

GETTING REAL ABOUT HOW MUCH YOU CAN AFFORD

The first step to take before you house-hunt is to determine what size mortgage payment you can comfortably afford. To qualify for a home loan, you must pass certain tests that lending institutions will impose. Therefore, it is helpful to apply those tests to yourself before you ever meet with a mortgage lender.

Loan approvals are based in part on *ratios*. The *front ratio* is used to give the lender a snapshot of what percentage of your gross monthly income can be prudently used for housing debt, which includes principal and interest, real estate taxes, homeowners insurance, and maintenance fees (for condomini-

Figure 3.1   Are You Ready to Buy a Home Quiz

Buying a home involves a major commitment of both time and money. Answer the 10 true-false questions below to determine if you're really ready to buy a home. Some of your answers are more important than others. When you're done, add up your points and see the results below.

1. If I buy a home, I don't plan on moving again for at least two years. (Worth eight points)

   _____ True   _____ False

2. My job is secure and there's little chance I will lose it. (Eight points)

   _____ True   _____ False

3. I've done some preliminary checking, and home prices in my area appear to be increasing. (Eight points)

   _____ True   _____ False

4. I have at least $5,000 or $10,000 available to use for a down payment and pay my sales-related closing costs. (Seven points)

   _____ True   _____ False

5. I'm willing to spend at least 40 hours looking for the best home that I can afford. (Four points)

   _____ True   _____ False

6. I'm willing to cut back on my other expenses if it's the only way I can afford to buy a home. (Four points)

   _____ True   _____ False

7. I pay my bills on time, and haven't made more than two late payments in the last two years. (Four points)

   _____ True   _____ False

8. My housing needs won't change much over the next two years. (Three points)

   _____ True   _____ False

9. I don't expect my first home to be my "dream house." (Two points)

   _____ True   _____ False

10. I'm willing to devote at least a couple of hours a week to keep my home looking nice and in good repair. (Two points)

    _____ True   _____ False

Source: *If You're Clueless about Buying a Home and Want to Know More* by David W. Myers.

Figure 3.1   (continued)

What Your Score Means

All questions answered "True" are worth the designated number of points. All "False" answers are worth zero points. Add 'em up and check out your score.

Score

43–50:   You're a great candidate to buy a house now.

35–42:   Your prospects are good, but double-check your finances and priorities.

28–34:   You can still buy a house, but it's going to take hard work and sacrifice.

 0–27:   Delay your homebuying plans until you can handle such a major commitment.

ums or neighborhoods with homeowners association dues). The *back ratio* includes all of the obligations mentioned above, plus other recurring debts that may extend beyond ten months or so, such as car payments, student loans, revolving lines of credit, credit card payments, and court-ordered child support. In general, ratios for a 10 percent down payment on a home follow the guidelines of 28/36, but those ratios can be manipulated by lenders with what are called *compensating factors,* which are other circumstances within your financial history that may permit lenders to stretch the limits considerably. Another way lenders look at this is as ratios, called the *debt ratio* and the *housing ratio,* as shown in Figure 3.2.

These factors are important ones to lenders when determining your ability to repay a loan. A perfect or near-perfect credit history, longevity and solid earning power within the same consistent line of work, or guaranteed, verifiable bonuses offered by your employer over time are all examples of compensating factors used by lending institutions. At the same time, spotty credit, constantly changing careers, and a fluctuating income may make qualifying a borderline call for any lender. The rule of thumb here is that the better your overall picture looks to a lender, the better the loan you can receive (such as a 30-year fixed-rate program) with a smaller down payment needed. For the purposes of helping you calculate whether you are a good candidate to obtain an approval for a mortgage loan, we should use the 28/36 scenario.

The monthly mortgage worksheet in Figure 3.3 will help you determine what size mortgage you can afford using these general ratios. The worksheet includes sample figures. To determine how much money you can borrow for the purchase of a home, you must assume an interest rate and a mortgage term. Figure 3.4 lists numerical factors for the two most popular term loans, 15 years and 30 years, at various *fixed* interest rates from 7 percent to 13 percent. When you have located the proper factor, multiply the loan amount by this factor to

Figure 3.2   Debt and Housing Ratios

Debt Ratio

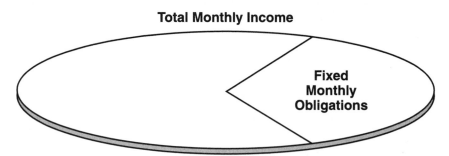

Debt Ratio = Fixed Monthly Obligations ÷ Monthly Income

Housing Ratio

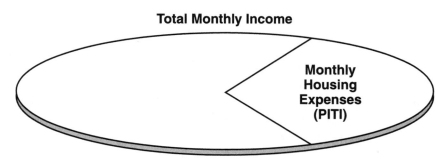

Housing Ratio = Monthly Housing Expense ÷ Monthly Income

Source: *The Mortgage Kit* by Thomas C. Steinmetz.

arrive at a monthly payment. For example, a $200,000 30-year loan at 8 percent interest would require $1,468 monthly payment ($200,000 × .00734 = $1,468). If item 10 on your monthly mortgage worksheet is greater than this monthly payment, you can afford the mortgage.

Using the factors in Figure 3.4, you can try different combinations of terms and interest rates to see how much money you can borrow. To do this, divide item 10 from the monthly mortgage worksheet by various factors to produce different loan amounts.

Figure 3.3   The Monthly Mortgage Worksheet

		Example	Your Loan
1.	Percentage of monthly income available for total mortgage payment, including principal, interest, real estate taxes, and homeowners insurance	28%	
2.	Percentage of monthly income available for real estate taxes and homeowners insurance	4%	
3.	Percentage of monthly income available for mortgage principal and interest payments	24%	
4.	Gross monthly income	$6,250	
5.	Multiply item 3 by item 4	$1,500	
6.	Percentage of monthly income available for principal, interest, real estate taxes, and homeowners insurance, plus other debts (subtract item 2 from 36%)	32%	
7.	Amount of monthly income available for principal and interest, plus other debts (multiply item 6 by item 4)	$2,000	
8.	Amount of monthly income available for other debts	$ 450	
9.	Subtract item 8 from item 7	$1,550	
10.	Enter either item 5 or item 9, whichever is less	$1,500	

Adjusting your worksheet figures to experiment with things such as paying off debt or increasing your down payment will help you arrive at a payment you can afford and one that fits into your long-term financial plan.

Notice that the longer the loan term and the lower the mortgage interest rate, the higher the loan amount you can afford.

Figure 3.5 will also help you determine what size mortgage you can afford. It displays examples of monthly mortgage payments based on various mortgage amounts and interest rates. All these payments are calculated for a 30-year, fixed-rate mortgage and include both principal and interest repayment.

Figure 3.4   Monthly Payment Factors

Interest Rate Percentage	30-Year Loan	15-Year Loan
7 %	.00666	.00899
7.5	.00700	.00928
8	.00734	.00956
8.5	.00769	.00985
9	.00805	.01015
9.5	.00841	.01045
10	.00878	.01075
10.5	.00915	.01106
11	.00953	.01137
11.5	.00991	.01169
12	.01029	.01201
12.5	.01068	.01233
13	.01107	.01266

Figure 3.5   Monthly Payment Table

Mortgage Amount	Interest Rates									
	7.5%	8%	8.5%	9%	9.5%	10%	10.5%	11%	11.5%	12%
$50,000	$350	$367	$384	$402	$420	$439	$457	$476	$495	$514
60,000	420	441	461	483	505	527	549	571	594	617
70,000	490	514	538	563	589	614	640	667	693	720
80,000	560	587	615	644	673	702	732	762	792	823
90,000	630	661	692	724	757	790	823	857	891	926
100,000	700	734	769	805	841	878	915	952	990	1,029

THE PRICE THAT'S RIGHT

Armed with the knowledge of what size mortgage you can handle and how much you must pay each month toward that mortgage, you can now determine what price you can pay for a home. It is safe to assume that closing costs—which include *points* (prepaid interest charged by the lender, one point is 1 percent of the loan amount), legal fees, title searches, transfer taxes, and other charges—will amount to between 2 percent and 4 percent of your mortgage amount. You should deduct all of these closing costs from the cash you have available for your down payment. You may be able to finance closing costs through your lender by adding them to your loan amount, assuming that you qualify for that loan amount, of course. You also may ask the seller of the home you intend to buy to cover these costs as a sales negotiation concession or incentive. This is a more common concession in the purchase of a new home than in the resale of an existing home, but not unheard of when the seller is motivated and wants to make the deal work for his buyer.

Many sellers and lenders prefer a 10 percent down payment, although 3 percent to 5 percent down loan programs have become increasingly popular for borrowers who lack ready funds but earn adequate incomes or those who prefer to hold on to their cash for other purposes. However, if you can make a down payment of 20 percent or more of the home's purchase price, you will save thousands of dollars in interest over the life of your mortgage as well as avoid the cost of private mortgage insurance (PMI) and increase the chance that your loan is approved more easily.

If you plan to make a 10 percent down payment, the purchase cost worksheet in Figure 3.6 will help you determine how much home you can afford. Sample numbers are provided.

Your mortgage analysis can change considerably if you are open to considering some of the more creative types of conventional loans. There are loan programs such as those fixed for a certain length of time which become variable at a certain point a number of years into the future (at which time you may be ready to sell or refinance). Adjustable-rate loans, which can offer easier qualifying terms and lower down payment options, adjust their interest rate on a regular basis annually. The rule of thumb on any loan program

---

Figure 3.6   Purchase Cost Worksheet

	Example	Your Purchase
Start with the mortgage amount qualified for (assuming $700/mo., 7.5%, 30 yr.)	$100,000	$
Add down payment cash	11,000	
Total price of home	111,000	
Add closing costs (at 4% of loan amount)	4,440	
Total Purchase Cost	$115,440	$

that does not have a fixed rate is to find out what the worst-case scenario could be during the life of the loan and then base your decision on whether you could handle the payment. Your mortgage lender's explanation of each program is a key to understanding these more complex types of mortgage loans (Chapter 4, Choosing the Best Mortgage, contains more loan program descriptions and terminology).

ASSEMBLING A DOWN PAYMENT

Buying a home depends on your ability to put together a down payment. The inability to do so is the single most common reason many people are shut out of the housing market. Many people have enough income to make mortgage payments (which can be less than rent in some areas) but are never able to assemble that up-front lump sum. If this is your dilemma, the following suggestions may help:

- *Borrow the money from your parents or other relatives.* If they are in better financial shape than you, Mom and Dad or another family member might lend you or even gift you the down payment, which you should be able to repay as you pay off your mortgage (or remain forever grateful). Be mindful that many lenders require that at least a certain percentage of down payment money be your own, and not a gift or loan from others. For that reason, try to arrange this transfer of funds as early as possible, placing it in an account and keeping it there for several months, so that your lender can verify "seasoned" funds when it comes time to do so.

- *Put securities or bank deposits in escrow to act as your down payment.* For example, in the Merrill Lynch Mortgage 100 program (800-854-7154; www.ml.com), if you can place a bit over 30 percent of the home's purchase price in escrow in the form of stocks, bonds, mutual funds, and certificates of deposit, Merrill Lynch will lend you 100 percent of your home's purchase price. One advantage of this system is that you do not have to sell securities and pay capital gains taxes on any realized gains to assemble your down payment. Over time, as you pay down the principal of your mortgage or the value of your home increases, you will be able to take securities out of escrow because you will have built up enough home equity.

  If you do not have enough securities to participate in the Mortgage 100 program, Merrill Lynch also offers the Parent Power Program, which permits parents to fund the escrow account with their securities or bank deposits, allowing their children to get 100 percent financing for their home. As the value of the home increases, the parents' securities can be released from the escrow account.

- *Take out a loan against your equity in your employer's profit sharing, thrift, or 401(k) plan.* Most firms allow you to borrow at the prime rate or at little more than prime and pay the loan back through payroll deduction over as many as ten years.

- *Make saving a priority.* The sooner you start putting money aside and investing it for growth, the sooner you will accumulate the down payment you need now or in the future. One path to increased savings is decreased spending, particularly frivolous spending on disposable items. Think of all those Chinese dinners that you pick up on the way home from work instead of cooking and those spur-of-the-moment vacations as assaults on your down payment fund.

- *Get a Federal Housing Administration (FHA) or Department of Veterans Affairs (VA) loan, either of which require lower or, in some cases, no down payments.* The maximum FHA loan amount varies greatly depending on the area (even by county) across country. Check with any local lender for FHA or VA loan limits in your area. VA loans are given to members of the armed forces, veterans, and widows of veterans. They are great not only for the low down payment required, but also because the seller is required to pay most of the costs of closing. Your intent to buy a home using VA financing should be contained within your eventual offer to purchase, so that the seller is not blindsided by this revelation.

- *Consider the Nehemiah Program®.* (Nehemiah Corporation of California, 1851 Heritage Lane, Sacramento, CA 95815; 877-643-3642; <www.nehemiahloan.com>) Created in 1997, this nonprofit, privately funded down payment assistance program is now available in many states nationwide. (Online, visit <www.getdownpayment.com> for information on this and other down payment assistance programs.) The program provides gift funds for down payment and closing costs of any resale or new property to qualified buyers using an eligible loan program (such as FHA). The gift funds of 1 percent to 6 percent of the contract purchase price can be requested, depending on the needs of the buyer. Because this program requires a hefty seller contribution, it may not be accepted on all purchase offers.

- *Check into your local banks' Community Reinvestment Act (CRA) programs.* Because lenders cannot limit their lending practices to certain geographical areas (called *redlining*), banks and savings and loans are required to reinvest a certain amount of their local capital into low-to-moderate income areas before they can expand their bases of operation (for information, see <www.federalreserve.gov/DCCA/CRA>). These CRA loan programs are available in HUD-designated target areas and require very little down payment from their borrowers. They also tend to offer generous qualifying ratios.

- *Look into the Fannie 97® Program offered by the Federal National Mortgage Association (known as Fannie Mae).* This program is designed for borrowers who have limited funds for down payment and closing costs. This program requires a down payment of only 3 percent and expanded debt-to-income ratios. There are income limits in some areas, but exceptions are made in high-cost areas such as parts of New England, New York, California, the Northwest, and Hawaii. Go to Fannie Mae's Web site at <www.homepath.com> to get the details.
- *Buy a foreclosed home.* Local lenders, as well as the FHA and VA, will usually accept low down payments to induce buyers to buy homes on which the lenders have foreclosed. You might have to fix up the property and it may not be located in a prime area, but the investment can get you into the housing market.

GETTING A LOAN PREAPPROVAL

One of the most important tasks to accomplish before looking for a home is to procure a letter or document of loan *preapproval* from a lender. This differs from a loan prequalification, which you may receive from real estate agents or on-site new home salespeople, who will query you as to income and debts in order to come up with the basic determination that you appear to qualify for a home loan. Even a cursory prequalification from a lender or cyberlender, who can ask more detailed questions by phone or over the Internet to offer you encouragement, does not have the power of a loan preapproval.

The loan preapproval is one in which a lender will investigate and verify your credit, assets, debts, and income. You'll come away with a written statement that the lender stands ready to make you a mortgage loan, assuming the house you choose meets the lender's standards, and that a last-minute snapshot of your financial status when you are about to close escrow shows that things have not changed. This appeals to a potential seller, who can be certain that you mean business, and it can even help you operate from a position of strength over other buyers who may not have taken the time to take this preemptive step with their lenders.

In these days of cyber-convenience, "desktop" underwriting permits loan consultants lightning quick speed for loan preapprovals. And although you will want to state in your purchase offer that you are fully preapproved for a loan, it is not advisable to actually show your preapproval document to a potential seller until after your offer has been accepted. The reason for this warning is that the document usually contains the highest priced home for which you can qualify, a piece of data you don't want potential sellers to see when you are negotiating the lowest possible purchase price. Figure 3.7 is a sample letter of lender preapproval.

FINDING THE RIGHT HOME

Once you have determined how large a mortgage you can afford, what home price is realistic, and how you will gather the down payment money, it's time to establish what kind of housing will best serve your needs, both today and in the future.

The Right Location for You

Before you explore the different homes available, determine where you want to live. For example, are you most comfortable in the city, the country, or the suburbs? Examine the trade-off criteria between different locations, not just for yourself but for your spouse and family as well, because they are a part of this equation. Would you exchange the convenience of your home and office for a pastoral setting miles away? Also evaluate shopping, public and private schools, recreational facilities, houses of worship, and transportation options, as well as the composition of the local population and cost of living in the area. Lifestyle considerations often outweigh financial ones when choosing a place to live. Check with the chambers of commerce for each area under consideration to get a more complete picture. Many of these organizations have Web sites that permit you to get an overview of these areas from the convenience of your home or office computer.

Determining How You Live

In addition to choosing where to live, you must determine what size home suits your current and future needs. How long will you plan to stay in the home you are about to buy? Do you prefer a newly built home, or will an established neighborhood appeal to you more? Many young couples prefer neighborhoods with new homes not only because of the "fresh slate" they provide, but also because they may have more in common with others who tend to buy there. Neighbors planning families and landscaping backyards at the same time can provide a kind of "birds of a feather" commonality lacking in older neighborhoods whose homes have cycled several times. Some young, childless couples might need only a small condominium or townhouse for now, but may want a larger home down the road when they begin

Figure 3.7   Letter of Lender Preapproval

December 23, 2002

To Whom It May Concern

RE: George and Connie Roberts

From: Joseph James, Great Granite Bank

Re: Property to be determined

Please be advised that the above mentioned loan applicant(s) have been approved for financing with the following conditions:

TERMS	CONDITIONS
Sales Price: $445,900	1. Appraisal
Loan amount: $423,600	2. Sales contract
Loan type: conventional	3. Funds to close
Loan term: 30 year/30 year fixed rate	

This approval is subject to reconsideration if there are any material changes in the financial status of the buyer. All information and property appraisal is subject to final underwriting review.

Sincerely,

Joseph James

Home Mortgage Consultant

a family. On the other hand, an empty-nester couple nearing retirement might find a large home a burden to maintain.

Next, establish a realistic picture of how much space you need, both now and in the future. If you plan to move in a few years, it might not make sense to buy more house than you need now because it will strain your budget. Conversely, a house in which you plan to live for the long term shouldn't be too small if it will be too cramped for growing children or the possibility of taking care of elderly parents.

Focusing on Lifestyles

Now it's time to assess what type of home suits your lifestyle. Here is some food for thought about the choices that may be available to you.

- New homes offer many state-of-the-art conveniences, including energy efficiency as well as the ability to customize the home from the ground up with items you deem important, such as structured wiring for home offices and home automation.
- You may find the charm of older homes irresistible. Although homes with experience cost more to maintain, they can possess owner-added features that can't be duplicated in today's new homes, as well as offer the beauty of mature landscaping.
- Do you want a traditional, single-family home? Or do you prefer the convenience of the turnkey lifestyle afforded by multifamily attached (an apartment home) or semi-attached housing, such as a townhouse or duplex, which can be later be used to generate rental income should you decide to hang on to it after you move? People who appreciate the freedom to take trips often and lessen their responsibility as a homeowner may find more freedom in attached or denser housing arrangements, which also offer security and lower maintenance. The traditional single-family home depicted with its white picket fence and grassy backyard, however, still tends to be the most common idea of home ownership.
- Perhaps the idea of room to roam on your own property is what you have always dreamed of. The purchase of a home situated on a larger parcel of land can have its plusses and minuses. Although it may seem idyllic to imagine life in the country, what degree of "neighborhood" and convenience will you realistically want for yourself and your family? By the same token, if having room for boats, RVs, a horse, or a huge vegetable garden has always been your idea of heaven, don't permit anyone to sway you towards higher-density areas.
- Finally, you may like the idea of purchasing an apartment in a cooperative or condominium building. The purchase of a *co-op* (most commonly found in the eastern United States) is one in which you actually

buy shares in the corporation owning the entire property, which grants you a proprietary lease to occupy an apartment. *Condos* allow you to buy the property outright, although you actually own the "air space" contained within the unit. In many cases, the cooperative or condominium board of directors must approve anyone to whom you want to sell the apartment, which can make the property difficult to sell. Both co-ops and condos assess a monthly maintenance charge to pay for such shared costs as the property's underlying mortgage, heat, elevators, electricity, water and waste management, grounds maintenance, security, and recreational facilities, such as swimming pools or tennis courts. If this type of property must undertake a particularly large repair job, like replacing a roof or a plumbing system gone bad, you will have to pay an extra assessment to cover your share of the bill.

Living in a well-run co-op or condo can liberate you from much of the maintenance of a single-family home. On the other hand, you must make sure that the homeowners association or board of directors runs the organization well, retaining enough funds within its budget to allow for regular maintenance of the complex. Also, try to find out if there is any pending litigation against a condo complex you are considering. This revelation could limit your ability to obtain a mortgage loan. Lawsuits are considered by many lenders to be a red flag signifying an increased investment risk. A poorly run organization or fears of litigation can also erode property values, ultimately making the property a less-than-desirable investment.

Conducting the Search

Now that you have zeroed in on location, size, and style of home that best suits your needs, you may begin your search. You have a wealth of ways in which to find your dream home.

Tell friends, family, and neighbors that you're in the market for a home. They might know of a good deal, a new neighborhood, a coworker who is ready to sell, or one who currently has a home on the market.

Contact a real estate agent. Unless you hire a broker who is from an Exclusive Buyer's Broker® agency, you will deal with an agent whose job it is to represent the seller, even though they may show you homes listed with other agents. Agents and brokers can be extremely helpful in showing you homes that fit your housing and budgetary needs, but always remember that the seller pays their commission, which is based on getting the highest price possible. You may consider working with a broker on a fee-for-services basis only, paying them for just the services that interest you.

Read classified ads in the newspapers. With practice, you will learn to scan the thousands of listings with an eye for a bargain. Your best chance to buy a great home at a good price occurs when the seller is under pressure to sell. He or she might be going through a divorce, on the verge of foreclosure, or relocating for a job in another city. Whatever the reason, look for what real estate professionals call *motivated sellers.* You might not only be able to get a good price, but also induce the seller to offer attractive financing terms, such as paying for your closing costs or giving you an allowance in escrow for new carpet or paint. This can offset what you may pay to a buyer's broker (if you use one) or in essence sidestep the listing agent's commission which is built into the price you are paying.

Search for a home on the Internet. A huge number of sites on which you can get advice and even purchase real estate exist on the World Wide Web. It is said that most Web surfers use the Internet for informational purposes only when it comes to big-ticket items, and there is no better time to let your mouse do the walking than now. Some of the more popular MLS-type listing sites for home buying are HomeStore.com, HomeAdvisor.com, and HomeGain.com. Also refer to the Resources section at the end of this chapter for more Web sites.

For-sale-by-owner (or FSBO) Web sites were predicted to transform home buying using the Web. The reason they have not proliferated as expected is that homebuyers can get easily frustrated with them, finding only one or two homes listed in a given area, without enough representative photos or information from the seller. Some survivors are helpusell.com, fizbo.com, fisbo.com, fsbo.com, homebytes.com, iown.com, ired.com, ziprealty.com, or oldhouses.com.

If your search is for a new home, try homebuilder.com, newhomesource .com, newhomesearch.com, nahb.com, or buildingahome.net. If cost-saving production (tract) homes are what you are looking for, most homebuilders now have their own Web sites, usually listed in your newspaper's weekend real estate section display advertisements, or linked to most common search engines. One new home site with a twist is iNest.com, which gives you a cash rebate at closing time if you walk into one of their participating builders' communities with an iNest coupon, printable from their Web site. Some of these Web sites do business all over the United States, while others cover a more area-specific base of clients.

Place a classified ad. If you can't find a home you like through newspaper classifieds, you can place an ad explaining what you are looking for. You may hear from a seller or real estate agent who can tell you about a property with which you are not familiar.

Look for vacant homes. By driving or walking through the neighborhood that interests you, you may spot a vacant home with an overgrown lawn, peeling paint, and a lot of junk mail in the mailbox. A For Sale sign may or may not be posted on the property. To determine who owns the home, you can look up records (a property profile) at the home's corresponding city hall, any title company, or the local county recorder's office with the property address or parcel number in hand. This can even be done on the Internet now by visiting dataquick.com, titleplus.com, or property-profiles.com. You can also question the neighbors or ask the post office if there is a forwarding address. The home may just be owned by a motivated seller who may be overjoyed to receive your offer.

It is also not unheard of to make up your own flyer-type notice asking if owners in the area know of anyone in the neighborhood who has recently mentioned selling their home. Stuff copies into every mailbox in the neighborhood that interests you and sit back to see if the phone rings or an e-mail pops up. You have nothing to lose by employing this inexpensive way of canvassing for a home, and perhaps something to gain, because many would love nothing more than to sell their home themselves, allowing them to keep as much of their equity as possible. Just be careful not to divulge the maximum price you are willing to pay for a home should someone get in touch with you as a result of your flyer. In other words, curb your enthusiasm if this is the neighborhood that puts stars in your eyes, or you will not put yourself in a good position to get the lowest price possible should you decide to make an offer.

Purchase real estate about to be or already foreclosed upon. The ultimate motivated seller is the person about to lose property to the bank because he or she has not kept up with the payments. You can buy from the owner before foreclosure, from the trustee at foreclosure, or from the bank that owns the property after foreclosure. If the FHA or VA insured the loan, it may also be involved in the foreclosure. Foreclosed properties are frequently offered at auctions; however, you will probably do better if you can buy the property directly from the owner before it gets to auction.

Use an Exclusive Buyer's Broker or agent to represent you. The traditional role of the real estate broker or agent has undergone many changes over the past few decades. As mentioned at the beginning of this section, because real estate commissions are paid by the seller or builder of a property, using the more traditional services of a real estate agent to represent buyers in the purchase of a home does not require any compensation by buyers for their services. At the same time, without formal agreements for homebuyers to use a particular real estate agent or broker to represent them exclusively, these hard-working professionals can spend weeks or even months running around previewing and showing properties that sound appropriate. They can then be left in the dust, receiving nothing for their time when home shoppers somehow end up buying property without them. The traditional buyer's real estate agent, however, cannot ignore an implied fiduciary agency responsibility to the seller, and must make known to the seller or seller's agent any material facts about you that would help the seller receive the highest price possible for their home when asked to do so. This means that they are duty-bound to reveal how motivated you are and how much house you can afford if asked about it by the seller's agent.

For that reason, the Exclusive Buyer's Broker (EBB) is a fairly new agent designation that is gaining popularity with the home-buying public. Agents and brokers from these fully licensed real estate agencies do not take any listings, stand armed and ready to represent you exclusively, and work to get you, the homebuyer, the best possible deal. They have access to all multiple-listed properties, as well as unlisted and for-sale-by-owner properties, and can assist you with the entire home buying process, if that is your wish. The buyer's broker will also help you define your wants and needs, make price comparisons, offer strategies, and help you look at a property's strengths and weaknesses. They can save you thousands of dollars by not having to disclose your highest price intentions or just how motivated you are to buy the house. An Exclusive Buyer's Broker can act as a liaison or intermediary with the seller, divulging only the information needed to seal the deal. Their allegiance and fiduciary responsibility is to you and you alone during the purchase of a home.

An EBB still may be paid a commission by the seller at closing (with many FSBOs they keep only their original retainer fee), which they will then credit to you the usually modest up-front fee they charge for their services. It is important to know that a traditional buyer's agent or broker may not have earned the National Association of REALTORS® official designation as an EBB, so not all real estate agents are authorized to operate under these terms. To find an EBB near you, contact the Buyer's Homefinding Network at 800-500-3569 for a free local referral, or read more about EBBs online at Realtor.com. An example of an EBB agreement appears in Figure 3.8.

Visit lots of open houses and model homes on weekends. You can't get a feel for the market, especially when looking on your own, unless you do your homework by sampling values in the various prospective areas that appeal to you. Resale home open houses generally take place on Saturdays or Sundays between noon and 5 PM. It's important to note that when real estate agents are involved, open house events are not only put on for the purpose of showing off the listed home to interested or curious buyers; they are also held for prospecting purposes of the listing or attending agent. An agent

Figure 3.8   Using an Exclusive Buyer's Broker

The following are examples of how the common provisions for each agreement might read. They are not suggestions nor are they recommendations. They are merely examples. Please seek legal advice before using as they are subject to applicable state and other laws.

Exclusive Buyer Representation Contract

Exclusive Buyer Representation/Workscope:

Buyer hereby grants _____ ("Broker") the sole and exclusive right during the duration of this agreement to assist Buyer in locating for purchase acceptable real estate ("Real Property") as indicated by Buyer signing an offer to purchase that is accepted by a seller.

Other duties & responsibilities as defined by state law.

Duration of Representation:

Duration of Agreement: This agreement shall commence on _____ and shall continue through _____ .

Property Description:

Description of Property Sought: Buyer wishes to purchase Real Property, which may include a lot and residence to be constructed, as follows:

A. Approximate Price Range: $ _____ to $ _____

B. General Description: _____

C. Preferred Location(s): _____

D. Preferred Terms: _____

Compensation Provision:

Compensation of Broker: As compensation for Broker's services, the Buyer agrees to pay the Broker as follows:

A. **On Listed Property with Commission Splits:** Commissions are generally paid by the seller or landlord. The Listing Agreement should specify who pays the Broker's commission. Broker, when the listing company, will split commissions with the cooperative brokerage company, because it is Broker's general policy to reciprocate compensation and cooperation with other brokers.

B. **On Other Property:** In the event that the owner of any Real Property with whom Buyer enters into an enforceable Purchase and Sale Agreement does not agree to pay Broker's real estate commission, or if the listing broker does not split commissions, then Buyer shall pay Broker a commission of $ _____ or _____ % of the purchase price of each Real Property purchased by Buyer (e.g., A "For Sale By Owner" property may fall into this category.) Broker shall credit against said commission any commission payments received by Broker from the Real Property seller. Buyer shall pay Broker said commission at the time Buyer closes any purchase of Real Property.

Figure 3.8   (continued)

C. Protection Period: In the event that during the period of _____ months following termination of this Agreement, Buyer purchases any Real Property shown or introduced to Buyer during the term of this Agreement, then Buyer shall pay Broker the commission as stated above in paragraph B.

Disclosed Dual Agency as a Possibly:

Possibility of Disclosed Dual Agency: You may want to be shown Real Property which is listed by your Broker. In that event, your Broker will undertake a dual representation (represent both the seller and the buyer for sale of the Real Property.) Representing more that one party to a transaction may present a conflict of interest since both clients may rely upon Broker's advice and the clients' respective interests may be adverse to each other. Broker will endeavor to be impartial between both parties and will not represent the interest of either party to the exclusion or detriment of the other party. Broker will act as a dual agent only with the written consent of ALL parties in the transaction. Parties are not required to participate in the Disclosed Dual Agency.

Consent to Show Properties to Other Buyers:

Other Buyers: Other potential buyers may be interested in the same properties as Buyer. It is agreed that Appointed Agent may represent those buyers, whether such representation arises prior to, during, or after the end of this Agreement. In such a situation, Appointed Agent will not disclose to either buyer the terms of the other's offer.

Payment of Charges for Services Performed by Others:

Costs of Services or Products obtained from Outside Services: The Buyer shall be responsible to pay immediately when due for all product or services from outside sources. (Examples: roof or mechanical inspections, pest inspections, surveys, title reports, etc.)

Provided with permission as a courtesy by Buyers Homefinding Network (800) 500-3569

or broker will be on hand to point out the good points of the open home, but will also ask you questions about what type of home interests you, just in case another of her listings or another listing with which she is familiar sounds appropriate. They will usually want to represent you in a home purchase, so be polite but minimal in terms of what information you offer to them about yourself unless you intend to sign up for their services.

Homebuilders generally have their model homes open seven days a week, often between the hours of 10 AM and 6 PM, depending on the season. It is the job of most on-site new home salespeople (in most states, these are licensed agents) to sell only their builder's homes. This means they represent the seller (builder) exclusively, and, although they must submit all offers, many homebuilders are reluctant to negotiate on the prices that appear on their handouts to prospective buyers unless they are closing out a neighborhood or have a move-in-ready inventory home on their hands. Even then, they may prefer to negotiate on terms rather than price to keep newly established home values in their communities as stable as possible. Builders operate on much smaller profit margins than one would surmise, relying mostly on volume to make their business viable.

As you evaluate various properties, write in a notebook the location, layout, features and financial details such as price, taxes, and maintenance costs of each home you consider. Create a folder for each home and include the marketing flyer or new home brochure that you have collected during your home search. Without keeping these records, you may have difficulty keeping all the details of each different home straight.

Making an Offer

Whether you deal directly with the seller or bargain through a real estate agent, you should know how much you can afford to bid, based both on your budget and on the mortgage for which you qualify. You should also determine whether it is you or the seller who has the stronger bargaining position. If the local market is active and many other buyers have expressed interest in the home, the seller is less likely to be flexible. On the other hand, if the market is glutted and the seller is desperate to move, you can expect to occupy the driver's seat and receive much better terms.

If you are not represented by an agent when making an offer, ask the seller or seller's agent to demonstrate to you just how they came up with their asking price. Then compare their criteria with what research you have already conducted on the area. Rely only on the information gleaned from closed sales made within the past six months or, if something has caused a cataclysmic effect on the local real estate market recently, within the past 60 to 90 days.

Your Serve, Their Serve

Once you have a figure in mind for the purposes of a purchase offer, it is important to understand how the game is played when beginning the offer process. Indeed, *game* is the appropriate word here, whether it is you or your agent that returns the proverbial volley once the negotiations have begun. To protect you, your offer should contain many safeguards that permit you to make a final, accepted contract contingent upon some important verifiable facts. These *contingencies* (conditions of the sale) can include an appraisal justifying the final price, a professional building inspection verifying that the house is not in worse shape for its age than you would have imagined, and a pest inspection to examine any active pest infestations or inform you of any red flags. Mortgage lenders require some or all of these terms, so rest assured that they are not uncommon requests in a purchase offer.

Although appraisals and inspections are not as pivotal in new home purchases (and pest inspections are usually not warranted at all), some homebuyers will opt to pay for the services of a structural inspection before drywall is applied, followed by another inspection just before closing or settlement. Buyers who do this may feel the need to be assured that they are purchasing the quality home originally represented by the builder. (See the inspection reports in the appendix.)

Your initial offer should contain all of these contingencies because the possibility exists that the initial offer could be accepted immediately with no counteroffers from the seller ever taking place. If you wait, thinking you can "beef up" your offer terms, it may be too late to do anything about these important contingencies. A written offer can become a binding contract once it is signed by the seller, and the *earnest money* (initial good-faith deposit) accompanying your offer to buy property may be at stake if you try to back out of your purchase after final acceptance has taken place.

The game itself is one of offer and counteroffer, much like the volley in a tennis game. When the ball is in your court, you must weed out the acceptable terms (those to which you need not respond) and those you wish to negotiate further, which are written on the counteroffer addenda after the initial contract has been presented.

Official Paperwork

It is possible to write up an offer to purchase a home in your own words and on your own paper. In fact, it is likely that many FSBO transactions take place without benefit of official forms or legal verbiage. There are, however, many caveats that could be issued in doing so. If this is the type of purchase you are considering, you may wish to write up your offer on a preprinted, fill-in-the-blanks type of purchase offer, available at many stationery shops or legal bookstores, or on a form that can be duplicated from one of the many do-it-yourself real estate books. Using these as a guide can help you make your offer without forgetting some important issues, such as the length of the escrow period (the lapse of time between the accepted offer and when the property records in your name), the type of loan you intend to obtain, and which items you want the seller to "throw in" on the deal. You may also be able to go to your local board of REALTORS® bookstore and buy a purchase offer. Always make sure you have allowed for addenda (additional fill-in-the-blank forms that become a part of the agreement) to the offer, upon which you can write additional terms and counteroffers.

Most real estate transactions within the United States take place with the aid of licensed real estate agents, whose job is to write up all the paperwork, interpret the verbiage to both you and the seller and act as a liaison between both parties. Because of the emotion involved in the purchase of a home, agents or brokers usually prefer that you not be present at the time the offer is presented. It is, however, your right to accompany your agent to the offer presentation if that is your wish.

Time Waits for No Offer

Time frames for responses should be written into every offer and counteroffer and everything should be presented in writing because verbal offers and representations are not considered binding in real estate transactions. If an offer or counteroffer's time frame lapses, the silence is usually interpreted as an offer going dead. Sellers can consider more than one offer at a time, sometimes pitting buyers against one another, resulting in a bidding war. It's easy to imagine that bidding wars are not enviable scenarios to buyers, and do not lead to getting the lowest possible price for the home. But take heart; sometimes a bidding buyer's terms, such as their time frame, loan worthiness, or lack of contingencies, look more attractive to the seller even if their offering price is lower. As they say, because everything is negotiable in real estate, it can be anybody's ball game.

Success Is in the Details

Be careful to put into writing any items you wish to have included in your purchase price, such the custom-cut area rug, the workbench in the garage, or the pool equipment. Items such as these could be perceived by homeowners as personal property (that which is not permanently affixed to the property), and may be packed up and taken away. Escrows have been known to go up in smoke when details like these are not tied down, with hurt feelings all around. It has been said that the emotions and stress of purchasing a home are second in impact only to a divorce or death of a loved one.

For that reason, be sure to have your detailed expectations put into writing within the purchase offer.

Once an offer has been accepted, get copies of everything that contains your endorsements and create a file for all your documents. Anything brought into question by buyer or seller during or after the escrow process will require hard-copy documentation to safeguard your claims and positions.

THE SALES CONTRACT

When you come to an agreement with the seller during the negotiation process, note all the terms in the sales contract. The formidable list of terms that follows may seem intimidating, but can serve as a guideline/checklist to protect the interests of both buyer and seller. The sales contract should include:

- Sales price
- Address and legal description of the property (including parcel number, if possible)
- Amount of your earnest money deposit, which reserves the house for you while the contract is prepared and executed and becomes part of your down payment monies at closing time. If your offer or terms include increasing this figure at certain milestones during the escrow process, such as the sale of your current home, final loan approval, or as more good-faith gestures toward the seller, it should be noted here as well.
- Amount of the intended down payment
- The terms of your mortgage, allowing you to withdraw from the sales contract if you cannot qualify for a mortgage or if interest rates rise so much that you can no longer afford to buy the home
- Terms of assuming the seller's mortgage, if applicable, which may allow you to obtain a lower rate than is currently available in the market
- Details of owner financing, if applicable, which should include repayment terms, interest rate, and down payment (The contract should not impose a prepayment penalty.)
- Closing details, such as when and where the closing will take place
- The date of occupancy, so that it is clear when you can move into your new home
- Type of deed required to be transferred from the seller to the buyer at closing
- Personal property and fixtures included with the house, such as appliances, carpeting, draperies, and lighting fixtures (The contract can define something as a fixture or as personal property, which thus establishes what stays with the property and what does not.)
- Inspections the seller agrees to permit and the repairs they intend to make before escrow closes, as well as which party pays for each (This

list should also include any required inspections by the city or county to ensure that the building has no code violations and has a valid certificate of occupancy.)

- Explanation of easement rights, which give someone else—such as a utility—the legal right to use your land
- The disclosure of any defects or material facts known by the seller or seller's agent that could adversely affect the value or future value of the home
- Amount of the real estate broker's fee, if any, and who will pay it (usually the seller, but this should be spelled out in the contract)
- Account where your earnest money and down payment will be kept, usually in escrow in a special bank account (Another clause should explain the conditions under which you can receive a refund.)
- Proration of home ownership costs specifying how property taxes, utility bills, and rent from tenants will be split during the period between the signing of the contract and the time you take possession of the home
- Provisions about title insurance specifying which title insurance company will issue a policy (Title insurance protects the buyer in case someone later challenges the seller's right to sell the property in the first place. If the title is unclear (called a *cloud on title*), the home cannot be sold easily. The contract should also specify who must pay for the title search—usually the seller, although in some areas of the country it is the buyer.)
- Warranty against liens stating that all renovation or repair bills and taxes have been paid (You don't want to take possession and then have to deal with a contractor trying to collect an unpaid bill dated several months or years ago.)
- Financing arrangements specifying that you will apply for a mortgage loan. The entire sale will usually be contingent on your obtaining financing. There should be a clause in the contract stating that if you can't get a mortgage, the contract is void. If the seller provides financing, its terms should be included in the sales contract. The seller has the right to run a credit check on you to ensure that you are creditworthy.
- The date by which you agree to provide formal loan approval to the seller
- An accompanying copy of the codes, conditions, and restrictions of the neighborhood, and the homeowners association budgets and by-laws, if they apply

As you can see by the volume of detail provided above, you may want to make sure all of these provisions are handled correctly by having an experienced real estate professional assist you or fully represent you in the sales contract process.

CLOSING THE SALE

The last step in buying your dream home is the closing or settlement, where the many players involved in the transaction come together and checks for thousands of dollars are distributed. You should enter the final leg of this house-buying marathon knowing the players that will be present, what legal documents you must bring, and how much money you must hand over to finish the deal.

The Final Performance

Depending on the part of the country in which your purchase is taking place, the cast of characters involved in a closing can include the buyer, the seller, real estate attorneys for both parties (mostly in the eastern United States), the buyer's mortgage loan consultant, the escrow agent, a representative of the escrow/title insurance company, and the real estate brokers for both parties. Customs for who attends and where the final paperwork is signed varies greatly by area. In California, for instance, sellers need not attend, having signed their grant deeds ahead of time by mail. In some states, attorneys are used for the formal paperwork and in others, only escrow officers are needed to explain things and point to where you are about to place what seems like hundreds of initials and signatures. This process is now also being streamlined by use of the Internet, making paperless closings possible and electronic signatures a reality. Cyber-closings have already taken place with entities such as CloseYourDeal.com. More information about these types of closings can be found on titleweb.com.

The entire settlement procedure is governed by a federal law called the Real Estate Settlement Procedures Act (RESPA) that helps you anticipate the costs of closing. Escrow services often arrange the details of a closing and, if you use such a service, you should shop around to get the best price on a closing cost package. Your real estate agent may have some suggestions.

Homebuilders, because they deal in volume, will usually have arranged bulk fee discounts for themselves as well as the buyers of their homes, so costs are generally lower than using separate escrow and title companies of your choice.

The following list names the most common closing costs:

- First mortgage payment
- Mortgage application fees (if any)
- Loan origination fees (fees the bank charges to process your loan)

- Points or prepaid interest charged by the lender (One point equals 1 percent of the loan amount. You may have to pay between 0 and 3 points, depending on what you have negotiated.)
- Loan assumption fee (if you are assuming the seller's mortgage)
- Mortgage insurance premiums (This insurance covers the lender's risk if the buyer fails to make loan payments.)
- Credit report fees
- Survey, inspection, and appraisal fees
- Recording deed fee
- Homeowners insurance premiums for the first year
- Escrow account reserves that the lender might require to cover insurance or property taxes over the coming year
- Property tax payments for the first year (prorated to the closing date)
- Legal fees for your lawyer and the bank's attorney
- Settlement (escrow) company fees
- Title search fees and title insurance premiums (usually paid by the seller)
- Down payment (which should include the earnest money you have already applied with your original offer)

Depending on the price of your home and the price you get for all these items, your closing costs may amount to between 2 percent and 4 percent of the cost of your home. Good faith figures are *estimates only,* so cushion your available funds to allow for some shortfalls. The figures can fluctuate according to the time of month you close, prorating many of the costs differently on the final paperwork you are presented. Any figure that looks significantly different than your original good faith estimate can be questioned at the time of signing.

If you purchased a new home and the builder has promised to pay all or part of your closing costs or design center upgrades, any incentive credits will be applied at closing, effectively lessening the amount of your funds to close.

RESOURCES

Books

All about Escrow and Real Estate Closings: Or How to Buy the Brooklyn Bridge and Have the Last Laugh, by Sandy Gadow and Dave Patton (Escrow Publishing Company, P.O. Box 2165, Palm Beach, FL 33480; 561-659-1474; www.escrowhelp .com). Leads the reader through the escrow and closing process, from opening the escrow to the closing statements.

Bob Vila's Guide to Buying Your Dream House, by Bob Vila (Time Warner, 3 Center Plaza, Boston, MA 02108; 800-343-9204). A practical guide to inspecting and buying a high-quality house from the man made famous by his TV renovation projects.

Buy Your First Home, by Robert Irwin (Dearborn Trade, Chicago, IL; 312-836-4400; 800-245-2665; www.dearborntrade.com). Will help first-time homebuyers navigate the homebuying process, from selecting a property to closing.

Buyer Beware: Insider Secrets You Need to Know before Buying Your Home— From Choosing an Agent to Closing the Deal, by Carla Cross (Dearborn Trade, Chicago, IL; 312-836-4400; 800-245-2665; www.dearborntrade.com). Explains how best to choose and screen an agent, why open houses are a waste of time for buyers and sellers, and advises on the right and wrong ways to negotiate a discount of an agent's commission.

Buying a Home When You're Single, by Donna G. Albrecht (John Wiley & Sons, 1 Wiley Drive, Somerset, NJ 08875; 212-850-6000; 800-225-5945; www.wiley .com). A one-stop how-to on homebuying for the unmarried.

Buying More House for Less Money, by Ceil R. Lohmar (McGraw-Hill, P.O. Box 543, Blacklick, OH 43004; 800-634-3961; www.mcgraw-hill.com). Techniques for house hunting and bargaining to get the best value for your housing dollar.

If You're Clueless about Buying a Home and Want to Know More, by David W. Myers (Dearborn Trade, Chicago, IL; 312-836-4400; 800-245-2665; www .dearborntrade.com). Full of tips to avoid hidden costs of home ownership, using Internet resources to learn about mortgages and the art of negotiation.

The Common-Sense Mortgage: How to Cut the Cost of Home Ownership by $50,000 or More, by Peter G. Miller (Contemporary Books, 4255 W. Touhy Avenue, Lincolnwood, IL 60712-1975; 800-621-1918; www.contemporarybooks.com). Shows how the lending system works, reviews dozens of individual loan programs, and raises questions for consumers to ask. Includes new information on loans for first-time buyers, and the pros and cons of finding loans on the Internet. Has lots of tables and examples.

The Common-Sense Mortgage: How to Cut the Cost of Home Ownership by $100,000 or More, by Peter G. Miller (Contemporary Books, 4255 W. Touhy Avenue, Lincolnwood, IL 60712-1975; 800-621-1918; www.contemporarybooks .com). Practical advice about using computerized mortgage loan shopping services, refinancing, and the different kinds of mortgages.

Dreams to Beams: A Guide to Building the Home You've Always Wanted, by Jane Moss Snow (National Association of Home Builders and nahb.com, 15th and M Streets, NW, Washington, D.C. 20005; 800-368-5242. www.builderbooks.com). Leads you through custom home design, construction, and remodeling processes. Features planning and design checklists, financial planning worksheets, and construction timetable, and gives you tips on cutting costs.

Essentials of Real Estate Finance, by David Sirota (Dearborn Trade, Chicago, IL; 312-836-4400; 800-245-2665; www.dearborntrade.com). Comprehensive reference for consumers and real estate practitioners on qualifying for and selecting the right loan for a home or investment property. Workbook format and questions increase its usefulness as a resource and self-study guide.

Finding and Buying Your Place in the Country, by Les and Carol Scher (Dearborn Trade, Chicago, IL; 312-836-4400; 800-245-2665; www.dearborntrade.com). Explains what the reader needs to know about due diligence on rural land being considered, contracts, negotiations, financing, etc.

The Frugal Homeowner's Guide to Buying, Selling, and Improving Your Home, by Julie Garton-Good (Dearborn Trade, Chicago, IL; 312-836-4400; 800-245-2665; www.dearborntrade.com). Advice on home ownership, mortgages, recouping remodeling costs, all in Q & A format.

Home Buyer's Checklist, by Richard M. Scutella and D. Heberle (McGraw-Hill, P.O. Box 543, Blacklick, OH 43004; 800-634-3961; www.mcgraw-hill.com). Provides helpful hints on buying a house.

The Home Buyer's Inspection Guide, by Warren Boroson (John Wiley & Sons, 1 Wiley Drive, Somerset, NJ 08875; 212-850-6000; 800-225-5945; www.wiley .com). Explains how to find and work with a home inspector and what to look for in a home.

The Homebuyer's Kit, by Edith Lank and Dena Amoruso (Dearborn Trade, Chicago, IL; 312-836-4400; 800-245-2665; www.dearborntrade.com). Furnishes would-be homebuyers with everything they need to know about buying a home, including using the resources on the Internet.

Home Buying for Dummies, by Eric Tyson and Ray Brown (IDG Books, 919 E. Hillsdale Boulevard Suite 400, Foster City, CA 94404; 650-653-7000; 800-434-3422; www.idg.com, www.dummies.com). Shows readers how buying a home fits into their financial picture, from saving for the down payment to selecting the best loan and figuring the after-tax cost of ownership.

The Home Inspection Troubleshooter, by Robert Irwin (Dearborn Trade, Chicago, IL; 312-836-4400; 800-245-2665; www.dearborntrade.com). Provides advice on how to hire and work with a home inspector or do some of the work yourself, from conducting a full-house investigation to evaluating various home systems.

Homesurfing.net, by Blanche Evans (Dearborn Trade, Chicago, IL; 312-836-4400; 800-245-2665; www.dearborntrade.com). Blends real estate information with the latest online sites and trends.

How to Buy the Home You Want, for the Best Price, in Any Market, by Terry Eilers (Hyperion, 77 W. 66th, 11th Floor, New York, NY 10023; 212-456-0100; www .hyperionbooks.go.com). Helps readers find their dream home as effectively and inexpensively as possible; includes tips on down payments and mortgages, checklists, and sample forms.

How to Buy Your Home . . . and Do It Right, by Sue Beck (Dearborn Trade, Chicago, IL; 312-836-4400; 800-245-2665; www.dearborntrade.com). Guidance on home styles, money and loans, house hunting, and contracts.

How to Buy Your Own Home in 90 Days: A 10-Step Plan for Finding and Buying a House in Today's Market, by Marc Stephen Garrison (Main Street Books by Doubleday, Bantam Doubleday Dell Publishing Group, Inc., 666 Fifth Avenue, New York, N.Y. 10103; www.doubleday.com). Step by step, the author uses a workbook-style format to take prospective homebuyers through the buying process.

How to Find Hidden Real Estate Bargains, by Robert Irwin (McGraw-Hill, PO Box 543, Blacklick, OH 43004; 800-634-3961; www.mcgraw-hill.com). Explains the process of purchasing attractively priced real estate from distressed sellers and foreclosures, among other techniques.

How to Get the Best Home Loan, by W. Frazier Bell (John Wiley & Sons, 1 Wiley Drive, Somerset, NJ 08875; 212-850-6000; www.wiley.com). Describes different types of home loans and how to choose the best one for you.

How to Negotiate Real Estate Contracts: For Buyers and Sellers: With Forms, by Mark Warda (Sourcebooks, Inc., PO Box 4410, Naperville, IL 60567; 630-961-3900; 800-432-7444; www.sourcebooks.com). Explains the pros and cons of each clause in the real estate contract. Lets you choose how you want to set up your own contract.

How to Save Thousands of Dollars on Your Home Mortgage, by Randy Johnson (John Wiley & Sons, 1 Wiley Drive, Somerset, NJ 08875; 212-850-6000; 800-225-5945; www.wiley.com). Describes all the different types of mortgages available to homeowners. Explains the terminology and the forms involved and how lenders make their profits.

Manufactured Houses: Finding and Buying Your Dream Home for Less, by Art Watkins (Dearborn Trade, Chicago, IL; 312-836-4400; 800-245-2665; www .dearborntrade.com). Provides a nontechnical overview of manufactured houses available and discusses their advantages. Photographs illustrate the range and styles of houses available.

The Smart Money Guide to Bargain Homes: How to Find and Buy Foreclosures, by James I. Wiedemer (Dearborn Trade, Chicago, IL; 312-836-4400; 800-245-2665; www.dearborntrade.com). A complete guide to finding quality homes in foreclosure with banks and government agencies. Describes how to evaluate foreclosed properties, obtain financing, and prepare the paperwork required by government agencies.

Starting Out: The Complete Home Buyer's Guide, by Dian Davis Hymer (Chronicle Books; 800-722-6657; www.chroniclebooks.com). Helps people find the perfect homes to fit their needs and budgets. There are charts, checklists, and sample contracts to help in the homebuying process.

Tips and Traps When Buying a Home, by Robert Irwin (McGraw-Hill, P.O. Box 543, Blacklick, OH 43004; 800-634-3961; www.mcgraw-hill.com). Reveals how to get a good deal on a home. Discusses how to inspect the home and negotiate for the best price.

Tips and Traps When Mortgage Hunting, by Robert Irwin (McGraw-Hill, P.O. Box 543, Blacklick, OH 43004; 800-634-3961; www.mcgraw-hill.com). Explains the pros and cons of different kinds of mortgages and helps you determine which is best for you.

The Unofficial Guide to Buying a Home, by Alan Perlis (IDG Books, 919 E. Hillsdale Boulevard, Suite 400, Foster City, CA 94404; 650-653-7000; 800-434-3422; www.idg.com, www.dummies.com). Provides guidance on such topics as how much home you can afford, how to find a real estate agent, where you should buy, what type of mortgage you should apply for, and what to know about all those fees.

The Well Built House, by Jim Locke (Houghton Mifflin Co., 222 Berkeley Street, Boston, MA 02116; 617-351-5000; www.hmco.com). The process of home building is explained from concept to finished product in terms a novice will be able to understand.

Your New House: The Alert Consumer's Guide to Buying and Building a Quality Home, by Alan Fields and Denise Fields (Windsor Peak Press, 436 Pine Street, Boulder, CO 80302; 800-888-0385; www.windsorpeak.com). Provides consumers with advice on how to research the best deals, save on a mortgage, and use the Internet as a valuable tool.

Web Sites

America's HomeNet. Links to databases of home listings in most areas of the country. Also includes data about local schools, businesses, and lenders. <netprop .com>

Cyberhomes. Listings of homes for sale over the Internet, including pictures, the listing agent's name and phone number, and e-mail addresses. <www.cyberhomes .com>

DoItYourself.com. This site provides a great deal of information about home building, home repairs, gardening, tools, codes, and where to get supplies with links to various commercial and retail sites. <www.doityourself.com>

eRealty.com. Online real estate brokerage. <www.erealty.com>

HomeAdvisor.com. A comprehensive all-purpose MSN (Microsoft Network) site with home listings, mortgages, insurance, and other tools. <www.homeadvisor.com>

Homebid.com. Lets a prospective homebuyer make an offer with contingencies followed by the homeowner's counteroffer. Gives agents and their clients the power to accomplish key steps of the homebuying and selling process via the Internet. <www.homebid.com>

HomeFair.com. If you are looking for a new home, this site will help with reports on cities, schools, crime, and home prices in the area in which you are interested. Offers calculators to help you calculate a mortgage payment and determine whether to rent or buy. Addresses temporary housing and offers comparisons of telephone, Internet, cable, and satellite services. <www.homefair.com>

Homeinspections-usa.com. Nationwide directory of home inspectors listed by state. <www.homeinspections-usa.com>

Homeseekers.com. This site offers a database of homes and other properties for sale throughout the country. Includes MLS listings in every state. <www.homeseekers .com>

Homestore.com. This is an all-purpose site with home listings, mortgages, insurance, and other tools. <www.homestore.com>

iNest.com. Online broker with co-op agreements with many homebuilders throughout the United States, if you are not already working with a broker. Offers you a cash-back rebate by printing up one of their coupons online and presenting the coupon upon your first visit to a participating builder's homes. May also be able to contact nonsubscribing builders for a similar rebate. <www.iNest.com>

Inspectamerica.com. Home inspection supersite offers free inspection checklists. <www.inspectamerica.com>

Kaktus.com. This site offers free real estate legal forms, a legal term glossary, links to brokers and agents, a loan amortization table, and calculators. <www.kaktus.com>

National Association of Homebuilders. Offers a great deal of statistical information about home building nationwide and includes a section on remodeling, with information and advice for the consumer. <www.nahb.com>

Owners.com. This site allows owners to display their homes without a real estate agent, using virtual 360-degree panoramic photos, descriptions, and maps, and allows buyers to peruse the site looking for a home. The site includes lots of help with online seller and buyer handbooks, newspaper advertising, insurance quotes, and, if you decide to use an agent, a selection of agents. <www.owners.com>

PestWeb.com. Information on pest control. <www.pestweb.com>

Real Estate ABC.com. Lists the 100 most-visited real estate Web sites. It also provides general information in its real estate and mortgage reading rooms, plus payment calculators. <www.realestate.com>

Realtor.com. National Association of REALTORS® site with comprehensive homebuying, selling, moving, and borrowing information. Includes sections on apartments, neighborhoods, insurance, home improvement, decorating, lawn and garden, and other home-related subjects. <www.realtor.com>

Realty.com. Offers advice on buying and selling, with home listings. <www .realty.com>

CHAPTER 4

Choosing the
Best Mortgage

The entire process of uncovering the appropriate loan program for your needs and qualifying for a mortgage is crucial to making the most of your real estate dollar. You must pay off this debt for years; therefore, to find the best possible deal, you should understand the various sources and types of loans available.

LOAN SOURCES

The first step in shopping for a mortgage is to identify loan sources. The following are the most likely lenders:

- *Savings and loans* (S&Ls) are the largest traditional lender to the home mortgage market. Despite the thrift crisis and subsequent bailout in the late 1980s and early 1990s, the S&Ls that survived are strongly committed to originating mortgages. They have great expertise in this area and frequently offer the lowest rates and some of the most generous qualifying terms.
- *Savings banks,* largely the same as S&Ls, are found mostly on the East Coast and specialize in mortgage lending.
- In recent years, *commercial banks* have been aggressively pursuing the S&Ls' bread-and-butter business of making mortgage loans. They may offer the best deal around, particularly if you combine your mortgage with your checking, savings, and investment accounts at the bank.

- Members of *credit unions* may be able to get the best mortgage terms from this nonprofit organization designed to serve its participants.
- *Mortgage bankers* borrow money from banks or investors, make mortgage loans, and resell the loans to investors at a profit. They may be able to tap into mortgage pools created by insurance companies, pension funds, and other institutional lenders you would not normally have access to on your own. Frequently, mortgage bankers will collect both your monthly payments and a fee from the lender for providing this service. You can find a mortgage banker through a local real estate agent, the Yellow Pages, or the Mortgage Bankers Association of America (1919 Pennsylvania Avenue, NW, Washington, DC 20006; 202-557-2700; www.mbaa.org).
- *Mortgage brokers* are capable of finding the most competitive rates for homebuyers for a fee paid by the lender. They get these good deals because they bring in many loans to a particular lender and therefore can obtain better terms than you, individually, could from the same lender. In addition to the loan fee, you normally must pay the mortgage broker an application fee. Generally, mortgage brokers do not lend any of their own money. You can locate a broker through a local real estate agent, the Yellow Pages, or the National Association of Mortgage Brokers (8201 Greensboro Drive, Suite 300, McLean, VA 22102; 703-610-9009; www.namb.org).
- Sellers may offer the best financing option if you are not able to qualify with another lender and the seller is desperate to move. The amount of *seller financing* rises sharply when interest rates at traditional lenders shoot up.
- Homebuilders frequently have their own (or in-house) lending operations for their homebuyers. They are generally owned by the same entity that owns the builder itself. The *in-house lender* (usually a mortgage banking operation) can be convenient and competitive as well, because they are accountable first and foremost to their builder-client. They are familiar with how the builder does business, already possess important paperwork required by the seller in a real estate transaction, and have performed "master" appraisals for the purposes of FHA or VA loans, just to make it easier for new homebuyers. Frequently, the homebuilder will offer an *incentive* (or monetary inducement, usually in the form of a credit or price reduction) to buy a home using the in-house lender. Some builders permit you to use this incentive towards nonrecurring closing costs or as a credit for your design center (upgrade) choices for your new home. The choice to take the builder up on this arrangement is still your decision, however, and a

careful analysis of what these lenders offer over the term of your loan should be balanced with the amount of the incentive being offered.

In addition to traditional home loans, most of these lenders will make loans guaranteed by the FHA or VA. These agencies set certain standards for the kinds and sizes of loans and borrower qualifications for their guarantees. For example, many VA loans require little or no down payment for qualified veterans. Many states also sponsor housing finance agencies that offer below-market mortgages for low-to-moderate-income homebuyers. These agencies usually raise the money for such loans by issuing municipal bonds backed by the home loans.

When you shop for a mortgage, compare not only the interest rate but also the closing costs (points and other fees) which can add to your total cost significantly. A few services such as the Home Buyer's Mortgage Kit run by HSH Associates (1200 Route 23N, Butler, NJ 07405; 800-873-2837; www .hsh.com) can, for a small fee, give you a current comparison of rates and terms for lenders in your area. Figure 4.1 charts both fixed and variable mortgage rates for the past ten years.

In today's mortgage market, many lenders do not retain the loans they make. They sell the loans in the multibillion-dollar *secondary market* to such quasi-governmental agencies as Ginnie Mae (Government National Mortgage Association), Fannie Mae (Federal National Mortgage Association), and Freddie Mac (Federal Home Loan Mortgage Corporation). Ginnie, Fannie, and Freddie then package these loans, guarantee them against homeowner default, and sell them as mortgage-backed securities. This secondary market continually brings in new dollars to the mortgage market for lending at the local level. So even though you continue to send your mortgage payments to the lender that financed your loan, your payments may very well be passed on to holders of mortgage-backed securities across the country.

KINDS OF MORTGAGES

Most lenders offer several types of mortgages. The most common options follow.

Fixed Rate

The traditional 30-year fixed-rate mortgage is still the industry standard because it offers long-term predictability. Your total payments are spread over so many years that your monthly payments are lower than they would be on a shorter-term loan. In the long run, however, you will pay thousands of dollars more in interest on a 30-year loan than on a less extended obliga-

Figure 4.1 Mortgage Rates—10 Year History

| 2.25 Yrs. | 2.75 Yrs. | ? |

30 Yr. Fixed

12/2001

1 Yr. Adjustable

1991 1992 1993 1994 1995 1996 1997 1998 1999 2000 2001

* Average conventional commitment
rate - WITH Closing Costs

Source: ArcLoan.com

tion. This interest is usually tax deductible, though, which lowers your actual after-tax cost of paying it.

Lately, 15-year loans have become particularly popular. They usually offer slightly lower interest rates than 30-year loans. If you want to prepay your mortgage on a faster schedule but not become tied to the higher payment of a 15-year program, contact your lender to arrange a prepayment schedule, and make sure that you will not be assessed any prepayment penalties. Because you pay off the loan balance faster, a smaller portion of your monthly payment goes for interest. This means that you will deduct less on your tax return but own your home sooner than you would with a 30-year loan. Some borrowers also choose to make one extra mortgage payment per year or tack on some extra funds to their payments when they can afford it in order to achieve a similar result. Making biweekly payments on a 30-year loan rivals making monthly payments on a 15-year mortgage.

In the early years of either a 30-year or a 15-year fixed-rate loan, you pay mostly interest. By the end of the loan, you pay almost all principal. Therefore, over time, ownership in your home gradually shifts from the lender to you.

Adjustable Rate

Instead of offering an interest rate fixed for the life of the loan, an adjustable-rate mortgage (ARM) features an interest rate that moves up and down with prevailing rates. Early in the ARM's term, its rate will almost always be less than that on a fixed-rate loan. Because the borrower agrees to risk fluctuating rates over the life of the loan, he or she is rewarded with a low initial rate.

ARMs come in many varieties. Some adjust their rates every year, while others alter them every three or five years. Loan rates are tied to a number of interest rate indexes. A bank will charge a margin, or spread, over the underlying index of up to two or four percentage points. The most popular loan rates include the national average mortgage rate as calculated by the Federal Home Loan Bank (FHLB) Board, U.S. Treasury bill rates, one-year constant maturity Treasury rates, the prime lending rate, and the 11th District cost of funds index rate (known as a COFI loan, this is the average cost that S&Ls must pay depositors for their money). Another rate used is the London Inter-Bank Offered Rate (LIBOR). Specifically, the LIBOR is the rate that international banks based in Europe charge each other for overnight funds. You can learn these rates from most lenders, from publications like *The Wall Street Journal* or from Web sites such as <www.bankrate.com>.

In general, the shorter the term of index to which your ARM is tied, the more volatile your payments can become. That's good if interest rates fall but can cause trouble if interest rates rise. Rates on T-bills and one-year Treasuries and the prime rate will fluctuate much more than the cost of funds rate or the national average mortgage rate. If you hesitate to take the risk of short-term rates, consider an ARM tied to the less volatile indexes.

Most ARMs offer two built-in *caps* to protect you from enormous increases in monthly payments. A *periodic rate cap* limits how much your payment can rise at any one time. For example, your loan agreement might stipulate that your rate cannot go up more than two percentage points a year. An *aggregate,* or a *lifetime,* cap limits how much the rate can rise over the life of the loan. The same loan that limits increases to 2 percent a year may also impose a 6 percent cap for the duration of the loan. Such caps can also apply to rate decreases. Therefore, the example loan may not fall more than two percentage points in one year or six points during its lifetime.

In addition to rate caps, many ARMs feature *payment caps,* which limit the amount your payment can rise over the life of the loan. Therefore, if the underlying index shoots up, your payment would increase only to the limit of the payment cap. Even though you do not pay the difference now, however, you owe it to the lender over the long term. When your mortgage payment does not cover the full interest and principal due, this is called *negative amortization.* The lender will apply more, and possibly all, of your payment to interest, which means that your home equity will grow more slowly or, in the extreme case, will actually shrink. To perform your own fixed rate vs. adjustable rate comparison, see Figure 4.2 or visit <partners.financenter.com>.

Automatic Rate Cut (ARC)

A newer type of loan program designed to help you take advantage of a drop in interest rates is the ARC loan. The interest rate and corresponding payment starts off ¼% to ⅜% higher than current fixed mortgage rates, but every time mortgage rates fall by a quarter point or more, you are allowed to adjust your rate downward with no closing costs, points, or fees. For FHA and VA borrowers, only your timely payment history is scrutinized each time your rate is lowered; for conventional loan borrowers, a short credit check, along with payment history and verification of income is required. With this system, your loan is "managed" internally. Although you must wait a minimum of 120 days for the first refinance opportunity, you may lock your rate before that time, and subsequent adjustments can occur as frequently as every 120 days. The program can be applied to fixed-rate or short-term fixed-rate programs. For more information about ARC loans, call 888-ARC-LOAN (272-5626) or log on to <www.arcloan.com>. See Figure 4.3.

Convertible

A convertible mortgage is an ARM that can be changed to a fixed-rate mortgage at a specified rate. You may have one chance or several to make the switch. The conversion feature gives you the opportunity to start with a low adjustable rate, then lock into a low fixed rate for a long time.

Balloon

A balloon mortgage requires a series of equal payments, then a large payment (balloon) at the loan's termination. The mortgage term may be from three to ten years. These can be called a "30 Due in 5" or a "30 Due in 7," indicating the length of years the rate remained fixed at the beginning of the loan. Usually, balloon mortgages are offered at the going fixed or slightly lower-than-fixed rates, though some adjustable-rate balloons are also available. Qualifying guidelines for these short-term fixed-rate loans may be more relaxed than for 30-year fixed rates, another reason they may be recommended in certain cases. The payments on a balloon mortgage generally

Figure 4.2   Fixed versus Adjustable Rate Mortgage Worksheet

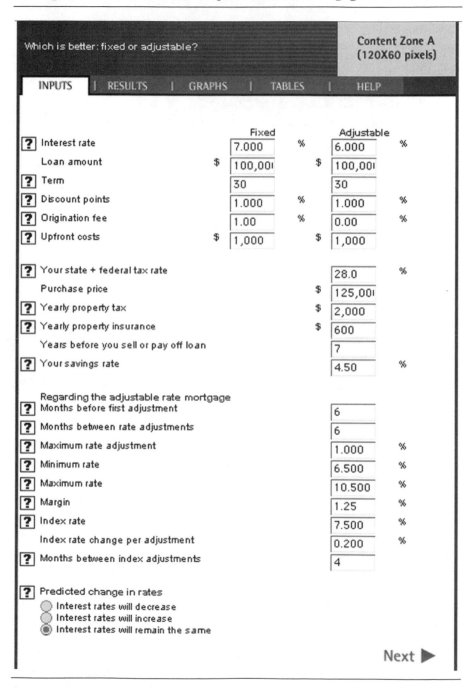

Figure 4.2   Fixed versus Adjustable Rate Mortgage Worksheet (continued)

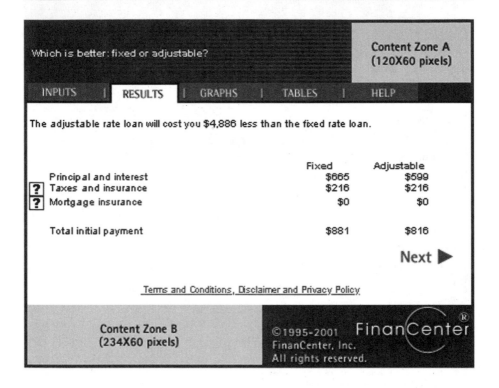

Screen capture from http://partners.financenter.com/financenter/calculate/us-eng/home04.fcs

cover interest only, so you do not build equity in the home over time. If you take on such a loan, you should know what you will do when the balloon arrives. Most homeowners refinance the payment. Some lenders will promise to refinance the loan when the balloon comes due, though they will not lock in an interest rate in advance. In many cases, home sellers offer buyers balloon mortgage options to help the deals go through.

Interest-Only Mortgage

Becoming increasingly popular in recent years are interest-only loans, where borrowers pay interest, but no principal on a loan during its early years, minimizing their monthly payments while recovering from down payment shock when buying a home. These types of loans have their risk factors, however. Because no equity is built up during the first 5 to 15 years, borrowers can get stuck owing more than their homes are worth if home

Figure 4.3   ArcLoan.com Web Site

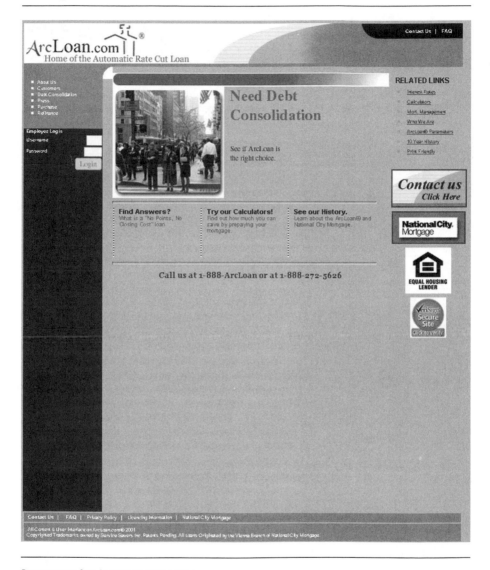

Screen capture from http://www.arcloan.com/

prices drop. They also may experience uncomfortable rate adjustments for at least a portion of the life of the loan if rates begin to rise rapidly. The beauty of this type of loan, however, may be that homebuyers can buy more house and qualify more easily than with other types of programs, often permitting up to a 42 percent debt-to-income ratio.

Figure 4.3   ArcLoan.com Web Site (continued)

Contact Us |
FAQ

ArcLoan.com
Home of the Automatic Rate Cut Loan

- About Us
- Customers
- Debt Consolidation
- Press
- Purchase
- Refinance

Employee Login
Username
Password
[Login]

ARCLOAN® PARAMETERS

Principles of a new innovative approach to your home financing.

ArcLoan® customers enjoy the unique benefits of Mortgage Management.

An ArcLoan® customer may inquirer at anytime as to the ArcLoan® adjustment rate for their mortgage by calling 1-888-ArcLoan. An ArcLoan® customer may lock-in an interest rate prior to the 120 days, however the customer must wait until 120 days have elapsed since their last ArcLoan loan before going to settlement on the new interest rate.

The ArcLoan® adjustment rate is based on current market rates for fixed rate mortgages and trend with the 60 - day FNMA index. The adjustment rate takes into account loan amount, and lender credit sufficient enough to allow all, or majority of, the closing costs associated with a streamlined portfolio refinance to be paid by the lender. These costs are not added onto the existing loan.

Now you can obtain a fixed rate mortgage that can Never Go Up, but can Go Down!

HERE ARE THE DETAILS

The ArcLoan® is available in all 50 states for conforming, non-conforming, VA and FHA Loans.

The ArcLoan® works the same as a standard fixed rate mortgage with the following added benefits:

- Save $$ up front with ArcLoan® Savings! Upon entry to the ArcLoan® program you will be shown options that allow you a closing cost credit. This credit may be sufficient to cover ALL CLOSING COSTS in your state.
- Save more money **When Rates Drop!** An ArcLoan® customer may reduce their mortgage interest rate whenever the ArcLoan® reduction rate falls by at least 1/4% provided:
  - 120 days has elapsed since entry to the program, or the last rate cut.
  - You may not have any late payments (over 30 days) in the previous 12 months, or since entry, if less than 12 months since entry.
  - Some updated income and asset verification documentation may be required which may need to be approved by an underwriter. Ask your ArcLoan® representative about your **ArcLoan® Mortgage Management Program** reduction details.

RELATED LINKS
- Interest Rates
- Calculators
- Mort. Management
- Who We Are
- ArcLoan® Parameters
- 10 Year History
- Print Friendly

Contact us
Click Here

National City.
Mortgage

EQUAL HOUSING
LENDER

Screen capture from http://www.arcloan.com/browse.asp?altfunc=5

Figure 4.3   (continued)

ArcLoan.com
Home of the Automatic Rate Cut Loan

- **About Us**
- **Customers**
- **Debt Consolidation**
- **Press**
- **Purchase**
- **Refinance**

Employee Login

Username

Password

Login

MORTGAGE CALCULATORS

Purchase Calculator	**Refinance Calculator**
To determine: Break Even Points between options	**To determine:** Break Even Points between options
This calculator will show you how long it will take to recoup the difference in closing costs between two interest rates in a purchase scenario.	This calculator will show how long it will take to recoup the difference in closing costs between two interest rates in in a refinance scenerio.
Perform Calculation	**Perform Calculation**
Prepay Mortgage	**Monthly Savings**
To determine: How much you can save by prepaying your mortgage.	**To determine:** How much you can save monthly
What will you save if you prepay your mortgage? This calculator will give you that approximation.	How much can you actually save monthly? This calculator will give you that aproximation.
Perform Calculation	**Perform Calculation**

Screen capture from http://www.arcloan.com/browse.asp?altfunc=2

Growing equity

A growing equity mortgage (GEM), often known as a rapid payoff loan, offers a fixed rate and a changing monthly payment. Formally, the loan term is 30 years but, in fact, it may be paid off in 15 years or less because your payments reduce the outstanding principal quickly. Your payment amount is usually tied to some index, such as the Commerce Department's per capita income index. In this case, as income rises, your payments increase. You can also create your own GEM by sending in extra principal payments or by paying your mortgage biweekly instead of monthly. All of these methods of payment will help you build equity faster and pay off your mortgage sooner.

Shared Appreciation

If you are willing to surrender to your lender some of your home's appreciation potential, you may want to opt for a shared appreciation mortgage (SAM). With this loan, you pay a below-market interest rate on your mortgage and, in return, offer the lender between 30 percent and 50 percent of the increased value of your home when you sell it in a specified number of years. If that day comes and you do not want to sell, you must pay the lender its share of the property's appreciation. If you don't have the cash to do so, you might have to sell the property anyway. On the other hand, if the property has not appreciated or has, in fact, decreased in value, you will owe nothing. SAMs were much more popular in the 1970s and 1980s, when housing appreciation was more assured. They are far trickier in the 2000s for both lenders and borrowers because of the unsettled real estate market.

Buy-Down

If you buy a new home from a developer, it may offer a buy-down, or mortgage subsidy, to help you afford the property. For example, to help you qualify, the developer may contribute enough of its own incentives to cut the interest rate on your mortgage by two or three percentage points for the first three years of your loan. While this may help you obtain the mortgage, you may not be able to afford the payments when the subsidy lapses. If you count on a higher income in the future to help you meet those higher payments, you could be in trouble if your income does not rise sufficiently. When interest rates are enticingly low, however, a buy-down can be an attractive way to start out in home ownership. The first two or three years after you move into a new home is when you are most likely to have hole-in-your-pocket syndrome, while you install landscaping, buy new furniture, and decorate your home. Just be sure to plan for the regular, full-rate payment that will be occurring down the road when taking a builder or seller up on a buy-down. Any loan program can be bought down, but fixed-rate programs are the most commonly used buy-down programs.

Choosing the best mortgage for you is a matter of weighing the pros and cons of each. For example, you might treasure the security of a fixed-rate mortgage, particularly if you lock in a favorable rate for a long time. However, the higher interest rate attached to a fixed loan can be a significant price to pay for that sense of security.

On the other hand, you might be better off taking the risk of an ARM and investing the difference between an ARM payment and a fixed loan payment. If you put the money in a few top-performing stocks, bonds, or mutual funds, your financial picture might improve far more with the adjustable mortgage, even if interest rates rise over time. If you don't plan to stay in the property you buy for long, adjustable-rate programs can make sense as well. If you do end up staying, it may always be possible to refinance to a fixed rate.

The other types of loans discussed here—convertibles, balloons, ARCs, graduated payment loans, interest-only loans, growing equity mortgages, shared appreciation loans, and buy-downs—all have their place, depending on your situation. As with adjustable-rate and fixed-rate loans, weigh the disadvantages against the advantages of each. Figure 4.4 provides a quick summary of the pros and cons of various mortgage types compared to a 30-year fixed rate loan.

As you shop around for the best mortgage, use the worksheet in Figure 4.5 to compare all of the terms of the mortgages against each other so you can figure out what is best for your situation.

No-Down-Payment Mortgages

Several mortgage lenders will now finance 100 percent of your home's purchase price if you can put a certain amount of securities in escrow to act as your down payment. For example, Merrill Lynch's Mortgage 100 program (800-854-7154; www.ml.com) requires that you place 30 percent of your home's purchase price in escrow in securities. If you were buying a $100,000 house, you would have to place a bit more than $30,000 worth of CDs, stocks, bonds, or mutual funds in escrow to get full financing. Merrill also offers the Parent Power program, which allows parents to place their securities in escrow for a bit over 20 percent of the purchase price for their children's home purchase. Because the securities put in escrow do not have to be sold, you can avoid the capital gains tax that would normally be required if you sold securities to assemble a down payment.

Figure 4.4   Comparing Different Types of Mortgages to 30-Year Fixed Rate

| | Fixed-Rate Mortgages | | | | | | |
| | Level Payments | | | Graduated Payments | | | FHA/ |
	30-Year	15-Year	Balloons	GPMs	GEMs	ARMs	VA
Lower Rates	0	+1	+1	−1	+1	+2	+1
Easier Qualifying	0	−2	+1	+2	0	+2	+1
Fast Payoff	0	+2	−1	0	+2	0	0
Low Down Payment	0	0	0	−1	0	0	+2
Low Initial Monthly Payment	0	−2	0	+2	0	+2	0

Legend: −2 = even less favorable compared   0 = similar to 30-yr.
              to 30-yr. fixed-rate mortgage   +1 = more favorable
              −1 = unfavorable   +2 = much more favorable

Source: *The Mortgage Kit* by Thomas Steinmetz

PREPARING TO QUALIFY FOR A MORTGAGE LOAN

It's important to be prepared for what may be requested over the phone or in hard-copy form by your lender to qualify for a mortgage loan. The following items are the most common documents needed to confirm the information on your loan application. Because of the proliferation of automated (desktop) underwriting, not all of these documents will be required, but you should know where to get a copy of any of the items listed below. Your lender will give you an accurate list of the items required for your individual loan.

- Residence addresses for the past two years (landlord's contact information, if you have been a renter)
- Names and addresses of each employer for you and your spouse for the last two years
- Current pay stubs for the last 30 days
- Names, account numbers, and balances for all checking, savings, money market, 401(k), and investment accounts with copies of the two most recent statements (all pages)
- Addresses and loan information on all real estate owned
- Estimated value of all personal property (autos, furniture, etc.)

Figure 4.5   Loan Comparison Worksheet

	Loan Type		
	Conventional	**FHA**	**VA**
Sale price	$_____	_____	_____
Interest rate	$_____	_____	_____
Down payment	$_____	_____	_____
Total loan to be amortized	$_____	_____	_____

Estimated Loan Costs

MIP (unless FHA included above)	$_____	_____	_____
Loan origination fee	$_____	_____	_____
Assumption fee	$_____	_____	_____
Credit report	$_____	_____	_____
Appraisal fee	$_____	_____	_____
Recording fee	$_____	_____	_____
Title (ALTA) policy (use loan amount)	$_____	_____	_____
Attorney fee	$_____	_____	_____
Escrow closing fee	$_____	_____	_____
Interest proration	$_____	_____	_____
Tax proration	$_____	_____	_____
Fire and hazard insurance first year	$_____	_____	_____
Lender's application fee	$_____	_____	_____
Purchaser's buydown points	$_____	_____	_____
Long-term escrow set-up fee	$_____	_____	_____
Tax service fee	$_____	_____	_____
Misc., LID, city code, reserves	$_____	_____	_____
Home inspection fee	$_____	_____	_____
Total estimated closing costs	$_____	_____	_____

Reserves and Prorates

Property taxes (minimum two months)	$_____	_____	_____
Fire and hazard insurance (minimum two months)	$_____	_____	_____
Mortgage insurance	$_____	_____	_____
Total reserves and prorates	$_____	_____	_____
Total cash outlay	$_____	_____	_____

Estimated Monthly Payment

Principal and interest	$_____	_____	_____
Tax reserves	$_____	_____	_____
Insurance reserves	$_____	_____	_____
MIP insurance (unless FHA included above)	$_____	_____	_____
Total estimated monthly payment	$_____	_____	_____

The undersigned hereby acknowledges receipt of a copy of this estimation.

By _____ Signed _____ Date _____

- Tax W-2 forms for the last two years. Signed federal tax returns required if you are self-employed or if your commission/bonus income is over 25 percent of salary
- Confirming documentation of regular or upcoming income bonuses, if they are being used to justify total income for qualification
- Bankruptcy papers with discharge, if applicable (all pages)
- Divorce decree, if applicable (all pages)
- Gift letter (if part of your down payment is a gift from a relative or friend)
- For FHA loans, proof of Social Security numbers is required
- For VA loans, your Certificate of Eligibility and DD214s are required
- Money for your credit report and the appraisal of the property, if applicable
- Contact information for your insurance agent who handles your homeowners policy

Proof of a steady income, job stability, and down payment funds, along with a what is considered to be a passable credit score, (which is discussed in detail in the next section), are usually enough to get you a fairly quick answer from most lenders these days, who take loan applications over the telephone and input them directly into their computers. They then follow up with requests for any or all of the information listed above after sending you a copy of the preprinted loan application (which includes the information you supplied to them) for signatures. To get quick sense of how much of a mortgage you should be able to qualify for, fill out the worksheet in Figure 4.6.

Understanding Credit Scores

Before the use of credit scoring, credit evaluation was a slower, more inconsistent, and sometimes biased process, forcing lenders to interpret and evaluate pages of information on a consumer's credit history. They would examine if the individual made good on promises to pay accounts on time and also take note of how frequently he or she applied for credit.

Consumers should look at credit scores just like a college hopeful looks at his or her scores on an SAT. That test doesn't always reflect what you really know; it just records how well you take the test.

Designed to take an entire picture of your creditworthiness into account, credit scores are meant to represent a mere "snapshot" of your experience as a credit consumer. When compiling the information regarding your creditworthiness, lenders will study credit scores such as those provided by FICO® (Fair, Isaac & Company), who developed the software and provides it to the three major credit reporting companies—TransUnion (800-916-8800), Equifax

Figure 4.6 Quick Qualifying Worksheet

	Column A	Column B
Annual gross income:	$_____	
Divide by number of months:	+ 12	
Monthly gross income (Record it in both columns. Perform operations only on figures in the same vertical column.):	=_____	=_____
Lenders allow 28% of monthly gross income for housing expenses.		× .28
Maximum monthly housing expense allowance (Column B):		=_____
Lenders allow 36% of monthly gross income for long-term debt:	× .36	
Monthly expense allowance for long-term debt:	=_____	

Calculate your monthly long-term
obligations below:

Child support	$ _____	
Auto loan	+ _____	
Credit cards	+ _____	
Other	+ _____	
Other	+ _____	
Total long-term obligations	= _____	

	Column A	Column B
Subtract total from your monthly expense allowance:	– _____	
Total monthly housing expense allowance:	= _____	
Look at the last amounts in Column A and B above. Record the smaller amount.	$_____	
About 20% of the housing expense allowance is for taxes and insurance, leaving 80% for payment of mortgage (principal and interest):	× .80	
Allowance monthly principal and interest (PI) expense:	= _____	
Divide this amount by the appropriate monthly payment:	+ _____	
	= _____	
Multiply by 1,000:	× 1,000	
Affordable mortgage amount (what the lender will lend):	$_____	

(800-685-1111), and Experian (formerly TRW, 888-397-3742). All three agencies may have different information on your credit history, and all three have different names for FICO scores, such as BEACON®, EMPIRICA®, and the Experian/Fair, Isaac Risk Model. Scoring does not consider gender, race, nationality, or marital status; all are prohibited by the Equal Credit Opportunity Act. It also ignores your salary, occupation, title, employer, length of employment, location of your residence, interest rates on credit, child or family support, certain types of inquiries on your report, information not found in your credit report, and any information that is not proven to be predictive of your future credit performance. As your data changes over time, your credit score will change according to new information that affects its status.

A FICO score will evaluate five main categories of information:

1. Types of credit in use
2. Payment history
3. Amounts owed
4. Length of credit history
5. New credit

When examining the *types of credit in use,* which account for 10 percent of your FICO score, this part of your evaluation will consider if you have what is referred to as a "healthy" mix. Although credit cards, retail accounts, installment loans, finance company loans, and mortgage loans will all be considered, it is *not* necessary to have one of each, and it is definitely not considered more advantageous to open credit accounts that you don't intend to use. The number of accounts will also be evaluated. A determination of whether you have too many in any given category differs for each credit profile. (See Figure 4.7.)

Your *payment history* is your most telling track record and takes up 35 percent of your total FICO score. The first thing any lender will want to know is if you paid a credit account on time. It will also examine public record and collection items, bankruptcies, foreclosures, lawsuits, wage garnishments, liens, and judgements. Delinquent payments are evaluated by how late they were, how much was owed, how recently they occurred, and how many there were.

Another whopping 30 percent of your score is based on the *amounts owed,* or the outstanding debt you have. A low score in this category does not necessarily mean that you are instantly considered a high risk. However, it does indicate that you can become overextended if you owe a great deal of money. It will take into account the balances owed on credit cards (if not paid in full each month), the amount owed on different types of accounts, how many accounts have balances, how much of the available credit you are using, and how much of any original installment loan accounts is still owed.

Figure 4.7   Credit Bureau Report

WHAT'S IN YOUR CREDIT REPORT?
Although each credit reporting agency formats and
reports this information differently, all credit reports
contain basically the same categories of information.

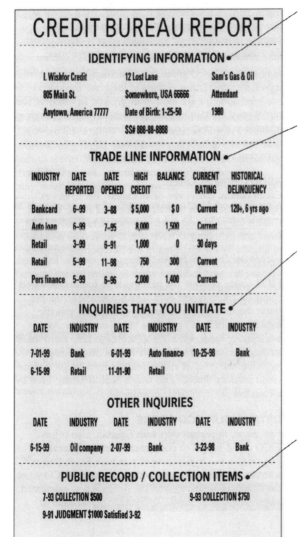

IDENTIFYING INFORMATION.
Your name, address, Social Security
number, date of birth and employment information are used to identify
you. These factors are not used in
credit bureau scoring. Updates to
this information come from
information you supply to lenders.

TRADE LINES. These are your credit
accounts. Lenders report on each
account you have established with
them. They report the type of account
(bankcard, auto loan, mortgage,
etc), the date you opened the
account, your credit limit or loan
amount, the account balance and
your payment history.

INQUIRIES. When you apply for a
loan, you authorize your lender to
ask for a copy of your credit report.
This is how inquiries appear on your
credit report. The inquiries section
contains a list of everyone who
accessed your credit report within
the last two years. The report you
see lists both "voluntary" inquiries,
spurred by your own requests for
credit, and "involuntary" inquires,
such as when lenders order your
report so as to make you a preapproved credit offer in the mail.

**PUBLIC RECORD AND COLLECTION
ITEMS.** Credit reporting agencies
also collect public record information
from state and county courts, and
information on overdue debt from
collection agencies. Public record
information includes bankruptcies,
foreclosures, suits, wage attachments,
liens and judgments.

Source: Fair, Isaac & Company

Figure 4.7   Credit Bureau Report (continued)

☹ **FALLACY:** Credit scoring infringes on my privacy.

☺ **FACT:** FICO scores evaluate your credit report alone, which lenders already use to make credit decisions. A score is simply a numeric summary of that information. In fact, lenders using scoring can often ask for *less* information about you. They may have fewer questions on the application form, for example.

Interpreting Your Score

When you or a lender receive your Fair, Isaac credit bureau risk score, up to four "score reason codes" are also delivered. These explain the top reasons why your score was not higher. If the lender rejects your request for credit, and your FICO score was part of the reason, these score reasons can help the lender tell you why your score wasn't higher.

These score reasons are more useful than the score itself in helping you determine whether your credit report might contain errors, and how you might improve your score over time. However, if you already have a high score (for example, in the mid-700s or higher) some of the reasons may not be very helpful, as they may be marginal factors related to the last three categories described previously (length of credit history, new credit and types of credit in use).

To see your own FICO score and reason codes with a detailed explanation on how you can improve the score over time, visit *www.myfico.com.*

COMMON SCORE REASONS

Here are the top 10 most frequently given score reasons. Note that the specific wording given by your lender may be different from this.

■ *Serious delinquency*

■ *Serious delinquency, and public record or collection filed*

■ *Derogatory public record or collection filed*

■ *Time since delinquency is too recent or unknown*

■ *Level of delinquency on accounts*

■ *Number of accounts with delinquency*

■ *Amount owed on accounts*

■ *Proportion of balances to credit limits on revolving accounts is too high*

■ *Length of time accounts have been established*

■ *Too many accounts with balances*

Figure 4.7   (continued)

Getting a Better Score

The next few pages give some tips for getting a better FICO score. It's important to note that raising your score is a bit like getting in shape: It takes time and there is no quick fix. In fact, quick-fix efforts can backfire. The best advice is to manage credit responsibly over time.

One general tip is to make sure the information in your credit report is correct. Check your credit report for accuracy at least 90 days before you plan any major purchases, such as applying for a mortgage. If you find errors, have them corrected by the lender and credit reporting agency. See page 16 for information on how to check your credit report.

For a more specific advice about your own FICO score, go to *www.myfico.com.*

What a FICO Score Considers

Listed on the next few pages are the five main categories of information that FICO scores evaluate, along with their general level of importance. Within these categories is a complete list of the information that goes into a FICO score. Please note that:

■ **A score takes into consideration all these categories of information, not just one or two.** No one piece of information or factor alone will determine your score.

■ **The importance of any factor depends on the overall information in your credit report.** For some people, a given factor may be more important than for someone else with a different credit history. In addition, as the information in your credit report changes, so does the importance of any factor in determining your score. Thus, it's impossible to say exactly how important any single factor is in determining your score—even the levels of importance shown here are for the general population, and will be different for different credit profiles. What's important is the *mix* of information, which varies from person to person, and for any one person over time.

■ **Your FICO score only looks at information in your credit report.** Lenders look at many things when making a credit decision, however, including your income, how long you have worked at your present job and the kind of credit you are requesting.

■ **Your score considers both positive and negative information in your credit report.** Late payments will lower your score, but establishing or re-establishing a good track record of making payments on time will raise your score.

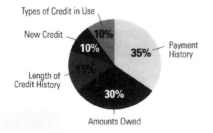

Types of Credit in Use
New Credit
10%
10%
35% Payment History
Length of Credit History
30%
Amounts Owed

How a Score Breaks Down

These percentages are based on the importance of the five categories for the general population. For particular groups—for example, people who have not been using credit long—the importance of these categories may be different.

Figure 4.7   Credit Bureau Report (continued)

MORE THAN ONE SCORE

In general, when people talk about "your score," they're talking about your current FICO score. However, there is no *one* score used by lenders to make decisions about you.

■ **Credit bureau scores are not the only scores used.** Many lenders use their own scores, which often will include the FICO score as well as other information about you. Some businesses will sell you credit scores that are not FICO scores and may not be used by any lenders at all. Such scores often include advice that may not apply to FICO scores and could actually hurt your credit standing with lenders.

■ **FICO scores are not the only credit bureau scores.** There are other credit bureau scores, although FICO scores are by far the most commonly used. Other credit bureau scores may evaluate your credit report differently than FICO scores, and in some cases a higher score may mean more risk, not less risk as with FICO scores.

■ **Your score may be different at each of the three main credit reporting agencies.** The FICO score from each credit reporting agency considers only the data in your credit report at that agency. If your current scores from the credit reporting agencies are different, it's probably because the information those agencies have on you differs. Today Equifax is the only credit reporting agency to make FICO scores available to consumers at *www.equifax.com* and at *www.myfico.com.*

■ **Your FICO score changes over time.** As your data changes at the credit reporting agency, so will any new score based on your credit report. So your FICO score from a month ago is probably not the same score a lender would get from the credit reporting agency today.

☹ **FALLACY:** Credit scoring is unfair to minorities.

☺ **FACT:** Scoring does not consider your gender, race, nationality or marital status. In fact, the Equal Credit Opportunity Act prohibits lenders from considering this type of information when issuing credit. Independent research has shown that credit scoring is not unfair to minorities or people with little credit history. Scoring has proven to be an accurate and consistent measure of repayment for all people who have some credit history. In other words, at a given score, non-minority and minority applicants are equally likely to pay as agreed.

How Do People Score?

Based on the general population's FICO scores.

The *length of your credit history,* which accounts for 15 percent, tells lenders how established you are in the credit game. In general, a longer credit history will increase your score, but other factors can come into play in this juggling act that can compensate for a short history. This category will consider the age of your oldest accounts and an average age of all the rest, it will look at each account individually, and it will evaluate how long ago your accounts were last used.

New credit indicates how much new debt you are taking on, which will add up to another 10 percent of your score. People tend to have more credit today than ever before, using it for Internet purchases, TV shopping channel goodies, and department store offers of discounts just to apply for credit. Be careful here. To a credit scoring agency, opening several accounts over a short period of time represents greater risk, especially for those who do not have a long credit history. This also applies to mere credit applications, called *inquiries* on your profile. They do, however, try to distinguish between rate shopping and new credit accounts.

As you can see, your credit scores represent a complex examination of your credit habits, and understanding what it takes to get a score that lenders look for is an important factor. Unlike a report card, though, what would be considered an *average* FICO score is not necessarily a bad thing. For facts and fallacies regarding credit scoring, visit <www.myfico.com>. It's a great place to get detailed information on how to "credit prepare" for a mortgage loan and contains fascinating information on how credit scores are obtained. Also useful is the PRIVISTA service at <www.guardmycredit.com>, where you can view both your credit score and your credit record.

A Word to the Wise after Qualifying

There are few more joyous phone calls than the one from your lender informing you that you have just been approved for the loan on your new home. This news means smooth sailing, as long as you supply the lender with whatever lingering requirements they request (these may be called *conditions* of the approval). But don't become complacent about this news. Your loan qualifying "picture" should become frozen in time until closing, or you may run the risk of losing your approval. Even when closing is just few days away, many lenders will verify credit scores to see that you have not suddenly gone crazy on credit card spending, and spot-check for employment verification to see that you haven't changed your line of work or income flow. If you are what is referred to as a "borderline" qualifier, don't risk your approval by applying for new credit, using savings to buy a car or take that much-needed vacation before the move, or trying your hand at a new career.

Once you get to the loan closing, you will be presented with what is known as the HUD-1, which is the Uniform Settlement Statement, laying out the entire sales and mortgage transaction, including where all the money is flowing and how much you will owe in fees and interest on your mortgage. See Figure 4.8 to see what is included in this form. Once the buyer and seller have verified that everything is correct, the checks change hands and the property is yours!

RESOURCES

Books

All about Mortgages: Insider Tips to Finance and Refinance Your Home (Second Edition), by Julie Garton-Good (Dearborn Trade, Chicago, IL; 312-836-4400; 800-245-2665; www.dearborntrade.com). Explains the complex process of getting a mortgage and provides practical know-how and lots of checklists and worksheets.

The Common-Sense Mortgage: How to Cut the Cost of Home Ownership by $50,000 or More, by Peter G. Miller (Contemporary Books, 4255 W. Touhy Avenue, Lincolnwood, IL 60712-1975; 800-621-1918; www.contemporarybooks.com). Shows how the lending system works, reviews dozens of individual loan programs, and raises questions for consumers to ask. Includes new information on loans for first-time buyers, and the pros and cons of finding loans on the Internet. Has lots of tables and examples.

The Common-Sense Mortgage: How to Cut the Cost of Home Ownership by $100,000 or More, by Peter G. Miller (Contemporary Books, 4255 W. Touhy Avenue, Lincolnwood, IL 60712-1975; 800-621-1918; www.contemporarybooks.com). Practical advice about using computerized mortgage loan shopping services, refinancing, and the different kinds of mortgages.

Essentials of Real Estate Finance, by David Sirota (Dearborn Trade, Chicago, IL; 312-836-4400; 800-245-2665; www.dearborntrade.com). Comprehensive reference for consumers and real estate practitioners on qualifying for and selecting the right loan for a home or investment property. Workbook format and questions increase its usefulness as a resource and self-study guide.

How to Get the Best Home Loan, by W. Frazier Bell (John Wiley & Sons, 1 Wiley Drive, Somerset, NJ 08875; 212-850-6000; www.wiley.com). Describes different types of home loans and how to choose the best one for you.

How to Save Thousands of Dollars on Your Home Mortgage, by Randy Johnson (John Wiley & Sons, 1 Wiley Drive, Somerset, NJ 08875; 212-850-6000; 800-225-5945; www.wiley.com). Describes all the different types of mortgages available to homeowners. Explains the terminology and the forms involved and how lenders make their profits.

Figure 4.8   Uniform Settlement Statement

| A. **Settlement Statement** | U.S. Department of Housing and Urban Development | OMB Approval No. 2502-0265 |

B. Type of Loan

| 1. ☐ FHA   2. ☐ FmHA   3. ☐ Conv. Unins. | 6. File Number: | 7. Loan Number: | 8. Mortgage Insurance Case Number: |
| 4. ☐ VA   5. ☐ Conv. Ins. | | | |

C. Note: This form is furnished to give you a statement of actual settlement costs. Amounts paid to and by the settlement agent are shown. Items marked "(p.o.c.)" were paid outside the closing; they are shown here for informational purposes and are not included in the totals.

D. Name & Address of Borrower:	E. Name & Address of Seller:	F. Name & Address of Lender:

G. Property Location:	H. Settlement Agent:	
	Place of Settlement:	I. Settlement Date:

J. Summary of Borrower's Transaction		K. Summary of Seller's Transaction	
100. Gross Amount Due From Borrower		400. Gross Amount Due To Seller	
101. Contract sales price		401. Contract sales price	
102. Personal property		402. Personal property	
103. Settlement charges to borrower (line 1400)		403.	
104.		404.	
105.		405.	
Adjustments for items paid by seller in advance		Adjustments for items paid by seller in advance	
106. City/town taxes to		406. City/town taxes to	
107. County taxes to		407. County taxes to	
108. Assessments to		408. Assessments to	
109.		409.	
110.		410.	
111.		411.	
112.		412.	
120. Gross Amount Due From Borrower		420. Gross Amount Due To Seller	
200. Amounts Paid By Or In Behalf Of Borrower		500. Reductions In Amount Due To Seller	
201. Deposit or earnest money		501. Excess deposit (see instructions)	
202. Principal amount of new loan(s)		502. Settlement charges to seller (line 1400)	
203. Existing loan(s) taken subject to		503. Existing loan(s) taken subject to	
204.		504. Payoff of first mortgage loan	
205.		505. Payoff of second mortgage loan	
206.		506.	
207.		507.	
208.		508.	
209.		509.	
Adjustments for items unpaid by seller		Adjustments for items unpaid by seller	
210. City/town taxes to		510. City/town taxes to	
211. County taxes to		511. County taxes to	
212. Assessments to		512. Assessments to	
213.		513.	
214.		514.	
215.		515.	
216.		516.	
217.		517.	
218.		518.	
219.		519.	
220. Total Paid By/For Borrower		520. Total Reduction Amount Due Seller	
300. Cash At Settlement From/To Borrower		600. Cash At Settlement To/From Seller	
301. Gross Amount due from borrower (line 120)		601. Gross amount due to seller (line 420)	
302. Less amounts paid by/for borrower (line 220)	( )	602. Less reductions in amt. due seller (line 520)	( )
303. Cash ☐ From ☐ To Borrower		603. Cash ☐ To ☐ From Seller	

Section 5 of the Real Estate Settlement Procedures Act (RESPA) requires the following: • HUD must develop a Special Information Booklet to help persons borrowing money to finance the purchase of residential real estate to better understand the nature and costs of real estate settlement services; • Each lender must provide the booklet to all applicants from whom it receives or for whom it prepares a written application to borrow money to finance the purchase of residential real estate; • Lenders must prepare and distribute with the Booklet a Good Faith Estimate of the settlement costs that the borrower is likely to incur in connection with the settlement. These disclosures are mandatory.

Section 4(a) of RESPA mandates that HUD develop and prescribe this standard form to be used at the time of loan settlement to provide full disclosure of all charges imposed upon the borrower and seller. These are third party disclosures that are designed to provide the borrower with pertinent information during the settlement process in order to be a better shopper.

The Public Reporting Burden for this collection of information is estimated to average one hour per response, including the time for reviewing instructions, searching existing data sources, gathering and maintaining the data needed, and completing and reviewing the collection of information.

This agency may not collect this information, and you are not required to complete this form, unless it displays a currently valid OMB control number.

The information requested does not lend itself to confidentiality.

Figure 4.8   Uniform Settlement Statement (continued)

L. Settlement Charges

			Paid From Borrowers Funds at Settlement	Paid From Seller's Funds at Settlement
700. Total Sales/Broker's Commission based on price $ @ % =				
Division of Commission (line 700) as follows:				
701. $	to			
702. $	to			
703. Commission paid at Settlement				
704.				
800. Items Payable In Connection With Loan				
801. Loan Origination Fee	%			
802. Loan Discount	%			
803. Appraisal Fee	to			
804. Credit Report	to			
805. Lender's Inspection Fee				
806. Mortgage Insurance Application Fee to				
807. Assumption Fee				
808.				
809.				
810.				
811.				
900. Items Required By Lender To Be Paid In Advance				
901. Interest from to @$	/day			
902. Mortgage Insurance Premium for	months to			
903. Hazard Insurance Premium for	years to			
904.	years to			
905.				
1000. Reserves Deposited With Lender				
1001. Hazard insurance	months @$	per month		
1002. Mortgage insurance	months @$	per month		
1003. City property taxes	months @$	per month		
1004. County property taxes	months @$	per month		
1005. Annual assessments	months @$	per month		
1006.	months @$	per month		
1007.	months @$	per month		
1008.	months @$	per month		
1100. Title Charges				
1101. Settlement or closing fee	to			
1102. Abstract or title search	to			
1103. Title examination	to			
1104. Title insurance binder	to			
1105. Document preparation	to			
1106. Notary fees	to			
1107. Attorney's fees	to			
(includes above items numbers:		)		
1108. Title insurance	to			
(includes above items numbers:		)		
1109. Lender's coverage	$			
1110. Owner's coverage	$			
1111.				
1112.				
1113.				
1200. Government Recording and Transfer Charges				
1201. Recording fees: Deed $; Mortgage $; Releases $				
1202. City/county tax/stamps: Deed $; Mortgage $				
1203. State tax/stamps: Deed $; Mortgage $				
1204.				
1205.				
1300. Additional Settlement Charges				
1301. Survey to				
1302. Pest inspection to				
1303.				
1304.				
1305.				
1400. Total Settlement Charges (enter on lines 103, Section J and 502, Section K)				

The Mortgage Kit, by Thomas C. Steinmetz and Phillip Whitt (Dearborn Trade, Chicago, IL; 312-836-4400; 800-245-2665; www.dearborntrade.com). Explains the intricacies of all the latest financing options in great detail. Includes Internet information, as well as the basics of the mortgage process, shopping for the right mortgage, and reverse mortgages.

Tips and Traps When Mortgage Hunting, by Robert Irwin (McGraw-Hill, PO Box 543, Blacklick, OH 43004; 800-634-3961; www.mcgraw-hill.com). Explains the pros and cons of different kinds of mortgages and helps you determine which is best for you.

Home Buyer's Mortgage Kit (HSH Associates, 1200 Route 23N, Butler, NJ 07405; 973-838-3330; 800-873-2837; www.hsh.com). For a nominal fee, provides a list of banks and savings and loans that might offer a mortgage on a property based on its location and your income. You are given a computer printout listing the lending institutions' latest interest rates, points, and fees, as well as other details. You then choose several mortgages that interest you, and the service has the banks or savings and loans contact you. Can save you an enormous amount of time and money and introduce you to lenders you might not find on your own.

Web Sites

America Online, Personal Finance-Real Estate. Has a nationwide electronic bulletin board accessible to Windows and Macintosh users. Members may ask real estate questions, check daily mortgage rates, read articles, and post messages on the AOL MLS to buy, sell, exchange, or rent property anywhere in the country. Open to brokers and nonbrokers. <www.aol.com>

Amortgage.com. A great place to look for a home lender. The site lets you search out the best deals by state and even apply for prequalification online. It also has many articles about the mortgage qualification and approval process. <www.amortgage.com>

ArcLoan. Offers a step-down mortgage. This is a mortgage that is allowed to follow descending market rates, with a .25 percent minimum increment and no-cost refinancing. Homeowners can activate the refinance with a phone call to the lender. (No more than one refinance is allowed within 120 days.) <www.arcloan.com>

Bankrate.com. Compares mortgage interest rates by lending company. Also compares different mortgage features as offered by different mortgage companies. <www.bankrate.com>

City Line Mortgage Company. Offers what is known as a step-down mortgage. This is a mortgage that is allowed to follow descending market rates, with a .5 percent minimum increment and no-cost refinancing. Homeowners can activate the refinance with a phone call to the lender. <www.citylinemortgage.com>

Consumer Mortgage Information Network. A great source to find the best mortgage. The site has links to many real estate agents and lenders around the country and hundreds of useful educational articles on the entire homebuying and mortgage-finding process. <www.mortgagemag.com>

Countrywide. Online home mortgage site. You can calculate and select the home loan that fits your situation, make an application, and get your home mortgage loan online. Current interest rates are available, along with all the information on the different types of loans offered. <www.countrywide.com>

E-Loan. Online broker for consumer loans, including home mortgages, using some 70 loan companies. Education about the different types of home loans available, online application, current interest rates, and online loan tracking. <www.eloan.com>

Fannie Mae's *Homepath.com.* This site lists and links to all Fannie Mae–approved lenders by state or by other factors you may select. Lists properties for sale and includes mortgage calculators. <www.homepath.com>

Finet.com. Online supplier of home mortgage loans. Site includes mortgage home loan calculator, interest rate tracker, and advisors. <www.finet.com>

Home Advisor. Online homebuying, homeselling, remodeling, financing, insuring, moving, or refinancing site. Offers access to MLS listings countrywide, tips on buying or selling, and links to 17 lenders with the loans and interest rates that they offer. Includes mortgage calculator. <homeadvisor.msn.com>

Home-equity-consolidation-loans.com. Rates and quotes for competitively priced home equity loans for the purposes of debt consolidation. Free quotes. <www.home-equity-consolidation-loans.com>

Home Loan Reviews. Compares several lenders for home loans, home equity and refinances as well as debt consolidation. <www.homeloanreviews.com>

HSH Associates. Publisher of consumer loan information, including home loans, interest rates, types of loan, and adjustable loan rate indexes. Includes mortgage calculator. <www.hsh.com>

Iown.com. Online home mortgage broker site. This broker will help you find a suitable loan from the many loan companies in its database. You can apply online and complete your loan. <www.iown.com>

Lendingtree.com. Permits borrowers to fill out one form and expect at least four lenders to bid on their loan. <www.lendingtree.com>

LoansDirect.com. Offers online mortgages. <www.loansdirect.com>

LoanWeb. Comprehensive loan site that includes home loans. The site asks the typical questions needed for a mortgage application, then passes the information on to a number of local mortgage lenders who will contact you in a few days with their competitive proposals. <www.loanweb.com>

MBAA.org. Mortgage Bankers Association of America. Articles about mortgages and listings of mortgage bankers complete with a glossary of mortgage terms and home buying tips Also check out MBAonline for estimators designed for converting loans to other loan programs. <www.mbaa.org/consumer>

Mortgage.com. Home mortgage site that walks you through the process of calculating your loan and application for the loan. Has a mortgage calculator that factors in interest rate changes and presents the information in a graph or a table. <www.mortgage.com>

MortgageBot.com. Online mortgage broker offering mortgages and home equity loans. Has comprehensive question and answer articles and offers a sophisticated set of online calculators. <www.mortgagebot.com>

Mortgage.Interest.com. A good general mortgage loan site with extensive background information on mortgages and how to lock in a mortgage interest rate. It has an online mortgage calculator. <www.interest.com>

MortgageIT.com. Online mortgage broker, offers 33 loan companies from which to select. Offers online mortgage advisors, instantaneous rate quotes, online tracking of your loan, and online loan applications. <www.mortgageit.com>

Mortgage Terms. A compendium of the language you will need to buy or sell a house. <www.yournewhouse.com/mtgterms.html>

Mortgages.com. Has links to over 20 online mortgage lenders and brokers. <www.mortgages.com>

Mycounsel.com. Legal site with advice on refinancing all kinds of consumer debt. <www.mycounsel.com>

National Average Mortgage Rates. A complete listing of national mortgage rates to help you can compare what you are considering against national averages. <www.interest.com/ave.htm>

Premierequity.com. Web site designed for those with good credit histories who wish to pay off high-rate debt. 888-321-7736. <www.premierequity.com>.

Priceline.com. Site that offers to match your home mortgage terms by auctioning your mortgage to a database of lenders. If no one can match the terms, offers will be made from the lenders. <www.priceline.com>

Quicken.com. Full-service online mortgage broker. Has mortgage loan advisors and many loans from which to choose. Includes loan calculators and equity loans. <www.quicken.com>

Trade Association

Mortgage Bankers Association of America (1919 Pennsylvania Avenue, NW, Washington, DC 20006-3438; 202-557-2700; www.mbaa.org). The trade group of mortgage bankers. Offers the following publications: *Applying for Your Mortgage; Closing on Your Mortgage and Your Home; Finding the Mortgage That Is Right for You; Get a Running Start on Good Credit; How to Manage Your Mortgage Obligations; Make Shopping Easier: See Your Mortgage Lender First; Refinancing: Does It Make Sense for You;* and *When Your Mortgage Loan Is Rejected.*

CHAPTER 5

Refinancing Your Mortgage

If you locked yourself into what you thought was a good fixed-rate mortgage and rates have since dropped, you may want to consider refinancing your loan to save what could total thousands of dollars over the long term.

THE CHANGING FACE OF REFINANCE ADVICE

The rule of thumb in the industry used to be that your new mortgage had to be at least two percentage points less than your existing mortgage for the transaction to be worthwhile. Recently, however, the competition among lenders has shaved closing costs significantly, and in many cases, it might pay off to refinance if the difference is one percentage point or even less. It all depends on how much the new bank charges in closing costs, and how long you plan to stay in your home. For an example of how much you could save in monthly payments on a $100,000 loan if your interest rate dropped from 10 percent to 8 percent, see Figure 5.1.

In order for you to refinance, your home must have enough value to justify a new loan. Many people who bought homes at peak prices in the late 1990s were disappointed to learn that they could not refinance their homes in the early 2000s when mortgage rates dropped so sharply because the worth of their homes had plunged as well.

If you apply to refinance with a lender that did not originate your loan, most lenders will make you go through the same application process you did when you applied for your original mortgage. Even though it doesn't seem fair

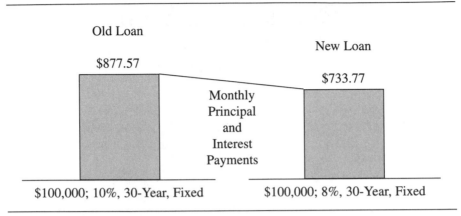

Figure 5.1   How a 2 Percent Difference in Interest Rates Can Lower Your Monthly Payments

Old Loan

New Loan

$877.57

$733.77

Monthly Principal and Interest Payments

$100,000; 10%, 30-Year, Fixed $100,000; 8%, 30-Year, Fixed

Source: *The Mortgage Kit* by Thomas Steinmetz (Dearborn Trade Publishing).

or necessary, you must again pay loan origination fees, credit report charges, appraisal charges, inspection fees, points, mortgage recording taxes, title insurance, and legal fees. Also, determine whether your current loan imposes prepayment penalties. If so, refinancing can be significantly more expensive.

To determine whether you should refinance your current mortgage, calculate your refinancing costs, then complete the refinancing worksheet in Figure 5.2. Sample figures are provided.

In the example in Figure 5.2, it would take the borrower ten months of lower payments to recover the $3,000 in up-front refinancing costs. Therefore, the borrower should plan to stay in his or her home at least ten months after the refinancing. In other cases, the savings would be less and the payback period would be longer. Again, it is worthwhile to refinance only if you live in your house for a significant amount of time after you refinance.

When you refinance, you will pay less interest on the new loan. That saves you money but means that you will receive fewer mortgage interest deductions to lower your tax bill. Also, any points you pay on the new mortgage can be deducted only over the life of the loan, not up front in a lump sum.

TRADING LOAN PROGRAMS

While most people refinance a fixed-rate loan with another such loan, you can also exchange a fixed-rate loan for an ARM or an ARM for a fixed-rate loan. When you convert a fixed-rate mortgage to an ARM, you should invest

---

Figure 5.2   Refinancing Worksheet

	Example	Your Mortgage
1. Present monthly mortgage payment	$1,000	
2. Mortgage payment after refinancing	$ 700	
3. Monthly savings (subtract item 2 from item 1)	$ 300	
4. Total fees, closing costs, and prepayment penalities	$3,000	
5. Time needed to break even (divide item 4 by item 3)	10 months	

---

your savings in stocks, bonds, or mutual funds that will give you long-term capital appreciation. Then, if interest rates on the ARM rise, you will have accumulated capital on which to draw to make the higher payments. One of the worst moves you can make is to convert from a fixed-rate loan to an adjustable-rate mortgage and spend the difference on a more extravagant lifestyle.

If rates drop low enough, it may make sense to exchange an ARM for a fixed-rate loan. Just realize that you are increasing your monthly mortgage payment in order to gain peace of mind. If you can live with a little more uncertainty, invest the money you save on an ARM in top-quality securities.

Another way to refinance is to convert a long-term loan, such as a 30-year mortgage, to a shorter-term loan, such as a 15-year mortgage. You might find that your monthly payment stays about the same, but you will pay off your mortgage many years faster.

A good way to determine whether refinancing makes sense and which refinancing options are best for you is to analyze your situation using calculators available on numerous Web sites listed at the end of Chapter 4. These include Quicken's Mortgage Tools at <www.quicken.com/tools/loan/products/loanquery.asp>, and Microsoft's MSN Home Advisor at <http://homeadvisor.msn.com/financing/overview.asp>.

IF THE MATH INDICATES A REFINANCE

Before being tempted to call the 800 number of the lender that blares its commercials on the radio during your daily commute to work, try your existing lender first. In order to keep your business, it will probably give you the best deal by offering you a "streamline" or "timesaver" refinance, waiving certain procedures, such as employment and income verification, or fees, such as the appraisal, credit report, or prepayment charges. Your lender should be particularly accommodating if you have made all your mortgage payments on time. Title company fees may be lower as well, once you inform them that you will be using your current lender (try to use the same title company you used originally for the optimum savings). Still, before you recommit to your lender, shop around to several other lenders to see whether you can obtain an even better deal.

SORTING OUT YOUR REFINANCE OPTIONS

Some real estate consultants or loan professionals specialize in equity management issues and can assist you in your refinance goals. He or she can assess what scenario might be best for you based on your long-range or short-term goals. For instance, if your plan includes selling your home in less than five years, up-front costs or prepayment penalties may deem refinancing not worthwhile. You may be advised to pay off revolving debt, such as credit cards, student loans, and cars in the refinance, so that you are free from these obligations if and when you are in the position to qualify for yet another mortgage. This may also work for disciplinary purposes, depending on your spending habits, so that you won't be tempted to take equity and spend it on recreation. The consultant can also show you how to maximize your build-up of equity with different loan terms, such as the shorter 15-year or 20-year varieties.

If you are among those contemplating retirement or semiretirement, for instance, your goals in refinancing may be based on how much income or savings you may have from Social Security, 401(k), pension plans, or eventual part-time income. If your goal is to remodel your home, however, a different approach may be suggested. Taking a good, hard look at your future plans can determine your refinancing goals and dictate what type of refinance is the most prudent for you.

RESOURCES

Books

All About Mortgages: Insider Tips to Finance and Refinance Your Home (Second Edition), by Julie Garton-Good (Dearborn Trade, Chicago, IL; 312-836-4400; 800-

245-2665; www.dearborntrade.com). Explains the complex process of getting a mortgage and provides practical know-how and lots of checklists and worksheets.

The Common-Sense Mortgage: How to Cut the Cost of Home Ownership by $100,000 or More, by Peter G. Miller (Contemporary Books, 4255 W. Touhy Avenue, Lincolnwood, IL 60712-1975; 800-621-1918; www.contemporarybooks.com). Practical advice about using computerized mortgage loan shopping services, refinancing, and the different kinds of mortgages.

Refinance Kit (HSH Associates, 1200 Route 23, Butler, NJ 07405; 973-838-3330; 800-873-2837; www.hsh.com). Explains how to calculate what different mortgages will cost you.

CHAPTER 6

Home Equity Loans

Once you have built up equity in your home, you have the privilege of applying for a *home equity line of credit,* which allows you to borrow against that equity inexpensively and conveniently. Most financial institutions—banks, savings and loans, brokerage firms, finance companies, credit unions, and others—have entered the home equity market, so you have plenty of options when you shop for the best loan.

In effect, a home equity loan is a second mortgage on your home. You usually get a line of credit up to 70 percent or 80 percent of the appraised value of your home, minus whatever you still owe on your first mortgage. For example, if your home is worth $100,000 and you owe $20,000 on your mortgage, you might receive a home equity line of credit for $60,000 because your lender would subtract your $20,000 owed on the first mortgage from your $80,000 worth of equity. You will qualify for a loan not only on the value of your home but also on your creditworthiness. For instance, you must prove that you have a regular source of income to repay a home equity loan. Because only the first $100,000 of home equity debt creates deductible interest, many people limit themselves to that amount, although banks will loan much more if you qualify.

Like other mortgages, the home equity loan requires you to go through an elaborate process to qualify for and open a line of credit. You will usually need a home appraisal and must pay legal and application fees and closing costs. Many banks also charge loan origination fees or points. In addition, they may collect an annual fee of up to $50 to maintain the account.

Because a home equity loan is backed by your home as collateral, it is considered more secure by lenders than unsecured debt, such as credit card debt. Further, because the loans are less risky for banks, you benefit by paying a much lower interest rate than you would on credit cards or most other kinds of loans. Typically, home equity credit lines charge a variable rate one to three percentage points more than the prime lending rate. In many cases, home equity lenders will start you off with an introductory rate of one-half to one percentage point below the prime rate for six months to as long as a year. Home equity loans can therefore offer extremely attractive rates when the prime interest rate is low, but subject you to much higher interest costs if the prime shoots up. You can tap the credit line simply by writing a check, and you can pay back the loan as quickly or as slowly as you like, as long as you meet the minimum payment each month. In theory, you must repay outstanding balances in five or ten years in one balloon payment. In practice, the bank will probably not require the balloon as long as you keep your minimum payment. (See Figure 6.1, Comparison Time Frames for Payoff of Home Equity Loans.)

DANGERS AND TEMPTATIONS

Home equity loans have become popular because they are flexible and offer attractive rates and tax deductions. However, you should be careful about how you spend the proceeds from your home equity loan. It is best if you use the money for major capital expenditures on which you might earn a return instead of on impulse items. For example, you might use home equity money to renovate your home, finance your children's tuition, buy a car or furniture, or pay off high-cost, nondeductible credit card debt. Don't, however, tap the credit line for a Caribbean vacation or a spin of the roulette wheel in Las Vegas.

Even though lenders' marketing campaigns may make recreational uses of your home's equity sound tantalizing, just remember that your home is on the line. If you spend the money frivolously and don't repay the loan, you'll lose your home quickly. If you know that you will be tempted to spend the money unwisely, it's best not to open a home equity credit line. Those equity checks the lender may send you can appear as safe as a normal checking account, but keep in mind that it comes with a much higher risk for misuse than your debit card.

The most dangerous type of home equity loan is the kind that taps even more than the existing equity itself. Sometimes called 125 percent loans, these *negative equity* type loans result in your owing more than your house is worth, spelling disaster if your financial picture forces you into having to sell your home. You would have to bank on being able to realize enough from the sale of your home to pay off this debt, or pay the remainder out of pocket.

Figure 6.1   Comparison Time Frames for Payoff of Home Equity Loans

The cost of a 9 percent home equity loan if paid off in 3, 5, 10, or 15 years.

Amount	Term	Required Payment	Total Interest	Total Cost
$5,000	3 Years	$159	$ 724	$ 5,724
	5 Years	104	1,227	6,227
	10 Years	63	2,600	7,600
	15 Years	51	4,127	9,127
$10,000	3 Years	318	1,448	11,448
	5 Years	208	2,455	12,455
	10 Years	127	5,201	15,201
	15 Years	101	8,256	18,256
$15,000	3 Years	477	2,172	17,172
	5 Years	311	3,682	18,682
	10 Years	190	7,801	22,801
	15 Years	152	12,385	27,385

Although these types of loans are not advertised as much as they once were, it is best to avoid them altogether.

BEHAVIOR MODIFICATION

One of the most popular reasons many Americans engage in equity-taking from their home investments is to consolidate debt. But if the practice of running up credit cards just to pay them off with your home equity becomes a habit, you will have defeated your entire purpose of purchasing a home as an appreciating investment.

Instead, consider keeping only one or two credit cards (those with low credit limits and low interest rates) for that rainy-day emergency and making scissor scraps of the rest. As you may have guessed, Americans lead the pack in credit card debt internationally, not only because of lenders and finance companies making it easier to obtain credit than in most other developed countries, but also because of the have-it-all mentality of the postwar generation. Your ability to discipline yourself by staying within a budget and making purchases backed only by serious rationale will go a long way in helping you keep the precious home equity you have worked so hard to establish.

If you do decide to take out a home equity loan, you may want to observe the following guidelines:

- Transfer only those credit card balances that you intend to close for good, and don't replace them with new ones.
- Never borrow more money than your home is worth.
- Be aware that you are, in essence, extending your loan another 10, 15, or 20 years.
- Study all the costs and fine print before signing on the dotted line, and understand precisely what your monthly payment will be.

RESOURCES

Art of Real Estate Appraisal, by William L. Ventolo, Jr. and Martha R. Williams (Dearborn Trade, Chicago, IL; 312-836-4400; 800-245-2665; www.dearborntrade .com). The complete reference on how to appraise the value of your home or evaluate appraisal reports. Up-to-date information on financing techniques, energy efficient construction, and home depreciation.

National Home Equity Mortgage Association (1301 Pennsylvania Avenue, NW, Suite 500, Washington, DC 20004; 202-347-1210; www.nhema.org). Group representing home equity lenders. Offers several free brochures for consumers about how to shop for a home equity loan.

Web Sites

Home-equity-consolidation-loans.com. Rates and quotes for competitively priced home equity loans for the purposes of debt consolidation. Free quotes. <www .home-equity-consolidation-loans.com>

Home Loan Reviews. Compares several lenders for home loans, home equity, and refinances as well as debt consolidation. <www.homeloanreviews.com>

MBAA.org. Mortgage Bankers Association of America. Articles and listings of mortgage bankers complete with a glossary of mortgage terms and home buying tips. Also check out the estimators designed for converting loans to other loan programs. <www.mbaa.org/consumer>

Moneybythebook.com. Discusses credit counseling, debt management, and the dangers of consolidated loans. <www.moneybythebook.com>

MortgageBot.com. Online mortgage broker offering mortgages and home equity loans. Has comprehensive question and answer articles and offers a sophisticated set of online calculators. <www.mortgagebot.com>

Mycounsel.com. Legal site with advice on refinancing all kinds of consumer debt. <www.mycounsel.com>

Premierequity.com. Web site designed for those with good credit histories who wish to pay off high-rate debt. 888-321-7736, <www.premierequity.com>

CHAPTER 7

Reverse Mortgages and Charitable Deductions

According to the Consumer Federation of America, the value of many consumers' homes can represent as much as 43 percent of their household wealth, if they have net assets of $100,000 to $250,000. If you are 62 or older and happen to be one of those disciplined (or lucky) homeowners and have paid down your mortgage considerably or own your home free and clear, you can now begin to pay yourself back without having to sell your precious asset by considering a reverse mortgage. In essence, your lender makes payments back to you.

A *reverse mortgage* permits you to convert your home equity into cash without selling the home or giving up title to it. It can provide funds to you (if you are available and willing to receive counseling or consumer education to prepare you) by a lump-sum, one-time payment, a line of credit (the most popular method), or fixed payments for life. The older you are, the more reverse mortgage money you can receive, but other conditions affecting the loan amount also apply, such as your equity in the property, the value and location of the home, and current interest rates. All single-family dwellings qualify, but a few programs also accept two to four unit owner-occupied, condominiums, and manufactured homes as well. (Co-ops do not qualify for reverse mortgages.) For a step-by-step explanation of the process of getting a reverse mortgage, see Figure 7.1.

Many older Americans have found a degree of financial security by obtaining a reverse mortgage, especially during their retirement years, with the money usable for any purpose whatsoever, from home improvements to

Figure 7.1   The Process of Getting a Reverse Mortgage

1. AWARENESS

Consumer (i.e., senior homeowner or adult child) learns about reverse mortgages or particular product from article, ad, direct mail, word of mouth, etc.

2. ACTION

Consumer seeks more information, by contacting a lender, HUD, Fannie Mae, AARP, National Center for Home Equity Conversion, or financial planner.

3. COUNSELING

If required, consumer gets counseling. For HECM loans, counseling is mandatory and must be received from a HUD-approved "housing agency" (nonprofit counseling agency). For Fannie Mae Home Keeper loans, consumer education is required. This is usually provided by a HUD-approved housing agency, or by a Fannie Mae HomePath specialist (telephone counseling). The counselor explains different options available to consumer and makes certain he or she is eligible for a reverse mortgage (i.e., generally age 62/65 or older). Most borrowers own their home free and clear or nearly so, but this isn't a requirement.

4. APPLICATION / DISCLOSURE

Consumer fills out application for reverse mortgage with lender, and selects payment option: fixed monthly payments for life, fixed monthly payments for finite period, lump sum payment, line of credit, or combination of monthly payments and line of credit.

Consumer decides (if option is available) whether to purchase deferred annuity as part of transaction. Lender discloses to consumer the estimated total cost of the loan, as required by federal Truth in Lending Act. Lender collects money for credit report (if applicable) and home appraisal. Consumer provides lender with required documents [i.e., photo identification, verification of Social Security number, copy of deed to home, information on any existing mortgage(s) on property, counseling certificate (if required)].

5. PROCESSING

Lender processes loan, ordering appraisal (to determine value of home), title work, lien payoffs, credit report, and verification of deposit (if required). Appraiser prepares appraisal report. If structural problems are noticed or suspected, physical inspection of home is ordered.

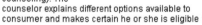

NEXT PAGE

medical bills, debt pay-offs, education, travel, long-term health care, repairs, or even eliminating the balances on their now-grown children's outstanding student loans. To get a sense of how much cash you may be able to get out of your house, fill out a loan calculator, such as the one shown in Figure 7.2. You can also log on to <www.rmaarp.com> to perform this calculation.

Your credit scores are of no consequence and your income is not considered for most types of reverse mortgages, nor do you need to reveal medical records or undergo a physical exam. And the loan does not have to be repaid until the death of the last surviving borrower. Even then, your heirs

Figure 7.1 (continued)

6. UNDERWRITING

After receiving all pertinent information and data, lender finalizes loan parameters with consumer (i.e., payment option, annuity or not, frequency of loan interest rate adjustments), packages loan, and submits package to underwriting department, for underwriting and final approval.

7. CLOSING

Following approval, closing (signing) of loan is scheduled. Initial and expected interest rates are set. These affect the amount of funds available to consumer, along with the age of borrower(s) and value of the home. Closing papers and final figures are prepared. Closing costs are normally financed as part of loan. Previous payments by a consumer for appraisal and credit reports may be refunded or used to reduce the closing costs financed. Lender or title company has consumer sign loan papers.

8. DISBURSEMENT

Consumer has three business days after signing papers in which to cancel the loan ("three-day right of rescission"). Upon expiration of this period, the loan is disbursed — consumer gets access to the funds, in the form of the payment option selected (i.e., monthly checks, etc.).

Any existing debt on the home is paid off. A new lien is placed on the home. The borrower may use the loan proceeds for any purpose. The interest rate charged on the loan generally is adjusted periodically (i.e., monthly or yearly). During the life of loan, servicer disburses monthly payments to the borrower (if this option is chosen), advances line of credit funds to the borrower upon request, collects any repayments by the borrower on the line of credit, and sends periodic statements to the borrower.

9. REPAYMENT

Consumer doesn't make any monthly mortgage payments to lender during the life of the loan. The reverse mortgage becomes fully repayable upon: the death of the borrower or last coborrower; the sale of the home by the borrower; a permanent move from the home by the borrower (i.e., to a nursing home, or another event after which the home is no longer the borrower's principal residence). The loan may be repaid by the borrower or borrower's heirs/estate, with or without a sale of the home. The repayment obligation generally can't exceed the home's value or sales price. If a deferred annuity has been purchased as part of the transaction, this will usually provide continued monthly income to the borrower even after the sale of, or move from, the home.

are not required to sell the home, but may choose to pay off the loan using other sources and retain title to the property. No payments on a reverse mortgage are due, however, until the borrower ceases to occupy the home as his or her principal residence.

Reverse mortgages are offered by thrifts, banks, and other financial institutions, and come in single-purpose, federally insured, and proprietary varieties. There are three types of reverse mortgage programs available today. They include the Fannie Mae Home Keeper, the privately offered Home Equity Conversion Mortgage (HECM), and some jumbo-type reverse mortgage

Figure 7.2   Reverse Mortgage Loan Calculator

AARP

home | what's new | search | join/renew | contact us | my aarp

Search [   ] [go]   Jump To [- select one & press go -] [↕] [go]

Reverse Mortgages

Shopping for Reverse Mortgages:

Loan Calculator

Reverse Mortgages

- Understanding Reverse Mortgages
- Shopping the Market
- Single-Purpose Loans
- HECM Loans
- Proprietary Loans
- Comparing Products
- Borrower Decisions
- Glossary
- **Loan Calculator**

Related Topics:

Money & Work

Related Links:

This calculator provides approximate estimates for two nationally available reverse mortgage programs. These estimates do not reflect local cost variables, are not an offer to make you a loan, do not qualify you to obtain a loan, and are not an official loan disclosure. AARP does not endorse any specific reverse mortgage product or lender.

How much cash could *you* get? To find out, answer these questions.

	Month	Year
1) When were you born? For example: type 5 for May.	5	192
2) When was your spouse (or other co-owner) born? Leave blank if you are the only owner.	Month	Year

3) How much is your house worth?   [120,00]
Type in your best guess.

4) What is your ZIP code?   [94115]
Just 5 digits, not ZIP+4.

Make your entries, then click [Calculate]

Screen capture from http://www.maarp.com/

products. Canadians can also take advantage of reverse mortgages with the Canadian Home Income Plan.

You should definitely look before you leap by researching which type of reverse mortgage is right for your situation.

SINGLE-PURPOSE REVERSE MORTGAGES

The name implies its use. These types of reverse mortgages are designated for one specific purpose, such as home repairs or improvements, payment of property taxes or special assessments or, in very limited areas, long-term care services. Single-purpose type programs are not available everywhere and many are not open to borrowers with higher incomes, but they are often the least costly type of reverse mortgage.

These types of reverse mortgage programs are typically offered by state and local governments and are approved mostly in a lump-sum form for the purpose for which they are designated.

FEDERALLY INSURED REVERSE MORTGAGES

Commonly known as HECMs (Home Equity Conversion Mortgages), these are any-purpose loans, available throughout the United States to any homeowners 62 years old or older, no matter what income they receive. Offered first in 1989, the HECM is the oldest nationally available reverse mortgage product, with tens of thousands of them currently outstanding.

These FHA-backed loans are more costly than single-purpose programs, but less expensive than proprietary loans. Offered through banks, mortgage companies, and other private-sector lenders, HECMs have the widest variety of loan-advance choices. Home Keeper® mortgages offer some different features than FHA HECM loans and can be for larger amounts, especially for couples.

Fannie Mae also offers a program called Home Keeper for Home Purchase®, which allows a senior to obtain a Home Keeper reverse mortgage on an existing home to help finance the purchase of a new home with less out-of-pocket cash, permitting the senior to keep more of the proceeds from the older home and avoid taking on a monthly mortgage payment.

PROPRIETARY REVERSE MORTGAGES

The most costly of the three varieties, proprietary reverse mortgages provide larger loan-advance amounts only if your home is worth a lot more than the average home value in your area. Backed by private companies (instead of government-related agencies), proprietary reverse mortgages can be used for any purpose, but are not available in every state. Although offered by banks and mortgages companies, the companies with ownership rights to these types of reverse mortgages can designate which mortgage companies offer their programs, unlike the FHA-approved variety, which are available through any lender.

AARP recommends that if you live in a home that does not qualify for an HECM loan, if your home's value is considerably greater than the average home in your area, or if you have the time to compare and research proprietary reverse mortgages in great detail, it may be worth a look into them.

However, the organization advises consumers that a number of proprietary programs that have been discontinued over the years because of their inherent complexities as well as their higher risks and costs.

MAKING YOUR HOME A CHARITABLE DEDUCTION

A tax-planning idea contributed by New York tax attorney Gerald Robinson is only for taxpayers who have genuine and major charitable objectives, and have reached an age where they want to do something significant about them. To make this work, the taxpayer has to own his or her own home free and clear and not be interested in passing it on to any children.

If you meet these conditions, good deeds and great tax results can ensue. The idea is for the taxpayer to donate a remainder interest in the personal residence to a charity. Because virtually all homeowners hold title to their home in *fee simple,* ownership can be split into other, smaller interests. Robinson cites the example of someone who transfers a fee interest in his or her home to another person, with the owner retaining the right to live in the home for the rest of his or her life or a period of years. By doing so, the owner creates a *life estate* or *term of years* for himself or herself, and creates a remainder interest in the home in the party to whom the transfer is made.

Giving your home to a charity under these rules can generate a substantial tax deduction from the value of the remainder interest. The use of this tax idea only makes sense in special situations, where transfer of a remainder of the interest is consistent with present tax and financial needs, as well as family living arrangements and estate plans—usually older homeowners who wish to permanently stay in their present homes.

RESOURCES

American Association of Retired Persons (AARP) (800-209-8085; www.aarp .org/revmort). Offers a hard copy or online booklet called *Homemade Money: A Consumer's Guide to Reverse Mortgages.*

Fannie Mae (800-732-6643; www.fanniemae.com). Get information about HECMs and Home Keeper mortgages, and a list of lenders who offer them.

Department of Housing and Urban Development (HUD) (888-466-3487; www .hud.gov). Offers reverse mortgage information specifically on the Home Equity Conversion Mortgage.

National Center for Home Equity Conversion (NCHEC) (651-222-6775; www .reverse.org). Offers calculators and other tools to help you decide on whether a reverse mortgage is right for you.

Financial Freedom Senior Funding Corporation (800-500-5150; www.ffsenior.com). Proprietary type (privately held) reverse mortgage company, offering programs such as Financial Freedom Equity Guard and Cash Account Plans, which are available in limited areas.

National Reverse Mortgage Lenders Association (202-939-1765; www.reversemortgage.org). Provides a list of reverse mortgage lenders in each state and has detailed information about reverse mortgages.

CHAPTER 8

Protecting the Value of Your Home

Y̲ou can help ensure the value of your home through regular maintenance, renovation, and home warranty. Just as a car reaps a higher price because of its maintenance records and overall condition, well-maintained and
improved homes can be priced higher than their comparable neighbors when
it comes time to sell.

MAINTAINING YOUR HOME

Because your home is probably your largest single asset, it pays to maintain and improve it over the years to enhance its value. It's great if you can
do much of the work yourself, but most people don't have the time or expertise to handle plumbing, electrical, and carpentry repairs, as well as mow
the lawn and paint occasionally. That is why you should assemble a team of
reliable plumbers, electricians, carpenters, lawn maintenance workers,
painters, and others to keep your home in tip-top shape. They not only solve
problems and perform regular maintenance to keep problems from occurring, but, if you employ them consistently, they know your home perhaps
better than you do.

As a homeowner, it is up to you to know when regular maintenance duties need to be performed. You may want to grab a 12-month calendar at the
beginning of each year and mark when heating filters may need to be
changed, gutters need to be cleaned, smoke detector batteries need to be replaced, and your air conditioner may need service. (See Figure 8.1, Mainte-

nance Checklist.) Homebuyers who purchase newly constructed homes should pay special attention to the explanations given by builder customer service personnel when attending their final walk-through orientation. Not adhering to some of the procedures outlined in their warranty programs may result in parts of their new home warranty being voided during those first few years.

Keep all product-related and maintenance paperwork for your home in a specially prepared folder, quickly accessible should any maintenance and repair issues arise.

REMODELING YOUR HOME

Renovating your home can cost thousands of dollars but can greatly add to the pleasure you derive from it—once the workers finally leave. In general, you should not expect to recoup all your money from most remodeling jobs when you sell, though some improvements hold their value better than others. The more customized your renovations, the more chance future buyers will not like what you have done. If you take on major remodeling, you should plan to stay in your home for at least five more years.

Remodeling jobs that pay off most include those renovations that add living space and those that improve kitchens and bathrooms. Figure 8.2 details what returns you can expect from your home inspection dollars. Buyers like large master bedrooms, many bathrooms (even half-baths), modern appliances, and open kitchen layouts.

Upgrading that costs the most and probably returns the least includes the addition of major recreational facilities like swimming pools, spas, or tennis courts. Similarly, decks and patios may be nice but often don't recoup the money it costs to build them.

It's important to avoid overimproving a home in relation to surrounding properties, as well as making improvements that render the home *functionally obsolete*. This means that the additions you are making are not in proper proportion to the rest of the dwelling. For instance, making a three-bedroom home into a five-bedroom layout may sound great. But when the home is served only by its one-and-a-half original bathrooms, the function of the plan becomes obsolete. Building a huge gourmet kitchen or a three-car garage onto a two-bedroom bungalow can also tip the balance of good sense.

When you take on a renovation project, obtain several written bids from qualified contractors before you choose one. The following list names some of the key items that should be included in the contract:

- Full name, address, and phone number of the company

Figure 8.1   Maintenance Checklist

Blue Ribbon Home Warranty, Inc.

MAINTENANCE CHECKLIST

Print and Save this checklist for easy use!

APPLIANCE/SYSTEM	MODEL	SERIAL NUMBER	LAST CHECKUP
Heating System			
Water Heater			
Garage Door Opener			
Electrical System			
Plumbing System			
Air or Evaporative Conditioning System			
Microwave			
Refrigerator			
Range/Oven			
Dishwasher			
Garbage Disposal			
Washer			
Dryer			
Trash Compactor			
Hot Tub			
Spa			
Pool			
Main Sewer Line			
Septic Tank (cleaning)			

Home | Apply On-Line | Home Warranty Benefits | Warranty Plans | Home Service Tips | Home Inspections
Colorado Real Estate and Services Information Center | Accomplishments and Client Letters
Questions, Comments, Problems, and Suggestions | Tell Your Friends! | Language Translator

Screen capture from http://www.blueribbonhomewarranty.com/checklist.htm

Figure 8.1   Maintenance Checklist (continued)

 HOME MAINTENANCE TIPS

Blue Ribbon Home Warranty, Inc.

Web Site Translator - English, Spanish, Japanese, Etc.

Print list or save in favorites and keep it handy!

APPLIANCE/SYSTEMS	TIPS
Heating Systems Gas, Boiler, Hot Water, Electric and Oil even Wood Stoves	✔ All Forced Air Systems: Conventional filters on forced-air systems should be checked monthly and cleaned or replaced as needed. Electronic filters should be checked monthly and cleaned as needed. Care should be taken to ensure the interior components are installed in the correct orientation after cleaning. Noisy blower sections should be brought to the attention of a technician. All types of furnaces and boilers should be inspected by a qualified technician every year to ensure that all the components are operating properly and no connections are loose or burned.
	✔ Gas Furnaces and Boilers: If gas odors can be detected, call the gas company immediately. Do not turn on any electrical equipment or use anything with an open flame. Gas furnaces and boilers should be cleaned and serviced annually. The exhaust pipe should be checked for loose or corroded sections. The heat shield (located where the burner enters the heat exchanger) should be checked to ensure that it is not loose or corroded. Burn marks around the heat shield or soot on the front may indicate a draft or combustion problem. A technician should be contacted.
	✔ All Hot Water Systems: Radiators and convectors should be inspected annually for leakage (particularly at the valves). Radiators should be bled of air annually, and as necessary during the heating season. Circulating pumps should be lubricated twice during the heating season. Expansion tanks should be drained annually.
	✔ Electric Heat: Electric furnaces and boilers should be inspected by a qualified technician every year to ensure that all the components are operating properly and no connections are loose or burned. The fuses or circuit breakers in some electric systems can be checked by the homeowner. Electric baseboard heaters should be inspected to ensure an adequate clearance from combustibles and they are keep clean. Baseboard heaters which have been mechanically damaged should be repaired or replaced.
	✔ Oil Furnaces and Boilers: Oil systems should be checked by a qualified technician on an annual basis. Oily soot deposits at registers of forced-air systems may indicate a cracked heat exchanger. A technician should be contacted. The exhaust pipe from the furnace or boiler should be checked for loose connections or corroded sections. The barometric damper on the exhaust pipe should rotate freely. The chimney clean out should be cleared of any debris. The oil tank should be inspected for leaks. Soot on the front of the furnace or boiler may indicate a draft or combustion problem. A technician should be contacted.
	✔ Wood Stoves: Wood stove chimneys and flues should be checked for creosote build-up and cleaned at least annually (more frequently depending upon use). Clearance to combustibles around wood stoves should be maintained at all times. If there is any doubt about the safety of a wood stove, contact the city building inspector immediately.
Heating Ducts	✔ Have your ducts cleaned at least every 5 to 6 years, this keeps your furnace clean and will increase life expectance.
	✔ Make sure your ducts have no cracks or leaks in the ductwork and tape were needed.
Water Heater	✔ Drain tank at least every year and flush it out.
	✔ Remove the elements and soak in vinegar, then scrape off scales.
Electrical System	✔ To prevent power outages, be sure there are not too many appliances plugged into one circuit.
Plumbing System	✔ Avoid flushing any paper products other than toilet paper down the toilets. Check for corrosion, leaks, and add a clean out compound to system once a year.

Figure 8.1   (continued)

Air Conditioning or Swamp Cooler System	✔ Check filters every month. ✔ Have annual system maintenance done one month before the air conditioning season begins. ✔ Keep the condensing unit free of debris.
Humidifiers	✔ Water levels in humidifiers should be checked and adjusted monthly. Interior components should be replaced on an as needed basis. The pad on drum type humidifiers should be replaced annually. The water supply to humidifiers should be shut off for the summer months and activated for the heating months. On systems with air conditioning or a heat pump, the damper in the humidifier ductwork should be closed during the cooling season.
Microwave	✔ Do not use pans or dishes that are metal or have a metallic trim. ✔ Only use mild soap and/or baking soda to clean the interior (abrasive cleaners or scouring pads can damage the lining).
Refrigerator	✔ Clean the interior shelves, shell and gaskets every 3 months. ✔ Once a year, clean the coils on the back or underneath.
Range & Oven	✔ To avoid damaging the burners, do not use extra-large and heavy cooking pots or pans. ✔ If you have a self-cleaning oven, do not use any other method to clean it.
Garbage Disposal	✔ To clean the disposal, push a full tray of ice cubes through it while running cold water. ✔ Always remember to run water during use and for at least two minutes after you finish. This prevents stoppages.
Washer & Dryer	✔ Clean the lint screen after each load of clothes has been dried and the unit is empty. ✔ To adjust the level of your washing machine, turn the legs clockwise to lower them or counterclockwise to raise them.
Hot Tub/Spa/Pool	✔ Keep a proper water level. ✔ Consult your pool and spa company for suggestions about maintaining your particular system
Structure or Structural	✔ Foundation Walls: Foundation walls should be checked for evidence of deterioration, dampness and movement. Limited dampness from slow moisture migration can be anticipated with most older foundation walls. This will often result in minor surface deterioration. Semi-annual inspections allow for monitoring of this situation. Cracks and voids should be filled. Filling cracks allows for easy monitoring of movement between inspections. Access hatches should be provided to all crawl space areas. ✔ Wood Framing: Exposed wooden structural components in the basement should be checked for evidence of rot and insect infestation. Deterioration usually results in sagging structural components. ✔ Wall and Ceiling Surface Cracks: Wall and ceiling surface cracks should be monitored for evidence of significant movement. Minor movement due to normal settling and shrinkage should be anticipated. ✔ Door Frames: Door frames should be checked to determine their square-ness. Door frames showing significant movement over a six month period are normally indications of more serious problems. ✔ Grading: The grading immediately adjacent to the house should be checked to ensure a slope of one inch per foot for the first six feet away from the house (where practical). Catch basins should be cleaned and tested.

Home I Apply On-Line   I About Warranties I Warranty Plans I Home Inspections I Maintenance Service Tips!
Colorado Information, Real Estate & Service Center I Accomplishments and Client Letter I Contact Us

Figure 8.2   Home Improvement Payback Estimates

Consider these payback estimates for the most typical home improvement projects.

Project	Cost	Average Payback
Add a new heating or air-conditioning system	$2,000 to $4,500	100% for heating; 75% for air-conditioning
Minor kitchen remodeling	$2,000 to $8,500	94% to 102%
Major kitchen remodeling	$9,000 to $25,000	90%
Add a bathroom	$5,000 to $12,000	92%
Add a family room	$30,000	86%
Remodel bathroom	$8,500	77%
Add a fireplace	$1,500 to $3,000	75%
Build a deck	$6,000	73%
Remodel home office	$8,000	69%
Replace windows	$6,000	68% to 74%
Build a pool	$10,000 and up	44%
Install or upgrade landscaping	$1,500 to $15,000	30% to 60%
Finish basement	$3,000 to $7,000	15%

Source: CEandR.com

- Contractor's name and license number
- Detailed specification of the job, including brand names, styles, colors, and model numbers of any materials or appliances being installed. The contractor should also agree in writing to give you a credit or refund for any materials not used.
- Start and completion dates, with a clause allowing you to withhold money if certain deadlines are not met
- Statement from the contractor stating that he or she will obtain all necessary building permits or variances before work begins

- Proof that the contractor carries liability and workers' compensation coverage
- Written warranty on all work performed
- Promise that the contractor will clean up the site when he or she is finished
- Statement that all changes to the contract must be approved and signed by you and the contractor
- Payment schedule specifying the deposit and progress payments

You should aim to pay contractors as slowly as possible, with perhaps a third of the money up front, a third after half the job is finished, and the final third when the job is completed to your total satisfaction. If you want a major overhaul of your home, you may need a general contractor to coordinate all the subcontractors. Otherwise, you must act as the general contractor and stay on top of the subcontractors to ensure that they keep to the schedule. The process usually takes much longer than you expect and costs far more (many times double) than you planned. But if the renovation turns out well, your home will give you many years of enjoyment.

Be wary of contractors that work only out of the back of their pick-up trucks and do not appear to have preprinted forms and paperwork. Their bids may sound wonderful, but you may be dealing with someone who starts the job only to leave you with an unfinished mess once he or she receives a little compensation. For a sample homeowner/contractor agreement, see Figure 8.3.

FINANCING HOME IMPROVEMENTS

There are several ways to finance the partial or entire renovation of your home using either your current equity or the estimated improved future value of the home.

Using part of all of the existing equity in the form of a *home equity loan* is usually done when you have an exact amount in mind before the project begins. The bank's rate is usually fixed, and the improvement may be paid out in a lump sum.

A *home equity line of credit,* on the other hand, is one that has no predetermined figure in mind and can be used over the longer term, almost in the form of an episodic "draw" over the longer term, for projects that will necessitate a ready source of cash. These loans are usually variable, and both types of home equity loans are usually tax deductible.

A *home improvement loan* may be offered when a homeowner does not have sufficient equity to cover the amount they want to borrow for future improvements. Some banks allow you to borrow up to 50 percent of the future

Figure 8.3   Homeowner/Contractor Agreement

Homeowner/Contractor Agreement

Owner's Name(s):	Contractor's Name:
Address:	Address:
Telephone Number: Work: Home:	Telephone Number:
Case No.:	License No.:

THIS AGREEMENT, *made this date_____, between the above mentioned Homeowner (Owner) and Contractor, is for the renovation/construction of the property located at_____*

that has been approved for FHA mortgage insurance under Section 203(k) of the National Housing Act, or Section 184 of the Housing and Community Development Act of 1992 or for Conventional Renovation financing. The Owner(s) shall pay the Contractor the maximum sum of $ _____ for completion of the work, including all sales tax due by law, together with such increases or decreases in the contract price as may be approved in writing by the Lender. The work will begin within 30 days of loan closing with the Lender and will be completed by_____ unless delayed beyond the Contractor's control. The General Provisions listed below are made a part of this Agreement. The contract documents consist of the architectural exhibits listed in the Construction or Renovation Loan Agreement between the Owner(s) and the Lender, or as described below (or on an attached sheet):

1. Contract Documents: *This Agreement includes all general provisions, special provisions and architectural exhibits that were accepted by the lender. Work not covered by this agreement will not be required unless it is required by reasonable inference as being necessary to produce the intended result. By executing this Agreement, the contractor represents that he/she has visited the site and understands local conditions, including state and local building regulations and conditions under which the work is to be performed.*

2. Owner: *Unless otherwise provided for in the Agreement, the owner will secure and pay for necessary easements, exceptions from zoning requirements, or other actions which must precede the approval of a permit for this project. If owner fails to do so then this contract is void. If the contractor fails to correct defective work or persistently fails to carry out the work in accordance with the agreement or general provisions, the owner may order the contractor in writing to stop such work, or a part of the work, until the cause for the order has been eliminated.*

3. Contractor: *The contractor will supervise and direct the work and the work of all subcontractors. He/She will use the best skill and attention and will be solely responsible for all construction methods and materials and for coordinating all portions of the work. Unless otherwise specified in the Agreement, the contractor will provide for and/or pay for all labor, materials, equipment, tools, machinery, transportation, and other goods, facilities, and services necessary for the proper execution and completion of the work. The contractor will maintain order and discipline among employees and will not assign anyone unfit for the task. The contractor warrants to the owner that all materials and equipment incorporated are new and that all work will be of good quality and free of defects or faults. The contractor will pay all sales, use and other taxes related to the work and will secure and pay for building permits and/or other permits, fees, inspections and licenses necessary for the completion of the work unless otherwise specified in the Agreement. The contractor will indemnify and hold harmless the owner from and against all claim, damages, losses, expenses, legal fees or other costs arising or resulting from the contractor's performance of the work or provisions of this section. The contractor will comply and perform the work in accordance with all rules, regulations, laws, ordinances and orders of any public authority or HUD inspector, Tribal Inspector and/or Lender selected inspector bearing on the performance of the work. The contractor is responsible for and indemnifies the owner against acts and omissions of employees, subcontractors and their employees, or others performing the work under this Agreement with the contractor. The contractor will provide shop drawings, samples, product data or other information provided for in this Agreement, where necessary.*

4. Subcontractor: *Selected by the contractor, except that the contractor will not employ any subcontractor to whom the owner may have a reasonable objection, nor will the contractor be required by the owner to employ any subcontractor to whom contractor has a reasonable objection.*

Signature Required on Page 2

Figure 8.3   (continued)

5. Work By Owner or Other Contractor: The owner reserves the right to perform work related to the project, but which is not a part of this Agreement, and to award separate contracts in connection with other portions of the project not detailed in this Agreement. All contractors and subcontractors will be afforded reasonable opportunity for the storage of materials and equipment by the owner and by each other. Any costs arising by defective or ill-timed work will be borne by the responsible party.

6. Binding Arbitration: Claims or disputes relating to the Agreement or General Provisions will be resolved by the Construction Industry Arbitration Rules of the American Arbitration Association (AAA) unless both parties mutually agree to other methods. The notice of the demand for arbitration must be filed in writing with the other party to this Agreement and with the AAA and must be made in a reasonable time after the dispute has arisen. The award rendered by the arbitrator(s) will be considered final and judgment may be entered upon it in accordance with applicable law in any court having jurisdiction thereof.

7. Cleanup and Trash Removal: The contractor will keep the owner's residence free from waste or rubbish resulting from the work. All waste, rubbish, tools, construction materials, and machinery will be removed promptly after completion of the work by the contractor.

8. Time: With respect to the scheduled completion of the work, time is of the essence. If the contractor is delayed at anytime in the progress of the work by change orders, fire, labor disputes, acts of God or other causes beyond the contractor's control, the completion schedule for the work or affected parts of the work may be extended by the same amount of time caused by the delay. The contractor must begin work no later than 30 days after loan closing and will not cease work for more than 30 consecutive days.

9. Payments and Completion: Payments may be withheld because of: (1) defective work not remedied; (2) failure of contractor to make proper payments to subcontractors, workers, or suppliers; (3) persistent failure to carry out work in accordance with this Agreement or these general conditions, or (4) legal claims. Final payment will be due after complete release of any and all liens arising out of the contract or submission of receipts or other evidence of payment covering all subcontractors or suppliers who could file such a lien. The contractor agrees to indemnify the owner against such liens and will refund all monies including costs and reasonable attorneys' fees paid by the owner in discharging the liens. A 10 percent holdback is required by the lender to assure the work has been properly completed and there are no liens on the property.

10. Protection of Property and Persons: The contractor is responsible for initiating, maintaining, and supervising all necessary or required safety programs. The contractor must comply with all applicable laws, regulations, ordinances, orders or laws of federal, state, county, tribal or local governments. The contractor will indemnify the owner for all property loss or damage to the owner caused by his/her employees or his/her direct or subtier subcontractors.

11. Insurance: The contractor/purchaser (circle one and initial here:) will purchase and maintain such insurance necessary to protect from claims under workers compensation and from any damage to the owner(s) property resulting from the conduct of this contract.

12. Changes in the Contract: The owner may order changes, additions or modifications (using form HUD 92577) without invalidating the contract. Such changes must be in writing and signed by the owner and accepted by the lender. Not all change order requests may be accepted by the lender, therefore, the contractor proceeds at their own risk if work is completed without an accepted change order.

13. Correction of Deficiencies: The contractor must correct promptly any work of his/her own or his/her subcontractors found to be defective or not complying with the terms of the contract.

14. Warranty: The contractor will provide a one-year warranty on all labor and materials used in the renovation of the property. This warranty must extend one year from the date of completion of the contract or longer if prescribed by law unless otherwise specified by other terms of this contract. Disputes will be resolved through the Construction Industry Arbitration Rules of the American Arbitration Association.

15. Termination: If the owner fails to make a payment under the terms of this Agreement, through no fault of the contractor, the contractor may, upon ten working days written notice to the owner, and if not satisfied, terminate this Agreement. The owner will be responsible for paying the contractor for all work completed.

If the contractor fails or neglects to carry out the terms of the contract, the owner, after ten working days written notice to the contractor, may terminate this Agreement. The owner may finish the job by whatever reasonable method the owner deems expedient. If the cost of completion exceeds the contract balance, the difference, as well as reasonable attorneys' fees if necessary, will be paid to the owner by the contractor.

Owner(s) Signature(s) and Date   _Owner(s) Signature(s) and Date_

Owner(s) Signature(s) and Date   _Owner(s) Signature(s) and Date_

Contractor's Signature and Date

NMFL #4264 04/01   Page 2 of 2

Figure 8.3   Homeowner/Contractor Agreement (continued)

CORF-4525

Cost of Renovation

Borrower Name:

Property Address:

Loan No:

I/We understand that, if my/our contractor's price is increased over and above the initially approved amount, and such increases will not be covered by executed and approved change orders with funding from my/our contingency reserve, I/we have the funds necessary to pay the contractor and complete the job. I/We further agree that I/we will furnish such excess funds directly to the lender to be placed in the contingency reserve account. I/We agree that these funds will remain irrevocably committed to this project and may not be withdrawn for any purpose.

EXECUTED AS OF THE DATE SHOWN BELOW:

_____   _____
Borrower   *Borrower*

_____   _____
Borrower   *Borrower*

_____
Witness   *Date*

NMFL# 4525 04/99

value of the qualified home improvement in addition to the current appraised value of your home, thereby increasing their financing ability. The most frequently approvable types of home improvements that banks will lend on are:

- Kitchen and bath remodeling
- Room additions
- In-ground pool or spa addition
- Garage addition
- Adding a deck or patio
- Replacing the home's siding
- Window replacement

Homeowners must usually have a firm contractor's bid as evidence of their qualifying home improvement value. Figure 8.4 shows examples of documents the lender will require the homeowner to sign.

Tax Shelters for Renovators

Gains are not limited only to those from market appreciation, according to Gerald Robinson, a New York tax attorney. If a homeowner can make improvements to their home that increase its value beyond the cost of the improvements, the increase in value can be realized tax-free when the home is sold.

Even if you bought, fixed up, and sold a fixer-upper every two years at a profit, as long as the home is your principal residence, your gain cannot be taxed under the current law. This loophole in the income tax laws may not last, once someone in Congress sees it as an "unintended benefit," according to Robinson, but in the meantime it is a perfectly legal tax savings technique, as well as a strong incentive to renovate run-down housing.

Home Warranties

Another way to protect your investment is through a home warranty. Most of the problems that surface after the purchase of a home occur within the first six months of move-in, and although a deductible usually applies when the items warranted fail, the amount you pay may be far smaller than the cost of the entire repair.

Warranties for New Homes

If your home was newly built at the time of your purchase, your homebuilder will have observed your state's building and inspection codes. Some states, like California, force builders to warrant their homes for structural

Figure 8.4   Renovation Loan Borrower's Acknowledgment

Renovation Loan Borrower's Acknowledgment

Condition of Property: I understand that the property I am purchasing is not Lender approved and neither Lender nor its investors, successors and assigns warrants the condition or the value of the property. I understand the plan review (where performed) and the appraisal are performed to determine compliance with the required architectural exhibits and to estimate the value of the property, but neither guarantees the house is free of defects. I understand I was responsible to have an independent consultant and/or a professional home inspection service perform an inspection of the property and the cost of the inspection was (or could be) included in the mortgage.

Loan Requirements

* I understand at the time of the loan closing of a Renovation Loan, for which I have applied to my lender, the proceeds designated for the renovation or improvement (including a contingency reserve, mortgage payments and any other fees, where applicable) are to be placed in an interest bearing escrow account. The Renovation Escrow Account is not, nor will it be treated as an escrow for the paying of real estate taxes, insurance premiums, delinquent notes, ground rents or assessments. I hereby request the Lender, after the Final Release Notice is issued, to:

☐ Pay the net interest income directly to me/us.
☐ Other: _____

☐ Apply the net interest income directly to the mortgage principal balance for an equal amount of principal reduction.

● I understand that the Renovation Escrow Account will cease paying interest to me if (1) the loan payments are delinquent for more than 30 days; or (2) the completion date (or an approved extension) has expired. During this period, the interest will be paid down on the mortgage principal. I understand if I clear up the delinquent or default status and/or the completion date has not expired or an extension has been approved, then the interest on the escrow account will begin again to be paid according to the request above.

● I understand no draws on the escrow account can be made until all permits have been issued by the local or state building departments, where required. I further understand I can only request monies for the actual cost of renovation. If any cost savings result on any line item of the Draw Request, form HUD-9746-A, the amount saved must be used to: (1) make further improvements to the property; (2) pay for cost overruns in other line items of the Draw Request; or (3) prepay the mortgage principal.

● I understand the contractor(s) is responsible to complete the work described in the architectural exhibits in a workmanlike manner. If I agree the work has been properly completed, I will sign the Draw Request, form HUD-9746-A, thereby accepting the responsibility that the completed work is acceptable and payment is justified. I understand there is a 10 percent holdback on each Draw Request to assure the work is properly completed and for lien protection.

● I understand I am responsible to negotiate any and all agreements with the contractor(s) I select and that the Lender, its investors, successors and assigns suggest that the Agreement with the contractor should include a provision for binding arbitration with the American Arbitration Association on any dispute.

* I understand if I change a contractor for any reason, I may be obligated under the terms of the original contractor's agreement and I should seek legal advice before taking such action. If I disagree with the contractor regarding the acceptable completion of the work, I can request an inspection by the fee inspector to determine if the work has been properly completed. If an agreement cannot be made with the contractor, the Lender may hold the money until such time as an agreement is reached or an arbitrator's decision is rendered.

* I understand the Lender, its investors, successors and assigns, does not provide a one-year warranty on the completed work on the property. I am responsible to obtain such warranty(s) from the contractor(s) and the warranty should be stated in the Homeowner-Contractor Agreement.

● I understand I am responsible to make the mortgage payments during the term of the loan, including the renovation period, to ensure the property will not go into default. The construction on the home must start within 30 days; if the construction ceases for more than 30 days, the Lender may consider the loan in default or the Lender can use the escrow money to have the work completed. If the work stops or is not progressing as it should, or if the work does not comply with the accepted architectural exhibits, the Lender may require additional compliance inspections to protect the security of the loan and I will be responsible to pay for the inspections and the cost of the inspection may be withheld at the next draw request.

* I understand no changes to the architectural exhibits can be made without the acceptance of the Lender, its investors, successors and assigns on form HUD-92577. The contingency fund is set up for changes that affect the health, safety, or items of necessity of the occupants of the property. If the contingency reserve is insufficient, I must place additional monies into the account for payment upon acceptance of the change. A change order will be made to assure the monies are available to the contractor upon completion of the changed work.

● I understand if there are unused contingency funds, mortgage payments, inspection fees or other monies in the Renovation Escrow Account after the Final Release is processed, the Lender, **must** apply those funds to prepay the mortgage principal, provided those items are a part of the mortgage.

● I understand the Lender may retain the 10 percent holdback, for a period not to exceed 35 days (or the time period required by law to file a lien, whichever is longer), to ensure compliance with state lien waiver laws or other state requirements. Upon completion of the work, I understand I will be provided: (1) the Final Draw Request; (2) the Final Release Notice; and (3) an accounting of the final distribution of all funds.

● I understand that under no circumstances may I act as the General Contractor or act in a "Self-Help" capacity.

This statement must be delivered to you prior to closing the loan. Return one copy to your Lender as proof you have read the entire document. Keep one copy for your records. You, the borrower(s), must be certain that you understand this information. Sign here only after you have read this entire document. Seek professional advice if you are uncertain.

Borrower's Signature & Date:	Borrower's Signature & Date:
X	X
X	X

I, the lender, certify this information was delivered to the borrower(s) prior to the time of loan closing.
Lender's Signature & Date:

X

NMFL# 4544 01/01

Figure 8.4 (continued)

203(k) Borrower's Acknowledgment

U.S. Department of Housing and Urban Development
Office of Housing / Federal Housing Commissioner

Condition of Property: I understand that the property I am purchasing is not HUD approved and HUD does. not warrant the condition or the value of the property. I understand the HUD plan review (where performed) and the appraisal are performed to determine compliance with the required architectural exhibits and to estimate the value of the property, but neither guarantees the house is free of defects. I understand I was responsible to have an independent consultant and/or a professional home inspection service perform an inspection of the property and the cost of the inspection was (or could be) included in the mortgage.

Loan Requirements

I understand at the time of the loan closing of an FHA-insured 203(k) Rehabilitation Loan, for which I have applied to my lender, the proceeds designated for the rehabilitation or improvement (including a contingency reserve, mortgage payments and any other fees, where applicable) are to be placed in an interest bearing escrow account. The Rehabilitation Escrow Account is not, nor will it be treated as an escrow for the paying of real estate taxes, insurance premiums, delinquent notes, ground rents or assessments. I hereby request the lender, after the Final Release Notice is issued, to:

☐ Pay the net interest income directly to me/us.

☐ Apply the net interest income directly to the mortgage principal balance for an equal amount of principal reduction.

☐ Other: _____

I understand that the Rehabilitation Escrow Account will cease paying interest to me if (1) the loan payments are delinquent for more than 30 days; or (2) the completion date (or an approved extension) has expired. During this period, the interest will be paid down on the mortgage principal. I understand if I clear up the delinquent or default status and/or the completion date has not expired or an extension has been approved, then the interest on the escrow account will begin again to be paid according to the request above.

I understand no draws on the escrow account can be made until all permits have been issued by the local or state building departments, where required. I further understand I can only request monies for the actual cost of rehabilitation. If any cost savings result on any line item of the Draw Request, form HUD-9746-A, the amount saved must be used to: (1) Make further improvements to the property; (2) Pay for cost overruns in other line items of the Draw Request; or (3) Prepay the mortgage principal.

I understand the contractor(s) is responsible to complete the work described in the architectural exhibits in a workmanlike manner. If I agree the work has been properly completed, I will sign the Draw Request, form HUD-9746-A, thereby accepting the responsibility that the completed work is acceptable and payment is justified. I understand there is a 10 percent holdback on each Draw Request to assure the work is properly completed and for lien protection.

I understand I am responsible to negotiate any and all agreements with the contractor(s) I select and that HUD suggests that the Agreement with the contractor should include a provision for binding arbitration with the American Arbitration Association on any dispute.

I understand if I am using the Escrow Commitment Procedure, I must sign form HUD-314. The funds deposited in an escrow, trust or special account will not be released until an assumption of the loan occurs by a creditworthy buyer or until the time allowed for such assumption has expired, thereby requiring the funds to be paid down on the mortgage principal.

I understand if I change a contractor for any reason, I may be obligated under the terms of the original contractor's agreement and I should seek legal advice before taking such action. If I disagree with the contractor regarding the acceptable completion of the work, I can request an inspection by the fee inspector to determine if the work has been properly completed. If an agreement cannot be made with the contractor, the lender may hold the money until such time as an agreement is reached or an arbitrator's decision is rendered.

I understand the lender or HUD does not provide a one-year warranty on the completed work on the property. I am responsible to obtain such warranty(s) from the contractor(s) and the warranty should be stated in the Homeowner-Contractor Agreement.

I understand I am responsible to make the mortgage payments during the term of the loan, including the rehabilitation period, to ensure the property will not go into default. The construction on the home must start within 30 days; if the construction ceases for more than 30 days, the lender may consider the loan in default or the lender can use the escrow money to have the work completed. If the work stops or is not progressing as it should, or if the work does not comply with the accepted architectural exhibits, the lender may require additional compliance inspections to protect the security of the loan and I will be responsible to pay for the inspections and the cost of the inspection may be withheld at the next draw request.

I understand no changes to the architectural exhibits can be made without the acceptance of the lender (or HUD) on form HUD-92577. The contingency fund is set up for changes that affect the health, safety, or items of necessity of the occupants of the property. If the contingency reserve is insufficient, I must place additional monies into the account for payment upon acceptance of the change. Additional improvements can be made after it is determined no further health and safety items exist. A change order will be made to assure the monies are available to the contractor upon completion of the changed work.

I understand if there are unused contingency funds, mortgage payments, inspection fees or other monies in the Rehabilitation Escrow Account after the Final Release is processed, the lender, in compliance with HUD regulations, must apply those funds to prepay the mortgage principal, provided those items are a part of the mortgage.

I understand the lender may retain the 10 percent holdback, for a period not to exceed 35 days (or the time period required by law to file a lien, whichever is longer), to ensure compliance with state lien waiver laws or other state requirements. Upon completion of the work, I understand I will be provided: (1) The Final Draw Request; (2) The Final Release Notice; and (3) An accounting of the final distribution of all funds.

This statement must be delivered to you prior to closing the loan. Return one copy to your lender as proof you have read the entire document. Keep one copy for your records. You, the borrower(s), must be certain that you understand this information. Sign here only after you have read this entire document. Seek professional advice if you are uncertain.

Borrower's Signature & Date:

X _____

Co-Borrower's Signature & Date:

X _____

I, the lender, certify this information was delivered to the borrower(s) prior to the time of loan closing.
Lender's Signature & Date:

X _____

-457 (9509)
VMP MORTGAGE FORMS - (800)521-7291

form HUD-92700-A (8/95)
ref. Handbook 4240.4

Figure 8.4   Renovation Loan Borrower's Acknowledgment (continued)

Notice to Contractor

There are no funds available for up-front start up costs.

This loan is in a mortgage program with set program requirements that must be followed.

All funds are disbursed after work has been completed in a workmanlike fashion and signed off on by the inspector.

All funds are released if work is completed as per the work write-up

Do not complete work unless outlined in the specification of repairs form(work write-up).

There will be no funds for changes unless approved by the Lender first.

All disbursements will be less a 10% holdback.

All disbursements will be made by two party checks to the contractor and borrower/homeowner.

All contractors must :
- *Complete the enclosed Homeowner/Contractor Agreement*
- *Attach a copy of your state business license or proof contractor by trade*
- *Complete the enclosed W-9 form*
- *Attach a copy of your insurance binder showing general liability and workers compensation if you have employees*

By signing this form you are acknowledging and agreeing to the above stated items. This notice does not supersede the Homeowner/Contractor Agreement.

Contractor's Company Name   *Contractor's Phone Number*

Contractor's Signature   *Print Contractor's Name*

NMFL# 4555 08/99

Figure 8.4   (continued)

Borrower's Identity-of-Interest Certification

Borrower's Name(s):	
Property Address:	
Telephone Number: Work: Home:	FHA Case No.:

"I hereby certify to the Department of Housing and Urban Development (HUD) and

(lender), that I/We do not have an identity-of-interest with the seller of the property. I also Certify that I/We do not have a conflict-of-interest with any other party to the transaction, including the realtor, lender, contractor, consultant and/or the appraiser. In addition, I certify that I am not obtaining any source of funds or acting as a "strawbuyer" for another individual, partnership, company or investment club and I/We ☐ will ☐ will not occupy the residence I/We are purchasing or refinancing."

Warning: HUD will prosecute false claims and statements. Conviction may result in criminal and/or civil penalties. (18 U.S.C. 1001, 1010, 1012; 31 U.S.C. 3729, 3802).

_____   Date: _____
Borrower

_____   Date: _____
Borrower

_____   Date: _____
Borrower

_____   Date: _____
Borrower

defects over a ten-year period, with the tolerances for those terms spelled out in their rules. Other states have yet to set sufficiently high standards, so it is important to examine the terms of the builder's new home warranty as well as research the builder's reputation and accountability within the areas they build.

In addition, most homebuilders will tell you that there is a one-year or two-year period up front that warrants appliances as well as major systems within the house. Most of these warranties hold either the product manufacturer or the subcontractors who installed the item accountable for its repair or replacement. It is important as a new homeowner that you follow the homebuilder's recommendation for maintenance to the letter or the builder may inform you that by neglecting their advice, you will have voided the terms of the new home warranty. More important, it is crucial that you complete and send in all warranty cards for systems or appliances (many companies now enable you to complete those tasks online) as soon as possible after taking possession of the new home.

Some builders of new homes buy separate warranties for the homes they build in addition to the structural warranty each state may require them to enforce. Home Buyers Warranty 2-10 insures a home against major system and structural defects for up to ten years. You can learn more about them at <www.2-10hbw.com>. With divisions set up all over the United States, each area has a toll-free number, however this organization is headquartered at 2675 South Abilene Street, Aurora, CO 80014 and can be reached at 720-747-6000.

Resale Home Warranties

Warranties also exist for previously occupied homes. Often, the seller of a home or the real estate agent involved in a transaction will offer to buy a warranty as a good faith gesture toward the homebuyer. If you have your home examined by a warranty inspector, you can get a policy to cover your major systems for several years. Policies issued without inspections restrict coverage greatly and usually are not worthwhile. The terms of these warranties can become very narrow when a major repair is called for, so ask plenty of questions about the type of warranty you purchase.

Home Buyer's Warranty 2-10 also has an existing home division and can be reached at 800-743-4210. Another very popular choice is American Home Shield Warranty (PO Box 2803, Memphis, TN 38101; www.americanhomeshield.com or call 800-735-4663).

Your home's professional inspection report is your best defense against the unknown on a used home. The inspector you hired will have cited, for example, how many years of service your roof has left, how soon your air conditioner may need to be replaced, or inform you of suspicious floor bulges found during his or her inspection. Becoming emotionally caught up in the home purchase, it is easy to ignore how serious and costly some of these repairs may become in a few years. Just be sure you proceed with both eyes wide open from the time of your initial purchase.

RESOURCES

Books

Dreams to Beams: A Guide to Building the Home You've Always Wanted, by Jane Moss Snow (National Association of Home Builders and nahb.com; 15th and M Streets, N.W., Washington, DC 20005; 800-368-5242; www.builderbooks.com). Leads you through custom home design, construction, and remodeling processes. Features planning and design checklists, financial planning worksheets, and construction timetable and gives you tips on cutting costs.

Find It, Buy It, Fix It: The Insider's Guide to Fixer-Uppers, by Robert Irwin (Dearborn Trade, Chicago, IL; 312-836-4400; 800-245-2665; www.dearborntrade .com). Reveals the ins and outs of buying and renovating your very own handyman's special. Shows homebuyers how to find the real bargains and how to avoid the moneypits.

The Frugal Homeowner's Guide to Buying, Selling, and Improving Your Home, by Julie Garton-Good (Dearborn Trade, Chicago, IL; 312-836-4400; 800-245-2665; www.dearborntrade.com). Advice on home ownership, mortgages, recouping remodeling costs, all in Q & A format.

The Homeowner's Property Tax Relief Kit, by Vincent and Laurence Czaplyski (McGraw-Hill, PO Box 543, Blacklick, OH 43004; 800-634-3961; www.mcgraw-hill .com). Describes how to lower your property tax bill through protesting assessments and other proven techniques.

The Kitchen Idea Book, by Joanne Kellar Bouknight (Taunton Press, 63 South Main Street, PO Box 5506, Newtown, CT 06470-5506; 203-426-8171; www.taunton .com). Detailed book displays photos and gives you ideas for kitchen design, storage possibilities, multiple work areas, and cabinet configurations.

Save a Fortune on Your Homeowners Property Tax, by Harry Koenig and Bob Lafay (Dearborn Trade, Chicago, IL; 312-836-4400; 800-245-2665; www.dearborntrade .com). Explains how to research and compare property values, check assessment records, file a claim, and appeal a property tax bill.

Tips and Traps for Saving on All Your Real Estate Taxes, by Robert Irwin and Norman Lane (McGraw-Hill, PO Box 543, Blacklick, OH 43004; 800-634-3961; www.mcgraw-hill.com). Explains all tax aspects of real estate. Discusses how to reduce property taxes, avoid taxes when selling a home, exchange properties to avoid taxes, and plan for tax consequences when you buy a home.

Web Sites

DoItYourself.com. This site provides a great deal of information about home building, home repairs, gardening, tools, codes, and where to get supplies, with links to various commercial and retail sites. <www.doityourself.com>

ImproveNet.com. Information for homeowners who want to remodel or find contractors and designers. <www.improvenet.com>

American Home Shield. Offers warranties for home appliances. <www .americanhomeshield.com>

CNA Warranty. Offers warranties for home appliances and extended warranties for home appliance purchases. <www.cna.com>

Home Buyer's Warranty Corporation. Offers warranties for home appliances. <www.2-10hbw.com.>

Professional Warranty Service Corporation. Offers warranties for home appliances. <www.pwsc.com>

Quality Builders Warranty Corporation. Online insurer for new homes. Will insure new home against defects in workmanship and materials for the first year; against defects in wiring, piping, and duct work, and performance of the home's systems and major structural defects in the second year; and against major structural defects for the third through the tenth years. <www.qbwc.com>

Residential Warranty Corporation. Warrants newly constructed homes. Will insure new home against defects in workmanship and materials for the first year; against defects in the major home systems in the second year; and against defects in the structural elements of the home for the third through tenth years. <www.rwcwarranty.com>

Trade Associations

National Association of Home Builders (1201 15th Street, NW, Washington, DC 20005; 202-822-0200; 800-368-5242; www.nahb.com). Represents single-family and multifamily home builders, remodelers, and others associated with the home building industry, such as those involved in mortgage finance and building products and services. Some local associations run consumer dispute resolution programs. The association's Home Builders Institute develops educational and job-training programs related to home building. Offers information on various homebuying issues, such as settling problems with builders and buying a new home. Sells books about home building, including *Building Your Home: An Insider's Guide and Remodeling Your Home: An Insider's Guide.* Also sells brochures, including "Choosing a Builder," "Designing Your New Home," "Paying for Your New Home," "Selecting Your New Home's Location," "The Building Contract," "The Building Process," "Moving into Your New Home," "The New Home Buyer's Workbook," and "Your New Home and How to Take Care of It."

United Homeowners Association (655 15th Street, NW, Suite 460, Washington, DC 20005; 202-408-8842; www.uha.org). Group representing American homeowners. It is a resource for helping homeowners save money when buying or selling a home, remodeling, financing or refinancing, and getting homeowners insurance. The UHA also lobbies for homeowner rights with the federal government. Members receive a great deal of educational material on buying, financing, and maintaining their homes and are eligible for discounts on appliances, insurance, and housing-related publications. Members also have access to UHA's Mortgage Rate Shopper, which is designed to help you get the most advantageous mortgage rate. The group's Web site, accessible through keyword UHA on America Online, explains its services in more detail and answers many questions you many have about home ownership.

CHAPTER 9

Selling Your Home

When the time comes to sell your home, you must do just as much homework as you did when you bought the property.

The first step in getting the highest price possible for your home is to obtain a realistic *appraisal* of its current value. If you have paid little attention to the market for the past several years, you may have an outdated sense of what your home is worth. You should get a feel for the market by scanning newspaper ads for similar properties and by visiting nearby open houses. Real estate agents will be glad to give you a free assessment of your home's strengths, weaknesses, and fair price range. For a fee, you can also obtain a professional appraiser's opinion.

If you want to avoid the real estate broker's fee, you can try to sell your home yourself with newspaper ads and a For Sale sign on your front lawn. Although you will have to deal with browsers and people unqualified to buy your property, you may be lucky enough to find someone who falls in love with your home, places a bid on it, and can afford to complete the purchase.

Before you let anyone past the front door, however, make sure your home is in tip-top shape. Add a fresh coat of paint. Locate plants and flowers strategically. Mow the lawn. Spruce up the exterior. Clean every room thoroughly. Remove excess clutter and furniture to maximize the appearance of living space. There are professional organizers and even professional "stagers" that you can pay to prepare your home for the best possible presentation, especially if you want a top-dollar asking price. For information on this, ask a real estate

broker for referral or visit <www.stagedhomes.com>, <www.homestagers
.com>, or <www.napo.net>.

Prepare and distribute a one-page fact sheet listing your home's selling
points and illustrating the layout, and add a photo for prospective clients to
take with them to remind them of your home during their home-shopping
tours. If you're located in an active real estate market, you might be able to
sell within a few weeks. It is always best, however, to sell your home before
you buy another property. You don't want to owe two mortgage payments if
your home sells more slowly than you had anticipated.

THE TRANSFER DISCLOSURE STATEMENT

More and more states require that you disclose all of your home's problems in writing to prospective buyers. The document covers a property's
structure, utilities (such as plumbing, air-conditioning, and water system),
and municipal status (such as building permits, zoning restrictions, certificate of occupancy, and property tax rates). If the buyer signs this sales disclosure form acknowledging that he or she has been informed of the home's
problems, the buyer has little right to sue you later if any problems crop up
for any of the items listed.

SELLING YOUR HOME BY YOURSELF

A growing percentage of homeowners are choosing to sell their homes
themselves, without the aid and expense of a licensed real estate agent. If you
have purchased and sold several homes in your lifetime, you may feel that
you have the expertise and time it takes to handle this job yourself. Of
course, there is no law that precludes you from selling your own home, but
you may want to go into this process with your eyes as wide open as possible so as not to have unrealistic expectations along the way.

A *for-sale-by-owner* is what is known in the real estate industry as a
FSBO (pronounced fizz-bo). The idea here is for a FSBO to sell his or her
home at full market value and pocket all the equity, including whatever they
would have had to pay out in a real estate agent's commission. In some cases,
these proceeds are absolutely essential for the FSBO owner to have enough
down payment money to get into another, perhaps more expensive home. In
other cases, it may just be a matter of wanting to go it alone, surmising that
they have the time, patience, and detached business acumen to do so. It is
possible for a FSBO seller to perform as well as industry professionals; it is
also possible for them to realize that the process of selling a home is much
more complicated and time consuming than they ever thought possible. Then

there are the realistic souls that pledge to try selling their homes themselves for a while, but name an arbitrary date by which they intend to engage some assistance if their own efforts prove fruitless.

The first thing to keep in mind is that although you as a FSBO seller may be lucky enough to save a bundle of money at closing, you will need to invest some money up front in order to successfully market a home. This includes signs, advertising, marketing materials (flyers), time off work to show the home, accessibility by phone around the clock, seven days a week, and the ability to view your home's value free of emotional attachment. In other words, you must possess the knack of regarding your home as venture capital instead of the place where many priceless memories have taken place. You must be able to make yourself fairly invisible (within the limits of home security) when potential buyers tour your home, and remain poker-faced when talking about selling terms. This is a tall order for some, though not for others who are able to keep their eyes focused on the prize they have in mind for their efforts.

A NEW TYPE OF REAL ESTATE AGENT

There is a middle road to selling your home that does not require a commissioned percentage of your final selling price, but gets you the professional services for which you may be willing to pay, while performing some or most of the home-selling tasks yourself. Just because the residential real estate business has been conducted pretty much the same way for the past hundred years doesn't mean that you have to settle for paying out the customary and gut-wrenching 4 percent to 8 percent broker commission.

Real estate agents and brokers have also had a vested reason to explore more avenues in home buying and selling for the consumer, because only the most seasoned veterans tend to make a consistent and reasonable living in the industry. For that reason, *fee-for-services real estate consultants* are becoming increasingly popular these days.

There are different models emerging in this menu-driven type of real estate service. Some are bundled packages, asking for a specific fee for the consultant in exchange for recommending an asking price and listing a home on the Multiple Listing Service, leaving you to do the task of advertising, showing, negotiating, and contracting the sale of your home. Others will permit you to hire them for the negotiation and paperwork end of the transaction; the part which may seem the most intimidating to many home sellers, experienced or not.

You may be committed to maximizing the proceeds from the sale of your home and don't feel the need for specialized training to handle many of the tasks that do not appear complicated. If so, you may find that many real estate agents will agree to focus exclusively on what services you want them to perform for an agreed-upon fee (far less than the usual real estate closing commissions). In the process, they can become an unbiased source of information while you remain in control of the entire process. For more information on fee-for-services real estate, check out <www.narec.com>, <www.ired.com>, <www.realtor.org>, or <www.helpusell.com>.

CHOOSING A REAL ESTATE PROFESSIONAL

If you cannot or you choose not to sell your home on your own, interview several real estate agents or brokers to compete for your listing. Unless you deal with a flat-fee or discount broker, you must pay the agent you choose a commission of 4 percent to 8 percent of your home's selling price, usually to be shared with the agent bringing them a ready, willing, and able buyer.

Deciding on just the right agent to get the job done should not be undertaken on impulse or merely on a referral basis, even though you may have seen a particular agent's name before. There are a number of very important questions you should ask regarding just what an agent is willing to do (and prove to you that they are doing) in order to procure the listing of your home.

Remember that during the entire time your home is on the market, your agent is your employee, so to speak. You have the final say in the details of the sale of your home, no matter what advice you may be given by various real estate professionals or well-meaning family or friends.

Any full-service agent you choose should be willing to provide you with:

- A complete market analysis; this always includes closed sales of comparable properties within the past six months.
- Pricing recommendations based on the strengths of detractors or your home compared to those that have sold recently. You must decide your own asking price, but if the agent thinks you are being totally unreasonable, he or she has the option of turning down your listing. Most often, however, the agent will try to get you to negotiate the terms under which you will attempt to get your price on the home before lowering it to what may be recommended as a more reasonable figure.
- Information about your property that will be offered to potential sellers, including easements, condition of the property, attractive amenities, and marketing strengths and apparent weaknesses of your home
- Suggestions for making the best presentation of your home (such as staging the home to appeal to the broadest range of potential buyers, applying new paint, adding fresh flowers, or removing clutter from rooms and storage areas)

- A pledge to supervise the showing and maintenance of your property if you are out of town or have already moved into another property
- Some of his or her own buyer/prospects, while being ever-vigilant in finding ways to attract other agents' clients
- The marketing of your home through the MLS, newspapers, the Internet, professionally prepared flyers, and holding broker tours and open houses
- Prospects that are financially qualified to buy your home; this means that looky-loos, tire-kickers, and non-loan-worthy prospects are eliminated from everyone's agenda.
- Appointment-scheduling expertise, clearing showing times with you in advance; even when a buyer's agent is involved, your agent should be willing to be on hand for the showing or have an assistant ready to do so.
- Regular bulletins on progress; this includes how often your home was shown, by whom, what impressions those showings produced, how many calls their office has received about your home, and what recommendations outside brokers may have had while offering feedback from the showing of your home.
- The negotiation of your contract with tact, diplomacy, and timeliness, so that you get the highest price possible; your agent should also insist on a full loan preapproval of your eventual buyer by a specified date in your accepted contract.
- Regular barometer checks on your escrow and your buyer's loan process, looking for any signs of nonperformance or cold feet, while readying you for the time frame agreed upon in the negotiated purchase agreement
- Attendance at closing; he or she is also required to keep copies of the all paperwork for any after-the-sale issues that may arise.

Real estate professionals depend on their reputations and track records to get prized referrals, the best kind of business for which they can hope. If your agent has done a particularly stellar job in helping you sell your home, remember him or her by word-of-mouth recommendations to friends, family, or business associates. A letter of praise to the office broker or the agent himself is always appreciated.

A FOOTNOTE ABOUT CLOSING COSTS

When you sell your home, either on your own or through a real estate agent, you must deduct all selling and closing costs from the gross sales price to arrive at your net proceeds. The worksheet in Figure 9.1 lists some of the

Figure 9.1   Net Proceeds Worksheet

Gross Equity	$ Amount	Total
Sale Price of Property	$ _____	
Minus Remaining Mortgage Balance	(_____)	
Minus Other Home-Related Debts	(_____)	
TOTAL GROSS EQUITY		$ _____

Selling and Closing Costs

Escrow or Other Fees	$ _____	
Legal and Document Preparation Fees	_____	
Title Search and Insurance Fees	_____	
Transfer Taxes	_____	
FHA, VA, or Lender Discounts	_____	
Mortgage Prepayment Penalties	_____	
Real Estate Taxes Owed	_____	
Appraisal Fees	_____	
Survey Fees	_____	
Termite and Other Pest Inspection Fees	_____	
Fees for Repair Work Required by Sales Contract	_____	
Home Protection or Warranty Plan Fees	_____	
Unpaid Assessments	_____	
Real Estate Commissions	_____	
Other Selling or Closing Costs	_____	
TOTAL SELLING AND CLOSING COSTS		$ _____
TOTAL GROSS EQUITY MINUS		_____
TOTAL SELLING AND CLOSING COSTS EQUALS		(_____)
NET PROCEEDS		$ _____

costs you might incur and helps you determine your profit. This worksheet will help you assess your gross equity in your home, deduct selling and closing costs, and arrive at a net figure as your final proceeds from the sale of your home.

At the closing, both the buyer and seller will receive from their lawyers a closing statement keeping track of all the money flowing back and forth, as well as a reconciliation statement showing how money was disbursed and received. A sample of these statements is shown in Figure 9.2.

RESOURCES

Books

All about Escrow and Real Estate Closings: Or How to Buy the Brooklyn Bridge and Have the Last Laugh, by Sandy Gadow and Dave Patton (Escrow Publishing Company, PO Box 2165, Palm Beach, FL 33480; 561-659-1474; www.escrowhelp .com). Leads the reader through the escrow and closing process, from opening the escrow to the closing statements.

Art of Real Estate Appraisal, by William L. Ventolo, Jr. and Martha R. Williams (Dearborn Trade, Chicago, IL; 312-836-4400; 800-245-2665; www .dearborntrade.com). The complete reference on how to appraise the value of your home or evaluate appraisal reports. Up-to-date information on financing techniques, energy efficient construction, and home depreciation.

If You're Clueless about Selling Your House and Want to Know More, by Bonnie Sparks (Dearborn Trade, Chicago, IL; 312-836-4400; 800-245-2665; www .dearborntrade.com). Helps you decide if selling is the best decision, and includes information on negotiating offers, closing deals, and finding the best agent. It demystifies the selling process.

Dress Your House for Success: 5 Fast, Easy Steps to Selling Your House, Apartment, Condo for the Highest Possible Price!, by Martha Webb and Sarah Parsons Zackheim (Random House, 400 Hahn Road, Westminster, MD 21157; 800-733-3000; www.randomhouse.com). Lots of ideas, checklists, and drawings to help the reader sell a property.

The For Sale by Owner Kit, by Robert Irwin (Dearborn Trade, Chicago, IL; 312-836-4400; 800-245-2665; www.dearborntrade.com). Explains how to set a realistic price; prepare a home for sale; promote the home with effective signs and advertising; find buyers; deal with documents, agents, and brokers; negotiate and finance.

The Home Buying and Selling Juggling Act: Timing the Process to Maximize Profits & Minimize Hassle, by Robert Irwin (Dearborn Trade, Chicago, IL; 312-836-4400; 800-245-2665; www.dearborntrade.com). Helps homeowners face the challenges of selling a house and buying another simultaneously.

Figure 9.2   Sample Closing Statement

SELLER'S STATEMENT			BUYER'S STATEMENT	
DEBT	**CREDIT**	**ITEM**	**DEBIT**	**CREDIT**
		Total Purchase Price		
		Binder Deposit		
		First Mortgage		
		Second Mortgage		
		Prorations and Prepayments		
		Rent		
		Interest (first mortgage)		
		Interest (second mortgage)		
		Prepayment penalty		
		Insurance		
		Mortgage insurance		
		Insurance reserves		
		Taxes (city)		
		Taxes (county)		
		Tax reserves		
		Expenses		
		Attorney's fees		
		Escrow closing fees		
		Escrow holding fees (long term)		
		State tax on deed		
		Recording mortgage		
		Recording deed		
		Title insurance		
		Brokerage		
		Miscellaneous		
		Total Debits and Credits		
		Balance Due		
		Seller and from buyer		
		Grand Totals		

RECONCILIATION STATEMENT

	RECEIPTS	DISBURSEMENT
Bank Loan (less points/origination fees)		
Deposit		
Check from Buyer at Closing		
Brokerage Fee		
Check to Seller at Closing		
Seller's Expense		
Buyer's Expense		
Grand Totals		

The Homeseller's Kit, by Edith Lank and Dena Amoruso (Dearborn Trade, Chicago, IL; 312-836-4400; 800-245-2665; www.dearborntrade.com). Tells how to list your house with or without an agent and how to price your property correctly.

The Homeseller's Survival Guide, by Kenneth W. Edwards (Dearborn Trade, Chicago, IL; 312-836-4400; 800-245-2665; www.dearborntrade.com). Identifies hazards associated with selling a home, describes them in some detail, and provides guidance to avoid them or deal with them.

How to Sell Your Home Fast, for the Highest Price, in Any Market, by Terry Eilers (Hyperion, 77 W. 66th, 11th Floor, New York, NY 10023; 212-456-0100; www.hyperionbooks.go.com). Takes the reader through every step of the sale process, from finding a qualified agent and establishing a list price, to marketing and advertising the house and managing details of the closing.

How to Sell Your Home without a Broker, by Bill Carey (John Wiley & Sons, 1 Wiley Drive, Somerset, NJ 08875-1272; 212-850-6000; 800-225-5945; www.wiley.com). Explains how to prepare your property for sale and how to find buyers so you can avoid paying the real estate broker's commission.

How to Sell Your House in 90 Days: A 10-Step Plan for Selling Your House in Today's Market, with or without a Broker, by Marc Stephen Garrison. (Doubleday, Bantam Doubleday Dell Publishing Group, Inc., 666 Fifth Avenue, New York, N.Y. 10103; www.doubleday.com). Step-by-step workbook that shows what it takes to sell a home in today's market.

Modern Real Estate Practice, by Fillmore W. Galaty, Wellington J. Allaway, and Robert C. Kyle (Dearborn Trade, Chicago, IL; 312-836-4400; 800-245-2665; www.dearborntrade.com). The reference book on every aspect of homebuying and selling: the sales transaction, real estate laws, leasing, financing, and appraising your home or real estate investment. Includes standardized forms for listing and sales contracts, deeds, appraisals, environmental assessments, and a sample mortgage. Also prepares you to become a real estate agent or broker. Available in 20 individual state editions or supplements.

Real Estate a la Carte: Selecting the Services you Need, Paying What They're Worth, by Julie Garton-Good (Dearborn Trade, Chicago, IL; 312-836-4400; 800-245-2665; www.dearborntrade.com). Cafeteria-style selections from which to choose for buying and selling your home designed to give consumers the power to pay for only those services they want, therefore putting them in control.

Seller Beware: Insider Secrets You Need to Know about Selling Your House—From Listing through Closing the Deal, by Robert Irwin (Dearborn Trade, Chicago, IL; 312-836-4400; 800-245-2665; www.dearborntrade.com). Tells readers how to navigate safely around the problems that can arise from an undisclosed defect in a home. Explains what defects to disclose (all), when to disclose them (up front), what to fix, and what to leave.

Sell It Yourself, by Ralph Roberts (Adams Media Corp., 260 Center Street, Holbrook, MA 02343; 781-767-8100; 800-872-5627; www.adamsmedia.com). How to sell your home without a broker.

Tips and Traps When Selling a Home, by Robert Irwin (McGraw-Hill, PO Box 543, Blacklick, OH 43004; 800-634-3961; www.mcgraw-hill.com). Offers strategies for getting the highest price possible for your home. Gives advice on sprucing up your property, using a real estate broker, and negotiating with buyers.

Web Sites

Domania.com. This site will list sale prices of properties in your neighborhood for the past three to four years. To obtain detailed information on those properties (number of bedrooms, baths, etc.), you must register and become a member. Members can also obtain a valuation of their own home, based on neighborhood sales. <www.domania.com>

Homebid.com. Lets a prospective homebuyer make an offer with contingencies; then the homeowner presents a counteroffer. Gives agents and their clients the power to accomplish key steps of the homebuying and selling process via the Internet. <www.homebid.com>

Homebytes.com. Home sale service that charges a flat fee instead of traditional commission. <www.homebytes.com>

Home Gain. This site specializes in making approximate appraisals of your home by looking up comparable, recent home sales in your area and using the information you supply about your home to reach a market value. The site also specializes in helping you prepare your home for sale and in finding an appropriate real estate agent for you. <www.homegain.com>

Kaktus.com. This site offers free real estate legal forms, a legal term glossary, links to brokers and agents, a loan amortization table, and calculators. <www.kaktus .com>

Owners.com. This site allows owners to display their homes without a real estate agent, using virtual 360-degree panoramic photos, descriptions, and maps, and allows buyers to peruse the site looking for a home. The site includes lots of help with online seller and buyer handbooks, newspaper advertising, insurance quotes, and, if you decide to use an agent, a selection of agents. <www.owners.com>

Realtor.com. National Association of REALTORS® site with comprehensive home-buying, selling, moving, and borrowing information. Includes sections on apartments, neighborhoods, insurance, home improvement, decorating, lawn and garden, and other home-related subjects. <www.realtor.com>

Realty.com. Offers advice on buying and selling, with home listings. <www.realty .com>

Trade Association

National Association of REALTORS® (430 N. Michigan Avenue, Chicago, IL 60611; 312-329-8200; 800-874-6500; www.realtor.com). The trade group for real estate agents. Has a Real Estate Q&A with hundreds of questions and answers on over 50 real estate subjects on its Web site.

CHAPTER 10

Investment Real Estate

Buying a home is the primary, but by no means the only, way to profit from real estate. Investing in real estate for profit is tricky and can take a great deal of time and expertise, but may offer lucrative rewards as well. Real estate has the advantages of appreciation potential, rental income, and tax benefits. On the other hand, it can be extremely *illiquid* (hard to sell) and management intensive. The real estate market is also subject to the influence of national trends, such as changes in tax laws and interest rates, as well as local trends in economic growth and supply and demand for similar properties.

When seeking advice about investing in real estate, make sure that you know or can research your source of knowledge. The field is rife with self-promoters promising instant riches for no money down. Their so-called seminars are, in fact, high-pressure sales pitches. These scam artists usually show off their wealth to impress you; however, they have probably earned their millions by giving bad real estate advice, not taking it. Some tout enormous riches to be made in foreclosed property. Others guarantee wealth through government loan programs. A few want you to believe your road to easy street is paved with multilevel marketing, another term for a pyramid or Ponzi scheme. Be extremely careful when dealing with these promoters. Their presentations are slick and convincing, but the chances that you will end up equally as rich are slim to nonexistent.

If you wish to invest legitimately in real estate, you have seven principal ways to do so. They are ranked and discussed below from the safest to the most speculative.

1. Real estate mutual funds
2. Real estate investment trusts
3. Real estate limited partnerships
4. Rental real estate
5. Exchanging property
6. Vacation homes and timeshares
7. Raw land.

REAL ESTATE MUTUAL FUNDS

Several mutual funds invest in publicly traded real estate–oriented stocks. As do all mutual funds, they provide a widely diversified portfolio of securities, professional management, and reasonable management fees of about 1 percent of your assets each year. Real estate funds tend to perform well when interest rates are low and when a glut of real estate exists on the market. Conversely, they tend to underperform during periods of rising interest rates and when gluts of real estate exist on the market. Some funds buy only U.S. real estate companies, while other global funds invest in real estate companies around the world.

Many real estate mutual funds buy stocks in homebuilders and suppliers to the home-building industry. It is important to note how closely home-building is tied to the economy at any given moment, with thousands of livelihoods dependent on its income generation. Homebuilding seems to be one of the industries historically least affected by an economic slowdown. Why? Perhaps because in times of uncertainty about the rest of the world, *home* is the place people tend to value most.

The popularity of real estate investing through mutual funds has spawned a profusion of funds. Some funds to research are

- ABN AMRO Funds, 800-443-4725
- Advantus Family of Funds, 800-665-6005
- AIM Family of Funds, 800-959-4246
- Alliance Funds, 800-227-4618
- Alpine Management and Research, 888-785-5578
- American Century Investments, 800-345-3533
- Brazos Mutual Funds, 800-426-9157, CGM Group, 800-345-4048
- Cohen and Steers Funds, 800-437-9912
- Columbia Real Estate Equity, 800-547-1707
- Advisors' Inner Circle Funds, 888-712-1103
- Davis Funds, 800-279-0279
- Delaware Investments, 800-231-8002
- Deutsche Asset Management, 800-730-1313

- DFA Investment Dimensions Group, 310-395-8005
- EII Realty Securities, 888-323-8912
- Excelsior Funds, 800-446-1012
- Fidelity Group, 800-544-8888
- First American Investment Funds, 800-637-2548
- Forward Funds, 800-999-6809
- Russell Funds, 800-787-7354
- Franklin Templeton Investments, 800-342-5236
- Fremont Funds, 800-548-4539
- Gabelli-Westwood Funds, 800-937-8966
- GMA LLC, 617-330-7500
- Goldman Sachs Asset Management Group, 800-621-2550
- John Hancock Funds, 800-225-5291
- INVESCO Family of Funds, 800-525-8085
- Johnson Mutual Funds, 800-541-1070
- Kensington Funds, 877-833-7114
- LaSalle Investment Management, 800-527-2553
- Lend Lease Funds, 877-563-5327
- Longleaf Partners Funds, 800-445-9469
- M.S.D.&T. Funds, 800-551-2145
- MFS Family of Funds, 800-225-2606
- Morgan Stanley Institutional Funds, 800-548-7786 or 800-869-6397
- The Munder Funds, 800-468-6337
- Phoenix Funds, 800-243-4361
- Pioneer Group, 800-225-6292
- Principal Mutual Funds, 800-247-4123
- Principal Investors Fund, 800-521-1502
- ProFunds, 888-776-3637
- Prudential Funds, 800-225-1852
- RREEF Funds, 888-897-8480
- Security Capital Real Estate Funds, 888-732-8748
- SSgA Funds, 800-647-7327
- Stratton Group, 800-634-5726
- T. Rowe Price Funds, 800-638-5660
- Third Avenue Funds, 800-443-1021
- UAM Funds, 877-826-5465
- Van Kampen Funds, 800-421-5666
- Victory Group, 800-539-3863
- Wells Real Estate Funds, 800-282-1851

For a list of regulatory agencies and investment research information, go to <www.greenjungle.com>.

REAL ESTATE INVESTMENT TRUSTS (REITs)

REITs were actually spelled out and created by the U.S. tax code back in the 1970s, as were mutual funds. When you buy shares in a REIT (which are traded on the stock exchange), you are actually investing in a company that invests in real estate. That company pools money together and builds a portfolio of real estate properties such as office buildings, apartment complexes, industrial facilities, shopping centers, regional malls, and other commercial spaces. They pay out almost all of their profit in the form of *dividends* to their shareholders, which, under current real estate law, exempts them from taxes at the corporate level as long as they distribute at least 95 percent of their earnings in this manner. Shareholders then pay taxes on the dividends as regular income. In some cases, a portion of the dividends may be considered a return of capital for tax purposes and therefore is not taxed.

The advantages of investing in REITs are that they tend to be diversified, offer liquidity, and are priced daily. A single REIT can offer as few as ten properties or as many as 100 or more for potential investment. Common wisdom tells us that the more diversified the portfolio, the lower the risk may be, in general, with special attention being paid to the REIT's past performance and reputation overall.

Investors may be able to further lessen their financial exposure in real estate investment by purchasing a real estate mutual fund that *buys* in REITs. Although a small fee will apply as in other mutual fund investments, these funds can pay high dividends, often with yields of 2 percent to about 5 percent.

Three primary types of REITs exist:

1. *Equity.* These trusts buy properties, fix them up, collect rents, and sometimes sell the properties at a profit. Equity REIT share prices greatly reflect the general direction of real estate values. Some equity REITs buy different kinds of properties across the country. Others specialize in a particular type of real estate. For example, several REITs, including Meditrust (197 First Avenue, Suite 300, Needham Heights, MA 02494; 781-453-8062) and Health Care REIT, Inc. (One Seagate, Suite 1500, P.O. Box 1475, Toledo, OH 43603; 419-247-2800), concentrate on health care facilities. Others buy properties in one region of the country. For example, Washington REIT (6110 Executive Boulevard, Rockville, MD 20852; 301-984-9400; http://ir .stockmaster.com/ir/wre) buys properties in the Washington, D.C., market, while Weingarten Realty Investors (P.O. Box 924133, Houston, TX 77292; 713-866-6000; www.weingarten.com) specializes in shopping centers in Texas and Louisiana. Equity REITs can provide some protection against inflation because they usually include rent

escalator clauses in their contracts with tenants so that price increases can be passed along in the form of higher rents.

2. *Mortgage.* This form of REIT originates or buys mortgages on commercial properties. Mortgage REITs offer yields of about 6 percent to 10 percent—much more than the 4 percent to 7 percent paid by equity REITs. But mortgage REITs offer little capital appreciation potential. If mortgages get into trouble or default, share prices can plunge.

3. *Hybrid.* These REITs combine equity and mortgage holdings. Hybrid trusts pay yields of 6 percent to 9 percent and offer some appreciation potential.

The REIT industry has become notorious for a boom and bust cycle. Its first boom occurred in the early 1970s, which led to an enormous bust in the 1973–1974 recession, when many REITs went bankrupt in the wake of massive overbuilding. The industry recovered and prospered for much of the 1980s until the real estate market again became glutted in the late 1980s and early 1990s. By the late 1990s and early 2000s, REIT shares were popular again as lower interest rates and tightening rental markets in many places boosted share prices.

Below is a list of the major REITs, the Stock Exchange on which they are traded, and their ticker symbols, courtesy of the National Association of Real Estate Investment Trusts.

New York Stock Exchange

Company Name	Ticker
Acadia Realty Trust	AKR
Agree Realty Corporation	ADC
Alexander's Inc.	ALX
Alexandria Real Estate Equities, Inc.	ARE
AMB Property Corporation	AMB
America First Mortgage Investments, Inc.	MFA
American Land Lease	ANL
American Residential Investment Trust, Inc.	INV
Amli Residential Properties Trust	AML
Annaly Mortgage Management, Inc.	NLY
Anthracite Mortgage Capital Inc.	AHR
AIMCO	AIV
Apex Mortgage Capital Inc.	AXM
Archstone-Smith	ASN
Arden Realty Group, Inc.	ARI

New York Stock Exchange

Company Name	Ticker
Asset Investors Corporation	AIC
Associated Estates Realty Corp.	AEC
AvalonBay Communities Inc.	AVB
Bedford Property Investors	BED
Boston Properties, Inc.	BXP
Boykin Lodging Company	BOY
Brandywine Realty Trust	BDN
Brookfield Properties Corporation	BPO
BRE Properties, Inc.	BRE
BRT Realty Trust	BRT
Burnham Pacific Properties, Inc.	BPP
California Preferred Capital Corp.	CFP
Camden Property Trust	CPT
Capstead Mortgage Corporation	CMO
CarrAmerica Realty Corporation	CRE
Catellus Development Corporation	CDX
CBL & Associates Properties	CBL
Center Trust Properties	CTA
CenterPoint Properties Trust	CNT
Chateau Communities, Inc.	CPJ
Chelsea Property Group	CPG
Chevy Chase Preferred Capital Corp.	CCP
Clarion Commercial Holdings Inc.	CLR
Colonial Properties Trust	CLP
Commercial Net Lease Realty	NNN
Cornerstone Realty Income Trust	TCR
Corporate Office Properties Trust	OFC
Correctional Properties Trust	CPV
Cousins Properties, Inc.	CUZ
Crescent Real Estate Equities, Inc.	CEI
CRIIMI MAE, Inc.	CMM
Crown American Realty Trust	CWN
Developers Diversified Realty Corporation	DDR
Duke Realty Corporation	DRE
EastGroup Properties, Inc.	EGP
Elder Trust	ETT
Entertainment Properties Trust	EPR
Equity Inns, Inc.	ENN

New York Stock Exchange

Company Name	Ticker
Equity Office Properties Trust	EOP
Equity One, Inc.	EQY
Equity Residential	EQR
Essex Property Trust, Inc.	ESS
Federal Realty Investment Trust	FRT
FelCor Lodging Trust Inc.	FCH
First Industrial Realty Trust	FR
First Union Real Estate Investments	FUR
Forest City Enterprises	FCE.A
Gables Residential Trust	GBP
General Growth Properties, Inc.	GGP
Glenborough Realty Trust Inc.	GLB
Glimcher Realty Trust	GRT
Great Lakes REIT	GL
Health Care Property Investors, Inc.	HCP
Health Care REIT, Inc.	HCN
Healthcare Realty Trust, Inc.	HR
Highwoods Properties, Inc.	HIW
Home Properties of New York, Inc.	HME
Hospitality Properties Trust	HPT
Host Marriott Corporation	HMT
HRPT Properties Trust	HRP
Innkeepers USA Trust	KPA
IRT Property Company	IRT
iStar Financial Inc.	SFI
JDN Realty Corporation	JDN
JP Realty, Inc.	JPR
Keystone Property Trust	KTR
Kilroy Realty Corporation	KRC
Kimco Realty Corporation	KIM
Koger Equity, Inc.	KE
Konover Property Trust, Inc.	KPT
Kramont Realty Trust	KRT
La Quinta Properties, Inc.	LQI
LaSalle Hotel Properties	LHO
LASER Mortgage Management, Inc.	LMM
Lexington Corporate Properties, Inc.	LXP
Liberty Property Trust	LRY

New York Stock Exchange

Company Name	Ticker
LTC Properties, Inc.	LTC
Macerich Company, The	MAC
Mack-Cali Realty Corporation	CLI
Malan Realty Investors, Inc.	MAL
Manufactured Home Communities	MHC
MeriStar Hospitality Corporation	MHX
Mid-America Apartment Communities, Inc.	MAA
Mid-Atlantic Realty Trust	MRR
Mills Corporation, The	MLS
Montgomery CV Realty Group	CVI
National Golf Properties, Inc.	TEE
National Health Investors, Inc.	NHI
Nationwide Health Properties, Inc.	NHP
New Plan Excel Realty Trust	NXL
Novastar Financial, Inc.	NFI
Omega Healthcare Investors, Inc.	OHI
Origen Financial, Inc.	OFI
Pacific Gulf Properties	PAG
Pan Pacific Retail Properties	PNP
Parkway Properties Inc.	PKY
Pennsylvania REIT	PEI
Phillips International Realt Corp.	PHR
Plum Creek Timber Company	PCL
Post Properties, Inc.	PPS
Prentiss Properties Trust	PP
Prime Group Realty Trust	PGE
Prime Retail, Inc.	PRT
ProLogis	PLD
Public Storage, Inc.	PSA
Ramco-Gershenson Properties Trust	RPT
Realty Income Corporation	O
Reckson Associates Realty Corp.	RA
Redwood Trust, Inc.	RWT
Regency Centers Corporation	REG
RFS Hotel Investors, Inc.	RFS
Rouse Company, The	RSE

New York Stock Exchange

Company Name	Ticker
Saul Centers, Inc.	BFS
Security Capital Group, Inc.	SCZ
Senior Housing Properties Trust	SNH
Shurgard Storage Centers, Inc.	SHU
Simon Property Group, Inc.	SPG
Sizeler Property Investors, Inc.	SIZ
SL Green Realty Corp.	SLG
Sovran Self Storage	SSS
Starwood Hotels & Resorts	HOT
Storage USA, Inc.	SUS
Summit Properties Inc.	SMT
Sun Communities, Inc.	SUI
Tanger Factory Outlet Centers, Inc.	SKT
Taubman Centers, Inc.	TCO
Thornburg Mortgage Asset Corporation	TMA
Town and Country Trust, The	TCT
Transcontinental Realty Investors, Inc.	TCI
Trizec Properties, Inc.	TRZ
U.S. Restaurant Properties	USV
United Dominion Realty Trust, Inc.	UDR
Universal Health Realty Income Trust	UHT
Urstadt Biddle Properties, Inc.	UBP
Ventas, Inc.	VTR
Vornado Realty Trust	VNO
Washington Real Estate Investment Trust	WRE
Weingarten Realty Investors	WRI
Winston Hotels	WXH

American Stock Exchange

Aegis Realty Inc.	AER
American Mortgage Acceptance Company	AMC
AmeriVest Properties Inc.	AMV
Anworth Mortgage Asset Corporation	ANH
Arizona Land Income Corporation	AZL
BNP Residential Properties, Inc.	BNP
Capital Alliance Income Trust	CAA
Commercial Assets Inc.	CAX

American Stock Exchange

Company Name	Ticker
FBR Asset Investment Corporation	FB
Golf Trust of America, Inc.	GTA
Hanover Capital Mortgage Holdings, Inc.	HCM
Hersha Hospitality Trust	HT
HMG/Courtland Properties, Inc.	HMG
Impac Commercial Holdings, Inc.	ICH
Impac Mortgage Holdings, Inc.	IMH
Income Opportunity Realty Investors	IOT
InnSuites Hospitality Trust	IHT
Mission West Properties	MSW
National Health Realty	NHR
One Liberty Properties, Inc.	OLP
Pacific Gateway Properties	PGP
Pittsburgh & West Virginia Rail Road	PW
PMC Commercial Trust	PCC
Presidential Realty Corporation (Class B)	PDL B
Price Legacy Corporation	XLG
PS Business Parks, Inc.	PSB
Resource Asset Investment Trust	RAS
Roberts Realty Investors, Inc.	RPI
Shelbourne Properties, Inc. I	HXD
Shelbourne Properties, Inc. II	HXE
Shelbourne Properties, Inc. III	HXF
Stonehaven Realty Trust	RPP
United Mobile Homes, Inc.	UMH
Wellsford Real Properties, Inc.	WRP

Nasdaq

Amresco Capital Trust	AMCT
Bando McGlocklin Capital Corporation	BMCC
Banyan Strategic Realty Trust	BSRTS
Capital Automotive REIT	CARS
Humphrey Hospitality Trust, Inc.	HUMP
Jameson Inns, Inc.	JAMS
Maxus Realty Trust, Inc.	MRTI
Monmouth Real Estate Investment Corp.	MNRTA
Pinnacle Holdings, Inc.	BIGT

REAL ESTATE LIMITED PARTNERSHIPS

Limited partnerships (LPs), which saw their heyday in the 1980s, raise money from limited partners and invest it in new or existing commercial real estate. A general partner makes decisions on what to buy and how to manage the properties.

Unlike real estate funds or REITs, LPs are not easy to buy and sell. When you buy, you must pay onerous sales charges and other fees that may amount to as much as 10 percent of your invested capital. On top of that, you remit annual management fees of 2 percent or 3 percent of your principal. If you want to withdraw from the partnership before it is liquidated, which occurs up to ten years after its launch, you must sell in a tricky secondary market where investors offer to buy your units at deep discounts.

In theory, a good real estate partnership produces high current income from rents and mortgage interest it collects. Upon liquidation, partners receive magnificent *capital gains* when the partnership's properties are sold for huge profits. The reality has been far from the hype, as many partnerships have suffered defaults, plunging property values, and declining rental income.

Another form of real estate partnership that offers more liquidity is a *master limited partnership* (MLP). These operate just like traditional partnerships except that they trade on exchanges like any other stock. In some cases, an MLP has been formed by combining the assets of several troubled illiquid partnerships into one giant, publicly traded vehicle. MLPs typically pay high dividends of 5 percent to 10 percent.

RENTAL REAL ESTATE

Becoming a landlord has its advantages and disadvantages. If you own a good property, it can appreciate handsomely over time and provide solid rental income. In addition, you can reap substantial tax benefits, such as writing off losses up to $25,000 against other income, if you meet certain IRS restrictions.

On the other hand, few people think being a landlord is fun. Tenants often complain. You are responsible if the plumbing breaks down in the middle of the night or the heat shuts off in the dead of winter. Not every renter pays his or her rent on time. You must constantly guard against vandalism. You must sometimes evict a tenant. Also, in some localities, rent controls prevent you from raising rents enough to cover increased expenses.

The key to successful rental real estate is to buy properties in good locations that attract the type of tenant who takes care of his or her unit and is so happy living on the property that he or she never objects to yearly rent hikes. Easier said than done!

When looking for profitable rental properties, you might begin in working-class neighborhoods, where prices are more reasonable and tenants are more reliable than in the elite neighborhoods of town. To find a bargain, you could focus on properties with problems that are relatively easy to resolve. The problem—be it asbestos, a leaky roof, or some other repair—might scare the current owner so much that he or she will sell at a large discount from the property's real value. Before buying, determine how much it will cost to resolve the problem and estimate the rent you could collect once the place is in tip-top shape.

Another way to get the best possible value when buying rental real estate is to look for a building that sits on a lot providing extra land that could be developed. You might be able to add onto the building, erect a new home, or even sell part of the land to offset your purchase cost. Before you contemplate such a strategy, however, determine whether you will need a zoning variance to subdivide the land.

EXCHANGING PROPERTY

Gerald Robinson, a New York–based real estate tax attorney and author of *Federal Income Taxation of Real Estate* says that owners of small rental properties can use the tax-free exchange provisions of I.R.C 1031 to buy vacation and retirement homes with tax free dollars. The idea is to sell the appreciated rental property, have the proceeds paid to a qualified intermediary, then reinvest those proceeds into a vacation or retirement home that is held temporarily for rental purposes. Properly handled, the swap is tax-free, according to Robinson, with one rental property having been exchanged for another. Then, if the target vacation or retirement home can be located *before* the rental property is sold, a simultaneous, rather than a deferred, exchange can take place.

VACATION HOMES

One of the more pleasurable forms of real estate investment is a vacation home because you can live there up to 14 days a year or 10 percent of the amount of time you rent it, whichever is less (according to the tax code) and still get a write-off on taxes. If you own a home in a desirable location near a beach, lake, ski resort, or tourist attraction, you should be able to rent out the property for at least part of the year. In the best of all worlds, your annual rental income would cover your expenses or even exceed them. That would mean that you could live in the house rent-free during your vacations. Unless your property is extremely popular, however, you should not expect to enjoy a positive cash flow.

A vacation home can provide tax benefits if it produces negative cash flow—in other words, costs more than it earns in rent. That's because the tax law allows you to deduct up to $25,000 of business losses from your adjusted gross income (AGI), as long as you actively rent and maintain the property. You qualify for the full $25,000 write-off if your AGI is less than $100,000. From $100,000 to $150,000 in income, the tax benefit is phased out. If you earn more than $150,000, you can deduct business losses only against rental income, not against regular income from your job or other investments. In calculating business losses, you can count all your expenses for maintaining the property, including depreciation, painting, yard maintenance, property taxes, insurance, and utility bills. You are also allowed to count any trips you take to inspect or repair the property. If you abuse this right of visitation, the IRS may consider your vacation home a personal, not a rental, property.

If you take out a mortgage to purchase a vacation home, you can deduct your mortgage interest on your tax return. While that deduction may be sizable, it also increases your expenses considerably and makes it more difficult to generate positive cash flow.

When looking for a vacation home to buy as a rental, you should hunt for a property that has already been rented for several seasons. This will earn you a return clientele and give you a realistic indication of the level of rent to expect. If you improve the property, you might even be able to increase the rent somewhat. If you're going to charge a hefty rent, though, the property must be in excellent condition, offer comfortable furnishings, and provide modern appliances that work. You might be able to rent the property yourself with ads in the local newspaper, but if that doesn't work, you will have to hire a rental agent, who might charge as much as 25 percent of the rent you collect.

In the end, you should not purchase a vacation home primarily as an investment that you expect will earn substantial capital appreciation. Instead, aim to generate a positive cash flow and maximize your tax benefits. If you get to live at the home two weeks every year for free, you've got yourself a good deal.

Timeshares

While they are often sold as real estate investments, timeshares are, in fact, not investments at all. When you purchase a timeshare, you own a specific block of time—usually a week—at a particular place—usually a condominium in a resort area. Before you buy, you must be convinced that you like the unit, development, and surrounding area so much that you will want to come back year after year on your vacation.

Owners of timeshare units built by developers that are members of the Resort Property Owners Association (PO Box 2395, Northbrook, IL 60062;

708-291-0710) can swap their units with other members at properties around the world. Another company that facilitates exchanges of timeshare units is Interval International (62 Sunset Drive, Miami, FL 33243; 305-666-1884; 800-843-8843; www.interval-intl.com). However, unless you own a share in a very popular resort at a highly desirable time of year, you may not be able to trade for a place to which you want to go. If you become ill or an emergency arises in your week for the timeshare, you probably will have to forfeit that week unless you can make a last-minute swap.

The high-pressure salespeople who sell timeshare units usually pitch the excellent resale potential of their developments. Don't believe it. Hundreds of thousands of people can't find buyers because the salespeople direct most potential purchasers to new units. If you still want to buy a timeshare, you will probably get the best deal by purchasing an existing unit at a deep discount in the secondary market. To see what is available, look at the Timeshare User's Group at <www.tug2.net>.

Be particularly wary of telemarketing firms that sell timeshares. Some of them claim to have extensive lists of sales agents and buyers lining up for their resale units. The more audacious promoters will even charge up to $500 for an "advance listing," promising that you can resell your unit for a quick profit. Some actually offer money-back guarantees.

Timeshare units are not only illiquid; they impose maintenance charges you must pay whether you use your unit or not. Even those who try to abandon their timeshares meet with little luck. The developer and timeshare owners association pursue them to collect the money due according to the contract.

Nevertheless, if you want to own a timeshare, begin by renting an apartment a few times in the development in which you are interested. If you really like the development and want to return frequently, it might be worth buying into it. However, try to buy into a development backed by a major, well-known corporation, such as Marriott, Disney, or Hilton, rather than some fly-by-night operation. Consider your purchase a way to lock in a long-term price for a vacation. It's unlikely to be an investment that grows in value over time.

To learn more about timeshares from the industry's point of view, contact the American Resort Development Association (1220 L Street, NW, Suite 500, Washington, DC 20005; 202-371-6700; www.arda.org).

RAW LAND

Picture the following: You buy a piece of raw land cheaply from owners who have been sitting on it for years, unaware of its true value. Knowing that the area is about to be developed, you sell the acreage to developers and reap huge profits. That's the dream. The reality of investing in raw land is usually quite different.

Most raw land is purchased by developers assembling a site for a housing project, a shopping center, a factory, or another commercial use. The land's value rises once utilities, roads, sewers, and other amenities are installed. The prospect of quick gains usually encourages investment houses to sponsor raw land (or predevelopment) limited partnerships, but most fail. The combination of high interest rates and a glut of commercial properties in many markets hurt the value of raw land throughout the United States in the 1990s.

Raw land is usually illiquid, meaning that it can be difficult to sell. In addition, unless you rent the land to someone, the property produces no income. Meanwhile, you incur expenses, such as maintenance and property taxes. If you borrow to buy the land, you must meet regular interest payments as well. This negative cash flow can drain your budget and makes sense only if you feel sure the land will rise in value soon.

Many factors affect the selling price of land, including the state of the local economy, the direction of interest rates, local zoning, environmental regulations, and changing tax laws. Any one of these factors can turn against the owner of raw land. For example, the property may be rezoned to a use with less commercial potential, hurting the land's value. The land may be classified as a wetland, making it unsalable. An inspector may find traces of toxic waste from a previous owner that you must clean up before you sell the property. Even if the land is clean, you should determine how difficult it will be to get water, electricity, sewage systems, and roads to the site. Before you buy, know everything about a piece of land, including its present condition and development potential.

In most cases, it has been difficult for raw land values to rise in the face of increasing property tax burdens, strict zoning enforcement, and slow economic growth. Buying raw land is therefore the most speculative real estate investment. You might hit it big with a combination of luck and inside knowledge, but don't count on it.

Getting a *land loan* is not as easy as procuring the garden variety mortgage offered on homes. Lenders incur a higher amount of risk because the object of value is not currently being used for anything. This fact alone makes it easier for an owner to default on or abandon his or her investment and results in much higher mortgage rates for land purchases. Because unimproved land (without sewers, utilities, or streets in place) spells speculative investment to a lender, it will require a higher down payment as well as a higher interest rate. A local lender who knows the land and the area's potential may be most approachable. He or she may want to know whether the services to improve the parcel are available, ask to see a staked-off survey of the property, and assess the easements and accessibility of the land you have in mind in order to seek loan approval. Land loans typically have a term of 10 to 15 years, and the interest on them may be deductible.

USING YOUR COMPUTER TO BUY AND SELL REAL ESTATE

The real estate market has always been considered local. But the advent of the home computer and the Internet is quickly bringing real estate into a national marketplace, making it easier for you to buy and sell your home and get financing from lenders anywhere in the country.

All of the major institutions involved in the home buying and selling business now have a significant presence on the World Wide Web. Mortgage lenders, real estate brokers, builders, relocation firms, home-oriented magazines, housing-related government agencies, and many others now have Web sites (listed in the Resources section of this chapter) that can educate you about real estate and help you go through much of the homebuying process online. Some things to remember:

- You can use various buy-versus-rent calculators to evaluate whether it makes sense for you to be buying in the first place. Other calculators help you determine how much of a mortgage you can afford based on your income and assets. Try <www.quickenloans.quicken.com>.
- You can shop for homes online through the many REALTOR®-sponsored Web sites. These sites offer information about various communities you may be interested in, as well as pictures and details about houses for sale. Just type in the name of your REALTOR®'s company to browse these sites.
- You can shop for the most competitive mortgage rate online. There now is a national market for mortgages, and you do not have to be limited to what your local lender is offering. These sites are constantly updated with the latest rates on fixed and adjustable loans, points, fees, closing costs, and even online applications. A few sample sites to help you tap into this market include: American Mortgage Online, <www.amo-mortgage.com>; HSH Mortgage Information, <www.hsh.com>; Mortgage Mart, <www.mortgagemart.com>; Mortgage-Net, <www.mortgage-net.com>.

One of the most complete online services to help you in your real estate decisions is the Real Estate section of America Online. Here is a sample of what it includes:

- *Apartments Plus.* An online listing of apartments for rent in most areas of the country. You can take a virtual tour of your choices, with pictures of the interior and exterior of the building and apartment and common areas like lobbies and pools. There are also listings of movers and relocation services to help you find the apartment you can afford.
- *Home Magazine Online.* A wealth of resources from *Home* magazine, including information on gardening, decorating, how to build your own home, and buyers' guides for home appliances and electronics. The site also hosts chat sessions with housing experts.
- *The Homeowner's Forum,* sponsored by the United Homeowners Association. This site includes sections on home improvement, how to sell your home without a broker, how to get the lowest-interest mortgage, how to find a good home inspector, and how to find a qualified remodeling contractor.
- *Homes.com,* sponsored by *Homes and Land* magazine. This site allows you to view homes for sale in almost every state in the country, as seen through free magazines distributed in those states. You can also advertise your home for sale on this site.
- *NAREIT Online.* The National Association of Real Estate Investment Trusts has a site giving you all the information you need on investing in REITs.
- *NARI Online.* The National Association of the Remodeling Industry promotes sound business practices for remodelers. Their Web site has sections on developing a budget, selecting contractors, what should be in a contract, and how to satisfy local zoning and housing code laws.

Other features of the AOL Real Estate section are Community Profiles by Century 21; Appliances Online, with links to major manufacturers and retailers like General Electric, Home Depot, and Whirlpool; and School Match, giving you details on the quality of schools in the district into which you are thinking of moving.

As in many other areas of personal finance, the computer is making the real estate market much more efficient. If you take advantage of the power of the computer, you can save thousands of dollars on financing and end up with the home of your dreams that you might never have found the old-fashioned way.

Investing in real estate—both in your home and in other investment property—will always hold great appeal for Americans. More people in this country have amassed fortunes in real estate than in any other asset. Although finding good sources of information before investing lessens your risk, real estate purchases do not require a college degree or superior intellect. By buying a home, you not only acquire pride of ownership, you also get real value out of your property by using it every day, even if its market value falls. Investment real estate offers potential capital appreciation, income, and tax breaks (as well as headaches).

The era of the 1970s and early 1980s, when almost every piece of real estate appreciated dramatically, has passed, probably forever. To succeed in real estate investment now, you must study the markets carefully and understand the complex financing options and tax laws that cause values to rise and fall. You need to depend less on luck and more on expertise.

RESOURCES

Books

All about Real Estate Investing: From the Inside Out, by William Benke and Joseph M. Fowler (McGraw-Hill, P.O. Box 543, Blacklick, OH 43004; 800-634-3961; www.mcgraw-hill.com). Practical guide to profitable real estate investing. Covers houses, apartments, and commercial real estate.

Buy It, Fix It, Sell It: PROFIT, by Kevin C. Meyers (Dearborn Trade, Chicago, IL; 312-836-4400; 800-245-2665; www.dearborntrade.com). A guide to developing a profitable, home-based home rehabilitation business.

Buying More House for Less Money, by Ceil R. Lohmar (McGraw-Hill, PO Box 543, Blacklick, OH 43004; 800-634-3961; www.mcgraw-hill.com). Techniques for house hunting and bargaining to get the best value for your housing dollar.

Buying Your Vacation Home for Fun and Profit, by Ruth Rejnis and Claire Walter (Dearborn Trade, Chicago, IL; 312-836-4400; 800-245-2665; www.dearborntrade .com). Provides readers with information to make a wise vacation home purchase.

Every Landlord's Legal Guide: Leases & Rental Agreements, Deposits, Rent Rules, Liability, Discrimination, Property Managers, Privacy, Repairs & Maintenance, by Marcia Stewart, Janet Portman, and Ralph E. Warner (Nolo Press, 950 Parker Street, Berkeley, CA 94710; 800-992-6656; www.nolo.com). Outlines what the law requires of a landlord and offers advice on how to be conscientious and profitable. Information on finding good tenants, on agreements and leases, liability issues, and terminations and evictions. Covers the law in all states.

Find It, Buy It, Fix It: The Insider's Guide to Fixer-Uppers, by Robert Irwin (Dearborn Trade, Chicago, IL; 312-836-4400; 800-245-2665; www.dearborntrade .com). Reveals the ins and outs of buying and renovating your very own handyman's special. Shows homebuyers how to find the real bargains and how to avoid the moneypits.

Finding and Buying Your Place in the Country, by Les and Carol Scher (Dearborn Trade, Chicago, IL; 312-836-4400; 800-245-2665; www.dearborntrade.com).

Explains what the reader needs to know about due diligence on rural land being considered, contracts, negotiations, and financing.

Getting Started in Real Estate Investing, by Michael C. Thomsett and Jean Freestone Thomsett (John Wiley & Sons, 1 Wiley Drive, Somerset, NJ 08875; 212-850-6000; 800-225-5945; www.wiley.com). Gives you information on everything from mortgage payments and property selection to financing options and landlording issues.

How to Find Hidden Real Estate Bargains, by Robert Irwin (McGraw-Hill, PO Box 543, Blacklick, OH 43004; 800-634-3961; www.mcgraw-hill.com). Explains the process of purchasing attractively priced real estate from distressed sellers and foreclosures, among other techniques.

How to Use Leverage to Maximize Your Real Estate Investment Return: Sensible Finance Techniques for Real Estate Investors, by John T. Reed (Reed Publishing, 342 Bryan Drive, Danville, CA 94526; 415-820-6292). Gives finance tips and describes how to use techniques like defeasance, prepayment bonuses, sunset clauses, interest rate futures hedging, substitution of bond collateral, cancellation of PMI, and rapid amortization.

Investing in Real Estate, by Andrew James McLean (John Wiley & Sons, 1 Wiley Drive, Somerset, NJ 08875-1272; 212-850-6000; 800-225-5945; www .wiley.com). Explains how to find properties worth buying, how to negotiate the best deal, how to obtain financing, and when to sell the properties.

Landlord and Tenant, by Steven D. Strauss (W.W. Norton, 500 Fifth Avenue, New York, NY 10110; 212-354-5500; www.wwnorton.com). Covers the rights, responsibilities, and duties of landlords and tenants, some ways of dealing with your landlord or tenant, and coming up with reasonable solutions to problems. The book includes sample scenarios of cases to illustrate the methods that can be used to deal with a variety of situations.

Landlording: A Handy Manual for Scrupulous Landlords and Landladies Who Do It Themselves, by Leigh Robinson (Express Publishing, PO Box 1639, El Cerrito, CA 94530; 510-236-5496; 800-307-0789; www.landlording.com). Describes the rights and responsibilities of landlords, including security deposits, leases, rent control, and other matters.

The Landlord's Handbook, by Daniel Goodwin and Richard Rusdorf (Dearborn Trade, Chicago, IL; 312-836-4400; 800-245-2665; www.dearborntrade.com). A complete guide to managing small residential properties. Features more than 50 forms and checklists covering everything from finding good tenants to maximizing tax deductions.

Modern Real Estate Practice, by Fillmore W. Galaty, Wellington J. Allaway, and Robert C. Kyle (Dearborn Trade, Chicago, IL; 312-836-4400; 800-245-2665; www .dearborntrade.com). The reference book on every aspect of homebuying and selling: the sales transaction, real estate laws, leasing, financing, and appraising your home or real estate investment. Includes standardized forms for listing and sales contracts, deeds, appraisals, environmental assessments, and a sample mortgage. Also prepares you to become a real estate agent or broker. Available in 20 individual state editions or supplements.

No-Nonsense Landlord: Building Wealth with Rental Properties, by James Jorgenson (McGraw-Hill, PO Box 543, Blacklick, OH 43004; 800-634-3961; www .mcgraw-hill.com). A helpful book if you are thinking of buying a building to generate income.

Profitable Real Estate Investing: Making Big Money, Finding the Right Properties, Investing on a Shoestring, by Roger Woodson (Dearborn Trade, Chicago, IL; 312-836-4400; 800-245-2665; www.dearborntrade.com). Focusing primarily on residential real estate investing, this book offers a step-by-step plan for the novice.

Real Estate Investing from A to Z, by William Pivar (McGraw-Hill, PO Box 543, Blacklick, OH 43004; 800-634-3961; www.mcgraw-hill.com). A step-by-step guide to successful real estate investing strategies. Describes creative financing techniques, foreclosure and tax sales, subdividing property, and managing real estate profitably.

Real Estate Investing from A to Z: The Most Comprehensive, Practical, and Readable Guide to Investing Profitably in Real Estate, by William H. Pivar (McGraw-Hill, PO Box 543, Blacklick, OH 43004; 800-634-3961; www.mcgraw-hill .com). Explains real estate investing in simple terms that are relevant to any investor. Outlines investing and financing techniques from the simple and straightforward to the more complex.

The Real Estate Investor's Survival Guide; Disaster-Proof Your Investments— Profit in Any Economic Climate, by Stuart M. Saft (John Wiley & Sons, Inc. Professional, Reference and Trade Group, 605 Third Avenue, New York, N.Y. 10158-0012, 212-850-6534, www.wiley.com). Techniques for avoiding problems and pitfalls of recession and recovery, including restructuring debt, defending against foreclosure, benefiting from bankruptcy (for investment real estate).

Real Estate on the Brink: Making Money in Distressed Properties, by Skip Lombardo (McGraw-Hill, PO Box 543, Blacklick, OH 43004; 800-634-3961; www .mcgraw-hill.com). Describes how to make money buying and selling distressed real estate.

The Smart Money Guide to Bargain Homes: How to Find and Buy Foreclosures, by James I. Wiedemer (Dearborn Trade, Chicago, IL 60606; 312-836-4400; 800-245-2665; www.dearborntrade.com). A complete guide to finding quality homes in foreclosure with banks and government agencies. Describes how to evaluate foreclosed properties, obtain financing, and prepare the paperwork required by government agencies.

Successful Real Estate Investing: A Practical Guide to Profits for the Small Investor, by Peter G. Miller (HarperBusiness, PO Box 588, Dunmore, PA 18512; 212-207-7000; 800-331-3761; www.harpercollins.com). Debunks the phony no-money-down strategies and offers guidelines for sensible, low-risk investments.

Tips and Traps for Making Money in Real Estate, by Robert Irwin (McGraw-Hill, PO Box 543, Blacklick, OH 43004; 800-634-3961; www.mcgraw-hill.com). Reveals the best techniques for buying when prices are low and selling as prices peak. Filled with practical advice for novice real estate investors.

Magazines

A.D. Kessler's Creative Real Estate Magazine (Drawer L, Rancho Santa Fe, CA 92067; 858-756-1441; adkessler.net). Covers the gamut of real estate investing issues. Features columns on mortgages, tax aspects of real estate, exchanging real estate, single-family homes, and distressed property. Includes a directory of real estate exchange groups and a listing of real estate seminars and home-study courses. Incorporates the Real Estate Observer and Investors Association newsletters. Published since 1972, this magazine is for anyone who wants to make money in real estate. Also sells memberships for the Tape-of-the-Month Club, which presents excerpts from seminars by renowned real estate experts on audiocassette. Offers the home-study course, "Your Key to Creative Real Estate Success." Also publishes Directory of Investors Associations, updated monthly, and has a weekly radio program, A.D. Kessler's Real Estate Roundtable, on America 1 Network.

Financial Freedom Report Quarterly (2450 Fort Union Boulevard, Salt Lake City, UT 84121; 801-272-5300). A quarterly magazine covering many areas of real estate investment, geared to the individual investor. Discusses property management, finance, negotiation strategies, distressed-property purchases, foreclosure, and discounted mortgage investment. Subscription includes an audiocassette featuring interviews with leading real estate experts, as well as membership in the META Institute, which is an academic institution granting a master's degree in real estate investing or professional certification through home-study courses.

Real Estate Portfolio (National Association of Real Estate Investment Trusts, 1875 Eye Street, NW, Washington, DC 20006; 202-739-9400; www.nareit.com). Covers the real estate investment trust industry.

Newsletters

Realty Stock Review (Rainmaker Media Group, LLC, 802 W. Park Avenue, Suite 3222, Ocean, NJ 07702; 732-493-1999; www.realtystockreview.com). Covers real estate investment trusts and recommends REITs to buy and sell.

John T. Reed's Real Estate Investor's Monthly (John T. Reed Publishing, 342 Bryan Drive, Danville, CA 94507; 925-820-7262; www.johntreed.com). Aimed at serious investors in real estate. Features such subjects as apartment conversion projects, bargain hunting, equity sharing, investment strategies, property exchanges, refinancing techniques, and tax laws. In addition to the newsletter, the publisher offers the following publications: *Aggressive Tax Avoidance for Real Estate Investors; Distressed Real Estate Times; Offensive and Defensive Strategy and Tactics: How to Buy Real Estate for at Least 20% below Market Value; How to Do a Delayed Exchange; How to Get*

Started in Real Estate Investment; How to Increase the Value of Real Estate; How to Manage Residential Property for Maximum Cash Flow and Resale Value; How to Use Leverage to Maximize Your Real Estate Investment Return; Office Building Acquisition Handbook; Real Estate Investment Strategy; Residential Property Acquisition Handbook; Single-Family Lease Options; and others.

Newspapers

National Mortgage News (1110 Plaza, New York, NY 10001; 212-967-7000; 800-535-8403; www.nationalmortgagenews.com). Covers the mortgage market and mortgage lenders, such as savings and loans and mortgage bankers.

Real Estate Weekly (555 Hillsdale Drive, Suite A, Charlottesville, VA 22901; 804-817-9330; www.therealestateweekly.com). The only weekly real estate newspaper in the United States. Concentrates on the New York real estate market.

Trade Associations

American Resort Development Association (1220 L Street, NW, Suite 500, Washington, DC 20005; 202-371-6700; www.arda.org). Represents the vacation ownership industry, including timeshares, lot sales, golf resorts, recreational vehicles, and campground resorts. Lobbies on issues related to timeshare resorts and provides information about buying and selling timeshares. The most popular publications offered by ARDA include *The Benefits of Timeshare Ownership: Results from a Nationwide Survey of Timeshare Owners; Consumer's Guide to Resort and Urban Timesharing; Financial Performance in the Timeshare Industry;* and *Vacation Ownership Industry Booklet.*

Commercial Investment Real Estate Institute (430 N. Michigan Avenue, Suite 600, Chicago, IL 60611; 312-321-4460; www.ccim.com). Represents those involved in commercial and investment-oriented real estate. Confers the Certified Commercial Investment Member (CCIM) designation on developers, brokers, property managers, corporate real estate executives, asset managers, institutional lenders, or others involved in any aspect of commercial real estate. Can help those interested in learning more about investing in commercial property.

Investment Program Association (1101 17th Street, NW, Suite 703, Washington, DC 20036; 202-775-9750; www.ipa-dc.org). The trade association for limited partnerships, many of which are real estate partnerships sold by brokerage firms.

National Association of Real Estate Investment Trusts (1129 20th Street, NW, Suite 305, Washington, DC 20036; 202-785-8717; www.nareit.com). Offers a free brochure titled "Most Frequently Asked Questions about REITs." Also produces the *REIT-Watch* newsletter, *REIT Basics, Real Estate Portfolio,* and *NAREIT Statistical Digest,* which names all publicly traded REITs and provides statistics on the industry.

National Real Estate Investors Association (111 S. Olive Street, Suite 451, Media, PA 19063). Provides a structure to help build effective real estate associations and is parent organization for independent chapters of real estate associations in large metropolitan areas around the United States.

Web Sites

America Online, Personal Finance-Real Estate. Has a nationwide electronic bulletin board accessible to Windows and Macintosh users. Members may ask real estate questions, check daily mortgage rates, read articles, and post messages on the AOL MLS to buy, sell, exchange, or rent property anywhere in the country. Open to brokers and nonbrokers. <www.aol.com>

Timeshare Users Group. This site includes reviews and ratings on more than 1,600 timeshare resorts, along with general information about restaurants and sights to see in or around these properties. Membership required. <www.timeshare-users-group.com.>

Appendix:
Sample Inspection
Reports

SUMMARY OF INSPECTION REPORT FINDINGS

The following is a categorized list of specific property defects noted in the attached home inspection report. It is provided as an addendum to the full report as an aid in evaluating the overall condition of the property. For a more detailed and comprehensive representation of property disclosures, parties to this transaction are advised to read the entire inspection report.

The subject property is a one story, stucco, single family dwelling, estimated to be approximately 12 years old. Deferred maintenance is apparent, as indicated by the numerous disclosures in the report. The property was inspected in accordance with the Standards of Practice of the American Society of Home Inspectors, and the following specific conditions were observed:

Note: The following legend designates the general categories of repair recommendations assigned to the various conditions disclosed in the report.

A **Health and Safety Item.** Should be evaluated and repaired by a qualified licensed contractor or tradesperson prior to close of transaction.

B **Defect or Functional Concern.** Should be evaluated and repaired by a qualified licensed contractor or tradesperson prior to close of transaction.

C **Routine Maintenance Item.** Can be repaired by a qualified handyman or home owner.

D **Upgrade Advised to Increase Safety or Improve Function.** Existing condition may have been acceptable at time of installation but does not meet current building or safety standards. Upgrade is advised but not required.

E **Recommend Evaluation of Property by a Licensed Pest Control Operator.** The presence of wood destroying organisms is suspected. In most states, only a licensed pest control operator can make this determination.

Apparent Addition:
The laundry room at the southeast corner of the building appears to be an addition to the original structure. Substandard conditions involving the roof, foundation, plumbing, and electrical systems in that area indicate that construction of the addition may have been done without a building permit. For verification, the local building department should be consulted prior to close of the transaction. Specific substandard conditions are included in this summary.

Site Conditions:
- The rear fence is leaning due to rotted posts. (C)
- A six foot section of the south fence is missing. (C)
- The gate is damaged at the side of the garage. (C)
- The large raised crack in the concrete driveway is a trip hazard. (A)
- Decayed wood was noted at the posts and framing of the deck cover. (E)
- The waterproof deck membrane is cracked and deteriorated. (B)
- The handrails are loose at the exterior stairs. (A)

page 1

Building Exterior:
- Decayed wood was noted at the eave corners at the front of the building. (E)
- Loose trim was noted at several of the south windows. (C)

Action Home Inspection Service
- Exterior wood trim is weathered and needs repainting. (C)
- Caulking is needed at gaps in stucco at various plumbing pipes. (C)

Foundation and Subarea:
- Earth to wood contact was noted at the access to the subarea. (E)
- Decayed wood and visible moisture were noted at the subfloor beneath the master bathtub, indicating active leakage and resultant damage. (E)
- The slab foundation at the added laundry has no apparent footing. This is one of the substandard conditions which indicate the lack of a building permit for the addition. (B)

Garage:
- The firewall between the garage and dwelling is incomplete. Openings between the roof rafters should be covered with 5/8 inch fire-rated drywall. (A)
- Holes in the drywall behind the water heater violate the firewall. (A)
- The tension rods are loose at the top and bottom of the garage door. (C)
- The automatic safety reverse function of the garage door opener is inoperative. (A)
- Decayed wood was noted at the bottom of the jamb at the garage side door. (E)

Roofing: (All roof repairs should be done by a licensed roofing contractor.)
- The composition shingles appear functional, with moderate signs of aging. Damaged shingles were noted at the front of the garage where the basketball hoop is mounted. (B)
- Ceiling stains were noted in the garage, directly above the water heater. This indicates leakage at the flue pipe flashing. Sealant is needed. (B)
- Seams are not adequately sealed at the rolled composition roofing on the addition. (B)
- Edge flashing has not been installed at the roof of the addition. (B)
- A drain gutter is needed at the south side of the building to prevent further soil erosion. (B)

Plumbing: All plumbing repairs should be done by a licensed plumber.
- PVC water piping is installed in the laundry. Not approved for use within a dwelling. (B)
- The laundry drain was installed without a trap or vent. (B)
- Flue pipe fittings at the water heater are not secured with screws. (A)
- The water heater lacks adequate protection from automobile impact in the garage. (A)
- The gas flex connector extends through the wall at the laundry addition. (A)
- Drain fittings at the kitchen sink are wrapped with duct tape. Substandard leak repair. (B)
- The drain hose at the dishwasher is not equipped with an airgap device. (D)
- The toilet in the hall bathroom is loosely attached to the floor. Darkened floor vinyl indicates active leakage at the seal. This may be causing damage to the subfloor. (E)
- Water volume is restricted at both shower heads due to apparent mineral deposits. (B)
- Leaking was noted at two of the front yard sprinkler valves. (B)

page 2

Action Home Inspection Service

Electrical: All electrical repairs should be done by a licensed electrician.
- The service connections at the roof need retaping. Refer to power company for repairs. (A)
- Double tapping was noted at one breaker in the main panel. This means that two wires are connected to a single-wire terminal. (A)
- No coupling device has been installed on the breaker switch handles for the 220 volt dryer circuit in the laundry. (A)
- Ground and neutral wires are not separated in the laundry subpanel. (A)
- A disconnected conduit was noted at the junction box beneath the kitchen sink. (A)
- The front porch light is wired with common lamp cord. (A)
- Exposed wire splices were noted in the subarea adjacent to the laundry. (A)
- Ungrounded outlets were noted in the laundry. (A)
- Outlets have reverse polarity in the dining room. (A)
- Weatherproof covers are needed at the deck outlets. (A)
- Bedroom ceiling fan is wired to a light dimmer. Humming indicates damage to motor. (B)

Heating: All heating repairs should be done by a licensed heating contractor.
- Furnace appears overdue for annual servicing, as indicated by excessive dust buildup at the blower and the return air plenum. (B)
- The flue pipe for the furnace is in direct contact with the plywood sheathing in the attic. One inch clearance to combustible materials is required for fire safety. (A)
- The air filter needs to be changed. (C)

Fireplace: Repairs should be done by a fireplace contractor or certified chimney sweep.
- Rust damage was noted at the spark arrestor and flue cap at the chimney top. (A)
- The chimney needs professional cleaning. (A)

Bathrooms and Kitchen:
- Drawers need adjustment to open and close freely at the hall bathroom. (C)
- Some wall tiles are loose at the master tub. (B)
- Loose counter tiles were noted in the hall bathroom. (B)
- The master tub whirlpool motor is not provided with an access opening. (B)
- The left rear burner did not ignite at the kitchen range.
- Bathroom and kitchen plumbing defects were noted above. (B)

Miscellaneous Interior Conditions:
- The vinyl floor seam is loose and uplifted in the master bathroom. (C)
- A hole was noted in the drywall near the front door (caused by door knob). (C)
- Rubbing and sticking were noted at the door to the hall bathroom. (C)
- The sliding glass door is difficult to operated at the patio, indicating faulty rollers. (B)
- Evidence of rain leakage was noted at the laundry room window. (B)
- Fogging at dual pane windows in kitchen and entry hall indicate leakage at seals. (B)
- Handrails are missing at garage stairs. (A)

page 3

© copyright 2000, Barry Stone

1

Goldring Home Inspections, Inc.

965 White Plains Rd., Trumbull, CT 06611
Connecticut's Original Home Inspection Company

Phone 203-261-9781   Fax 203-268-5174

Date:
October 20, 1999

Address inspected:
100 New Street
Old Town, U.S.A.

Inspection for:
Mr. & Mrs. John Doe
Present Address
Anywhere, U.S.A.

Inspected by:
John Ghent

Who was present:
Broker

"Know The Home You Buy"

2

PLEASE NOTE:
This report is based upon the observable unconcealed structural conditions of the residence reported on below at the time of this inspection. Inspectors cannot and do not move furniture or pull up wall-to-wall carpeting, puncture, perforate, lift or remove wall, floor, sidings or roofs to observe conditions behind or under them or do anything which would or could damage or alter the condition of the property. This report does not expressly or impliedly warrant or guarantee the condition of the residence in any respect, nor is any inspection done to determine if appliances of any kind are in proper working order. It does not expressly or impliedly represent in any manner that the land or structure to which this report refers is in compliance with any of the laws rules and regulation, of any government authority, nor does it make any representation, guarantee or warranty as to the existence or condition of sewer, septic or water systems, or any other underground system. This report does not attempt to describe, locate, identify, detail or warrant the absence or presence of any materials which may be hazardous or toxic, including molds or mildews, whether located in accessible or inaccessible areas.

GENERAL:
This is a stone constructed home which is built in the style of a French country residence and was originally constructed in the 1920s, according to my information. The construction is of very high quality. At some point in the 1970s a contemporary addition was built on the left side. Some additional renovation may have taken place to the main part of the house at the same time. The house is occupied by a tenant at this time and cosmetic maintenance on the house has been good. Overall, general maintenance to the house and its systems has been average with no significant major upgrading of the systems. It would appear that generally as items failed, they were repaired. I inspected this house for another client earlier this month and this report is an upgrade to the original inspection.

At the time of this inspection some items were noted which are in need of attention and these points as well as other items will be brought out in this report for the benefit of the buyer. Items which are discussed in this report may have a financial impact on the cost of the house and repair estimates should be obtained prior to signing final contracts.

There is an in ground pool which is winterized and is not included as a part of this inspection. The buyer should obtain a statement from the owner or the pool servicing company as to the condition of the pool and its equipment. A separate pool inspection is also advisable.

Surface drainage around the house is slightly away from the foundation. The house is situated on a generally level lot.

FOUNDATION:
The foundation is constructed of stone and mortar. Foundations of this type are porous by nature and some seepage would not be unusual. Periodic pointing may be needed to mortar joints as normal deterioration occurs. This is considered to be routine normal maintenance. The foundation has no signs of abnormal deterioration and is functional at this time.

3

Some poured concrete and block are used on the newer addition in satisfactory condition. Some of the interior slab areas have some cracking which is normal based on the age of the house.

BASEMENT:

A small section of the house is built over a limited height utility basement which has a sump pump at the base of the bilco stairway. The sump pump is functional. There is evidence that there has been wetness on the floor of the basement in the past but I see no signs of any recent water problems. It appears that the sump pump is controlling any seepage that may occur. It should be pointed out that any basement that is built into the earth can be susceptible to seepage under unusual conditions. Proper surface management of runoff, including gutters and leaders, is critical in keeping a basement area dry. Operation of a dehumidifier in the summer months will assist in keeping humidity levels to a minimum. The owner should be questioned as to any past water problems that may have been encountered.

There is an expansive dirt floored crawl space. The entrance to the crawl space was blocked with wood storage and debris and broken glass and I was unable to enter the crawl space. As far as I could see into the crawl space area there are no signs of any structural issues, however, there is a good deal of poor plumbing which will be discussed later. Some type of vapor barrier should be placed over the dirt to minimize moisture levels. Insulation is recommended for this area. There should be exterior ventilation and it should be open in the summer and closed in the winter. Elevated radon levels are present and a radon mitigation system will probably include covering the dirt crawl floor with plastic. This should be discussed with the contractor selected to do the mitigation.

There is a wine storage area and the interior is finished with some hard asbestos material. This material is not generally considered to be a problem and is still in use in some applications. However, it should not be sanded or cut, and when and if it is removed, it should be disposed of properly. Painting it will also encapsulate the surface.

FRAMEWORK:

Framework wherever seen is of a quality which is consistent with normal building practice for this area. There are no signs of any unusual settlement or movement to the house. Framework which is not visible is not being reported on.

WOOD DECAY:

Some of the exterior fascia boards and vertical corner trims are decayed on the addition at the left side. There is decay to a few garage window trims on the right front side. The right side of the house has decay and what appears to be some insect activity to the garage door jambs and to some of the vertical siding which goes directly down to the ground. You should consider some other type of trim in this area so that the siding does not continue to decay due to its proximity to the soil.

Any exposed wood should be kept either painted, stained, or treated with wood preservative to prevent decay. Wood decays rapidly and periodic inspections of the exterior are recommended. See the "Maintenance" brochure for a schedule of homeowner inspections.

TERMITES:

It appears that this house is being treated for termites by the use of a termite bait system. This type of treatment requires periodic attention and inspection by the treating company. The buyer should obtain the name of the treating company and call them regarding the reason for treatment, the length of the existing treatment contract and the cost of continued use of the bait system. Although no current termite activity is seen, a reinfestation is always possible. A warranty should have been issued with the original treatment and the buyer should check with the owner regarding

4

current warranty protection. Because the house is being treated our termite guarantee is not in effect and periodic future inspections are advised. The exterminator can be consulted to develop a program of regular future inspections. There may be some concealed damage associated with this past infestation which is not apparent due to the visual nature of this inspection.

Inspection for termite activity also includes searching for other wood destroying insects, and none were found at this time. We do not offer a guarantee for these other wood destroying insects. Periodic inspections are a proper preventative measure against any future infestation. Information regarding other wood destroying insects is contained in our booklet.

Firewood is being stored at the back of the house adjacent to the bilco hatchway and it is also being stored in the basement. All firewood should be moved to a location away from the house as it presents an invitation to wood destroying insects.

Our inspection for wood destroying insects does not include infestations from fleas, roaches, rodents or other common pests, although we will report on such when clear evidence of any type of infestation is present.

ELECTRICAL:
A 200 amp 120-240 volt service is provided through a circuit breaker panel. Service is brought to the house by underground cables. Main service wire is aluminum and the panel is located in the basement. The system is properly grounded and outlets which were randomly checked were found to be properly grounded. Branch circuit wiring within the panel is copper properly sized to the circuit breakers and no signs of over fusing are found. Lighting fixtures and switches where randomly checked are working normally. No signs of branch circuit aluminum wire were seen in those areas which were inspected.

The upgraded electric service feeds a number of sub panels throughout the basement and the remainder of the house, all of which are older. It also appears that there was portable generator setup in the past but there is no generator present. If any expansion takes place to the house, an upgrade of the electrical service should be considered because the system is being used to a maximum capacity at this time.

Ground fault interrupter protection is now required in new construction for kitchen, bathroom, basement, garage and exterior outlets, as well as other damp locations such as pools or spas. Although this may not have been a requirement when this house was built, it would be beneficial to upgrade outlets in these areas to incorporate G.F.I. protection.

Many of the sconces and light fixtures are still operated by older style manual switches. A few areas are lacking outlets.

There is an alarm system, however, we did not operate this due to the possibility of setting it off. You should spend some time with the owner, or have the alarm company explain the operation of the system to you. When you move in, you should have all the codes and passwords changed for your personal security.   You should also determine the cost involved with the monthly maintenance of the system, if any.

HEATING:
Heat is provided by three separate systems. The primary heat for the main part of the house is from an H. B. Smith, gravity feed, manifold cast iron boiler which is the original with the house. The boiler has been converted from oil to gas and was functional at this time. In my opinion, although the system is functional, it is not very efficient. It also has a significant amount of rust

5

on some of the manifold connections both at the top and at the bottom. You should consider a planned replacement of this boiler as soon as possible for better efficiency and prior to its failure.

This boiler and a number of the adjacent heating pipes in the basement are covered with asbestos material that has been encapsulated. When the boiler is replaced, the asbestos material should be removed as repairs which might be needed to the piping cannot be made until the asbestos is removed.

The second system is a small gas fired, Lennox, forced warm air furnace which I believe heats the newer addition at the left side only.   This furnace fired satisfactorily at this time, however, because of its age, future longevity cannot be predicted. The furnace air supply was tested with a Carbon Monoxide Analyzer to determine if there was any heat exchanger leakage. The results of this test were negative and the heat exchanger is apparently sound at this time. This test would also indicate elevated levels of carbon monoxide in the occupied space and levels were within acceptable limits. The heat exchanger should be routinely tested by your service company when the furnace is cleaned and serviced. It is important to understand that a heat exchanger can crack or develop a pinhole rapidly. This will lead to a potential health problem and will require the furnace to be replaced. Good maintenance and periodic inspections will usually pick up heat exchanger failure. Normal life expectancy for a furnace of this type is 15 to 20 years and this furnace appears to have been installed in 1973 when the addition was constructed. You should consider a planned replacement of this furnace.

The third heating system is a gas fired, Utica, cast iron, hot water boiler which has a single circulator and is used for heating the caretakers apartment. This is a good quality system which is in need of routine cleaning and servicing. Otherwise, it is in satisfactory condition. It was installed in 1983 and has a normal life   span of 25 to 35 years.

All heating equipment should be kept on a service contract so that it receives routine preventative maintenance. Cleaning and servicing is recommended at least once each year to maintain operating efficiency and to help prolong its life.   As a routine safety precaution, one should consider installing a carbon monoxide detector.

When replaceable air filters are used, they should be changed on a monthly basis for regular sized filters and quarterly for oversized heavy duty filters. Properly sized, clean filters should always be used to obtain maximum efficiency of the system.   Electrostatic air cleaners need periodic maintenance.

The humidifier on the gas furnace is not working. Humidifiers require periodic cleaning to prevent a buildup of minerals which will impair proper operation. All humidifiers should be cleaned, drained and turned off during the summer months. Humidifiers are also prone to leak and any leakage should be corrected promptly to prevent deterioration to the ductwork or to the heat exchanger.

Domestic hot water is provided by a commercial, 30 gallon, gas fired water heater with 190,000 BTUs. This heats water then stores it in an 80 gallon aqua booster storage tank. This also has a recirculating system that moves hot water through the house at all times. It provided adequate amounts of hot water during the inspection and is visually in satisfactory condition with no signs of leakage or excessive rust. The normal life expectancy for a unit of this type is approximately 15 years. This unit appears to have been installed in 1993.

The heating system originally was oil fired. There are oil lines which leave the back foundation of the house that are no longer in use but have not been properly terminated and capped as is

6

normally done when an oil tank is removed. It is of major concern that you clarify whether the oil tank is still in the ground at the rear or if it was removed. If removal is confirmed the lines in the basement should be properly terminated to avoid confusion in the future.

PLUMBING:

There are some older brass and galvanized lines still in use that are showing signs of normal aging. Because of this older plumbing some replacement should be anticipated on a continuing basis until the older pipes have been replaced. This is considered to be a normal process in older homes. At this time, most of the waste lines which were visible in the basement and crawl space are badly corroded. Some have been patched with tape and all of these should be replaced at this time. The third floor bathroom appears to be suffering from older plumbing in that there is very poor water pressure to the toilet and the sink and tub water ran dirty.

Throughout the basement old plumbing waste lines are patched and there has been some replacement of water lines with newer copper tubing. But no major upgrade of the plumbing has been done in general and it appears that there may be a good deal of older piping still used in the walls. It is my opinion that this is a primary issue of concern and a plumber should be brought in to provide estimates for upgrading the entire house plumbing system.

While this report does not deal with underground systems such as the water supply, the septic system, sprinkler systems, pool piping or other underground services which may be present, the following should be noted. The house is connected to city water. The main water supply line as seen in the basement is the original, large diameter galvanized pipe. One must be aware that 80 years is an extremely long life for this type of pipe to remain in place underground without showing signs of any deterioration. The plumber should also provide an estimate for brining in a new main water supply. The main shutoff is located in the basement.

The septic system was replaced about 2 years ago according to my information. It is a pump-up system. The warning bell in the basement does not have a test button or shutoff switch other than the ability to turn it off at the circuit breaker. You should obtain a copy of the "as-built" plan of the septic for future reference. If it has not been cleaned since it was installed, it should be done at this time. A separate inspection of the system when it is opened for cleaning is recommended. A large tank is located at the left front according to a drawing made available to me. This is the primary tank which drains by gravity into a smaller pump tank. There is considerable settling of soil around the larger tank and there may be some underground seepage or leakage which is causing this. It needs to be investigated by a septic contractor.

INTERIOR:

Doors throughout the house are in satisfactory condition. Some doors will periodically need minor adjustment and trimming.

Flooring consists of oak, fir, carpeting and tile. Floors throughout the house are generally firm and level. This evaluation is based on the visible sections of flooring which are not concealed by furniture or carpeting. Where carpeting is present, it was not lifted to determine the type of flooring or condition of the finish of the floors. No major areas of deterioration were noted. Floors should be reinspected before the closing when furniture or carpeting was present. Some settling is noted in the second floor bathroom floor tile which appears to be within normal limits for a house this age.

Walls are mostly plaster in satisfactory condition. Some sheet rock is also used. There are a few settling cracks in the caretakers apartment above the garage. Some acoustical tile is used on the first floor and this is somewhat uneven in a few places.

7

Smoke detector protection is present. It was not tested. These safety devices should be kept in working order at all times.

There seven full and two half bathrooms. Many of the bathrooms are older and although there is some corrosion on some of the fittings, none of the fixtures were leaking at this time. The third floor toilet does not fill rapidly because of some type of restriction. The bathroom to the left of the master bedroom has a painted tub and some of the paint is peeling around the tub drain. The master bath has a crack in the shower base. One of the bathrooms has a tub only with no shower. The third floor modern bathroom has a cracked basin. Both half bathrooms are in satisfactory condition.

The kitchen has an adequate supply of cabinets and counter space in satisfactory condition. The kitchen appliances were turned on to determine only that they are operational. This operation does not include testing of any self-cleaning features or the accuracy of temperature settings. We only report on obvious operational problems with these kitchen appliances such as a burner not working or a leak in a dishwasher. This is not a statement on the condition of the appliances and we will not operate any appliance which is presently in use by the owner. It is important that the buyer operate all appliances prior to the closing to make sure they are in normal operating condition at the time of the closing. If a washing machine and dryer are included in the sale, these should also be operated prior to the closing. The kitchen in the caretakers apartment is functional.

Fireplaces appear to have good drafts and operational dampers. Chimney flues should be cleaned routinely to prevent a buildup of soot or creosote. I would be concerned about using the chimney at the left front until the vines are cleared away.

The attic was entered through a doorway on the upper level. The roof is wet on the underside of a valley. Attic insulation consists primarily of 2" to 4" of mineral wool which is less than desirable. It should be upgraded to 6" or more, where possible, to prevent heat loss in the winter and keep the house cooler in the summer. Insulation should always be placed against the heated surface. When original insulation exists, supplemental insulation should be of an unfaced type to prevent trapping of moisture between layers. Attic ventilation is required to be open year round to prevent moisture buildup in the winter and excessive heat buildup in the summer. There is an attic space above the finished third floor but there is no access.

Stairs and rails are in satisfactory condition. We cannot evaluate the condition of the treads where they are covered with carpeting or other materials.

EXTERIOR:
Windows consist of the double hung type with combination storms and screens. A random number were operated and were in satisfactory condition. The storm window weep holes should be kept open to prevent moisture build-up and subsequent decay. As mentioned, some of the sills are starting to soften and some of the trims have minor spot decay. But basically, the windows have been well cared for. Some of the windows are being affected by vine growth. In the contemporary portion of the house there are a number of fixed and sliding thermal glass door panels. Some seals have failed on the thermal glass panes in this area. It is impossible to detect the extent of all seal conditions unless the windows are cleaned and closely inspected. A glass company needs to be brought in to provide estimates for repair or replacement of the window glass which has failed prior to signing final contracts. They should also reinspect all of the window panels to determine if any other seals have been compromised.

8

Siding is mostly stone with some vertical tongue and groove wood. The stone is in good condition. Some pointing is needed over the garage area to a few cracks which have developed. The steel lintels over the garage doors have rusted and sagged slightly. These are exposed so that they can capture water and continue to deteriorate. A mason should be consulted about sealing these with mortar to prevent further rusting. If these deteriorate to any major degree they will have to be replaced but I did not see this as a necessity at this time. There is extensive vine growth on the siding of the house and some has encroached on the roof edge and crept under the shingles. The vines are also growing around the chimney at the top and chimney flues. It has also affected some windows. On the back of the house there are a number of dead vines which should be removed. Some of these have insect damage. Shrubs should be kept trimmed back away from the house to allow free air flow. Tree branches should not be allowed to come in contact with roofing or siding material.

Paint is generally satisfactory. Some touch up painting is needed on the garage side of the house when repairs are made to the wood decay. There is a steel fire escape at the rear which needs to be scraped and painted as it is starting to rust.

Roofing consists of slate which appears to be the original layer. There have been numerous repairs to valleys between the dormers and the roof itself. Slate roofs are laid over a paper barrier that deteriorate with time and you should anticipate periodic leakage through the roof. It is necessary to make repairs on an ongoing basis. It is quite obvious at this time that roof repairs are needed and there is an active leak in the valley adjacent to the third floor attic. A slate specialist should be brought in to provide estimates for bringing the roof up to good condition as it is in fair to poor condition at this time. At the front of the house a birch tree has damaged the edge of the slate over a dormer and the tree should be pruned back or removed.

The flat roof over the addition is in need of stripping and replacement. A small section of it has been repaired with a rolled asphalt material which is a low cost material. This roof should be redone as soon as possible.

The stone chimneys appear to be in sound condition. Flues were viewed from below and were not completely visible. As mentioned, the vines are affecting one of the chimneys and the vines needs to be removed.

Gutters are half round copper in fair condition. Some leaders go into underground piping. The buyer should make sure that during heavy rains all pipes are flowing freely. If blockage occurs to underground pipes, then the leaders should be directed away from the house by surface piping. Some leaders empty water directly on the ground at the foundation. They should be piped away as far as possible to prevent water seepage during heavy rains. There are also some built in gutters which appear to be functional.

The two-car garage is heated and is in satisfactory condition. There are two electric openers which operated normally at this time. Both automatic return/stop mechanisms also operated normally. Automatic doors should not be operated unless you can see them to avoid accidental injury to children or pets. It appears that there was a third garage bay which has been converted into the side entry and small utility room.

LABORATORY TESTS:
A lead-in-water analysis was requested and a two-bottle sample was taken. The test results showed no lead detected on either sample.

9

A continuous monitoring radon device was used to provide a readout of radon gas levels. The test results are attached. The elevated levels of radon indicate the need for a mitigation system and estimates should be obtained.

FOR YOUR INFORMATION:

We do not perform an inspection for toxic or hazardous materials. While the following information may not apply to all houses, we feel it is important that you be made aware of these environmental concerns.

Until the recent past, most solder used on copper tubing in residential and commercial installations contained a mixture of lead and tin, with as much as 60% lead content in some solder. Lead content has generally been reduced to 5% in solder used on water supply piping due to the health problems associated with lead. The change to a lower lead content took place about 1987 and all homes built after that should have the lower lead solder. If you have concerns about this, a separate test can be arranged through a testing laboratory.

Lead was also used in paint through the years but was eventually removed from all paint in 1978. Tests are available from independent laboratories to determine if lead is present in older paint on the interior of a house but one should assume that if your house is older, some lead paint may be present. Where lead paint is the exposed layer, or where it is exposed from peeling or chipping, it must be professionally removed or encapsulated. If the house is older we strongly recommend testing of the interior and exterior paints for lead content.

Through the years asbestos has been used in a number of products. Your inspector cannot and does not identify these uses of asbestos as in most cases a laboratory test of each item is needed to identify the asbestos. Following are some of the most common uses of this material, and the last year in which it was generally known to be used (but it does not represent the entire list); Appliance parts-1980, door gaskets-1984, drywall patching compounds-1978, flooring-1981, furnace insulation and furnace cement-1985, pipe insulation (still found but no longer installed), roofing and siding-present, textured paint-1978 and wall and ceiling insulation-1950. A spray coating of asbestos containing material was also commonly used on some metal sinks to deaden sound. To determine if any of these specific products are in use in this home a separate investigation would be required and can be obtained from a testing laboratory.

Fiberglass insulation, which is widely used, has been found to present a potential health problem due to skin contact and breathing fibers. The use of fiberglass insulation should be done in accordance with label instructions. Disturbing fibers in existing fiberglass may also pose a potential problem and any work done with existing insulation should only be done with proper precautions.

The opinions of this inspector regarding the above property are based on the observable conditions in readily accessible areas at the time of inspection. These conditions can change and this inspection report can only represent the condition of the property on the day of the inspection. It is the buyer's responsibility to return to the property prior to the closing to determine if conditions are substantially the same as found on the day of this inspection. This report is not a warranty or guarantee of the property, its systems or appliances which may be included in the sale. The cost of repair for any of the items or conditions mentioned in this report should be estimated by local repair people prior to the closing so that the buyer is fully aware of these repair costs and therefore the true cost of the home. The buyer should also read the information contained in our "Know The Home You Buy" booklet which is a part of this report.

Glossary

abstract of title The condensed history of a title to a particular piece of real estate and certification by the abstractor that the history is complete and accurate.

addendum An addition to the contract.

adjustable rate mortgage (ARM) A loan with an interest rate that is periodically adjusted by the lender according to its governing index.

agency The relationship between a principal (buy or seller) and an agent (brokerage firm or salesperson) when the agent is authorized to represent the principal in certain transactions, such as marketing the home.

agent One who acts or has the power to act for another. A fiduciary relationship is created when a property owner, as the principal, executes a listing agreement authorizing a licensed real estate broker to be his or her agent.

amenities Special features in a home or housing development. Central air-conditioning, pools, built-in appliances, or maple cabinetry throughout a home are examples of amenities.

amortization The process of paying the principal and interest on a loan through installments.

appraisal An estimate of the quantity, quality, or value of something. The process through which conclusions of property value are obtained; also refers to the report that sets forth the estimation and conclusion of value.

appreciation an increase in the worth or value of a property due to economic or related causes, which may prove either temporary or permanent; opposite of depreciation.

back-end ratio The ratio, or percentage, that a lender uses to compare a borrower's total debt (principal, interest, property taxes, and insurance plus other monthly debt payments) to gross monthly income. (See also *front-end ratio.*)

back-up offer A secondary bid for a property that a seller agrees to accept if the first offer from a different buyer fails.

broker One who acts on behalf of others for a fee or a commission.

built-ins Appliances, cabinetry, or fixtures that are framed into a home or permanently attached to its walls. Built-ins cannot easily be removed, which is why they are usually included in the sale of a home unless otherwise specified and agreed to by buyer and seller.

buyer's market A slow real estate market in which buyers have advantage over sellers. When inventory (supply) exceeds demand.

cancellation clause Sometimes referred to as "liquidated damages" in a purchase agreement, the clause that details the conditions under which either buyer or seller can terminate the contract.

cap A limit on the amount that the interest rate or monthly payment can increase in an adjustable rate mortgage. Most ARMs have two caps: One prevents the rate or payment from rising above a preset level at each adjustment period, while the other prevents the rate or monthly payment from climbing above a specified limit over the life of the loan.

capital gain Profit earned from the sale of a property.

certificate of title A statement of opinion on the status of the title to a parcel of real property based on an examination of public records.

certificate of eligibility A document issued by the Department of Veterans Affairs that verifies the eligibility of a veteran of the armed forces to take part in the VA's special mortgage programs.

closing statement A detailed cash accounting of a real transaction showing all cash received, all charges and credit made, and all cash paid out in the transaction.

commission Payment to a broker for services rendered such as in the sale or purchase of real property, usually a percentage of the selling price of a property.

comparables (comps) Properties used in an appraisal report or competitive market analysis that are substantially equivalent to the subject property. Similarities would include location, style, square feet, and amenities.

comparative (or competitive) market analysis A comparison of the prices of recently sold homes and current comparable homes that are similar to the seller's house in terms of location, size, style, and amenities.

condominium An individual unit in a building or development. The homeowner holds title to the interior space and shares ownership of common areas (such as parking lots, pool, tennis courts, or common areas) with other owners in the building or development.

contingency A provision in a purchase agreement that requires a certain act to be done or a certain event to occur before the agreement becomes binding. A buyer may have to secure a mortgage or sell their existing home, or a seller would have to find a home of his or her own choice before releasing the contingency.

contract a legally enforceable promise or set of promises that must be performed and for which, if breach of the promise occurs, the law provides a remedy (such as those promises agreed to between buyer and seller in a purchase agreement).

conventional loan A loan that requires no governmental guarantee or insurance.

counteroffer A response to an offer that may contain changes to the original offer. Until all terms of the buyer and seller are agreed to and endorsed, there is not a binding contract. The offer/counteroffer process can go on indefinitely, but usually contains time frames for response for each party or it is deemed dead, and the process must be started over.

credit (in closing a transaction) On a closing statement, an amount entered in a person's favor—either an amount the party has paid or an amount for which the party must be reimbursed.

credit report A report from a credit bureau that shows a loan applicant's history of payments made on previous debts. You can get a copy of your credit report from the three national credit bureaus, Equifax, Experian, and TransUnion.

debit (in closing a transaction) On a closing statement, an amount charged; that is, an amount that the debited party must pay.

deed of trust A document that gives a lender the right to foreclose on a property if the borrower defaults on the loan.

discount point A unit of measurement used for various loan charges; one point equals 1 percent of the amount of the loan.

documentary stamps/transfer tax Tax stamps required to be affixed to a deed by state and/or local law. Often paid by the seller when the deed is recorded.

dual agency Representing both buyer and seller in a transaction. It is illegal in many states and in others must first be agreed to by both parties.

earnest money Money deposited by a buyer under the terms of a purchase agreement, to be forfeited if the buyer defaults, but is applied to the purchase price when the sale is closed. It accompanies a written purchase agreement.

encumbrance A right or interest that someone else holds in a homeowner's property, such as a mortgage, tax, or judgement lien; an easement or restriction on the use of the land that may reduce the value of the property.

Equal Credit Opportunity Act (ECOA) The federal law that prohibits a lender or other creditors from refusing to grant credit based on an applicant's sex, marital status, race, religion, national origin, or age, or because the applicant receives public assistance.

equity The interest that an owner has in a property above what he or she owes on a mortgage. When the property is sold, this may also include any accrued appreciation the home may have reaped after all selling costs are subtracted.

escrow The closing of a transaction through a neutral third party called an *escrow agent* or escrowee, who receives funds and documents to be delivered upon the performance of certain conditions outlined in the escrow instructions.

exclusive agency listing A listing contract under which the owner appoints a real estate broker as the exclusive agent for a designated period of time to sell the property, on the owners stated terms, for a commission. The owner reserves the right to sell without paying anyone a commission if he or she sells to a prospect who has not been introduced or claimed by the broker.

Fannie Mae Formerly called the Federal National Mortgage Association, a publicly held company that buys mortgages from lenders and resells them as securities on the secondary mortgage market. The process ensures that lenders always have enough cash to make new loans.

Fair Housing Act This act generated the federal law that prohibits discrimination based on race, color, religion, sex, handicap, familial status, and national origin.

FHA loan A loan insured by the Federal Housing Authority and made by an approved lender in accordance with FHA regulations. It is a government loan often requiring discount points customarily paid by the seller.

fiduciary One in whom trust and confidence is placed; this person can be any broker employed in a transaction or a loan consultant with proprietary financial information about the borrower, which produces a *fiduciary relationship,* as between attorney and client.

first mortgage The primary mortgage on a property that has priority over all other mortgages.

fixed-rate mortgage A home loan with an interest rate that will remain at a specific rate for the term of the loan.

Freddie Mac Nickname of the Federal Home Loan Mortgage Corporation, which buys mortgages from lenders and resells them as securities on the secondary mortgage market. The process ensures that lenders always have enough cash to make new loans.

front-end ratio The ratio, or percentage, that a lender uses to compare a borrower's monthly housing expense (principal, interest, property taxes and insurance) to gross monthly income. (See also *back-end ratio.*)

FSBO (for sale by owner) A property for sale, but one in which an owner has no outside agent, broker, or other representation.

good faith estimate An estimate that a lender must provide to a prospective borrower that shows the costs the borrower will incur for loan processing charges, fees, etc.

half-bath A room that contains only a toilet and sink, but no tub or shower. Sometimes called a *powder room.*

home equity loan A loan (sometimes called a line of credit) under which a property owner uses his or her residence as collateral and can then draw funds up to a prearranged amount against the property.

homeowners association A group that sets and enforces rules in a condominium or town house development or a planned community of single-family homes. In a new housing development, the builder remains the enforcer of the neighborhood's rules and regulations until mostly sold out, when the transfer is made to the homeowners themselves.

homeowners insurance policy A standardized package insurance policy that covers a residential real estate owner against financial loss in the event of fire, theft, public liability and other common risks. Usually required by the lender for protection of both lender's and owner's equity.

home warranty A type of insurance that covers repairs to certain parts of a house and some fixtures after a buyer moves in.

impounds The portion of a monthly mortgage payment that the lender places in a special account to pay for hazard insurance, property taxes, or other bills as they come due. Not all loan programs require borrowers to have an impound account, but some borrowers prefer them as a type of disciplined, forced payment of these fees, and an account can be set up for this purpose.

inspection report A report, usually prepared by a professional inspector, that summarizes the condition of a home's various components.

jumbo loan A loan that exceeds the limits set by Fannie Mae and Freddie Mac.

listing agreement A contract between the owner (as principal) and a real estate broker (as agent) by which the broker is employed by the owner as agent to find a buyer for the owner's real estate on the owner's terms. The owner then agrees to pay a commission to the broker when the party sells and closes on the transaction.

loan-to-value (LTV) ratio A technical measure lenders use to assess the relationship of the loan amount to the value of the property. For example, a borrower seeking a $90,000 loan to purchase a home valued at $100,000 would have an LTV of 90 percent.

low documentation loan A mortgage that requires only minimal verification of the borrower's income and assets. Many "low-doc" loans require a down payment of at least 20 percent to 25 percent.

margin A lender's retail markup on an adjustable-rate mortgage. If an ARM's index is 5 percent and the lender charges a 2.5 percent margin, the borrower's actual loan rate will be 7.5 percent.

market value The most probable price property would bring in an arm's length (objective) transaction under normal conditions in an open market.

mortgage A conditional transfer or pledge of real estate as security for the payment of a debt. Also the document creating a mortgage lien.

mortgage banker A company that provides home loans using its own money. Typically, the company then sells the loans to investors. Many homebuilders' "in-house" lending operations are mortgage bankers.

mortgage broker A person or company that helps borrowers find a lender. The broker does not make the loan, but receives compensation from the lender for its services.

Multiple Listing Service (MLS) A marketing organization composed of member brokers who cooperate to share their inventory of properties in the hope of procuring a pool of ready, willing, and able buyers more quickly than they could have on their own. Most Multiple Listing Services accept exclusive-right-to-sell or exclusive agency listings from their broker members.

negative amortization Arrangement under which the shortfall in a mortgage payment is added to the amount borrowed, gradually increasing the debt.

net listing A listing based on a specific sum or net price the seller will receive if the property is sold. The broker can offer the property for sale at a higher price obtainable to increase the commission. This type of listing is illegal in many states because of its vulnerability to abuses.

note The legal document that requires a borrower to repay a mortgage at a certain interest rate over a specified period of time.

offer and acceptance Two essential components of a valid contract; a "meeting of the minds." An agreement between buyer and seller on the provision of the purchase agreement.

open house A marketing event held by the seller or listing agent of a home in which prospective buyers can walk through the house to determine if they would like to buy it.

PITI Lender's acronym for principal, interest, property taxes, and insurance.

points Fees a lender charges to a borrower when a loan is issued. One point equals 1 percent of the loan amount. Points can be paid up front, absorbed into the loan amount, or paid by the seller, essentially making it a "zero-point" loan.

portfolio lender A lender that makes loans with its own money and then keeps the loan on the company's books, or inside its "portfolio," rather than selling it on the secondary market.

prepayment penalty A charge lenders can levy on borrowers who pay off their loan early, whether the home is sold or the property is refinanced. Most fixed-rate mortgages include prepayment penalties, but many adjustable-rate programs do not.

principal (1) A sum loaned to the purchaser of a home in a mortgage note. (2) The original amount (as in a loan) of the total due and payable at a certain date. (3) A main party to a transaction—the person for whom the agent works—usually a buyer or a seller.

private mortgage insurance A special type of loan insurance that many lenders require borrowers to purchase to protect the lender against default in higher LTV scenarios (generally less than 20 percent down payment).

prorations Expenses, either prepaid or paid in arrears, that are divided between buyer and seller at closing. Property taxes are typically a prorated item.

REALTOR® A registered trademark reserved for the sole use of active members of local REALTOR® boards affiliated with the National Association of REALTORS®.

recording The act of entering or recording documents affecting or conveying interests in real estate in the recorder's office in each county (usually housed in the courthouse).

"time is of the essence" A phrase in a contract that requires the performance of a certain act within a stated period of time or the contract can be voided.

title (1) The right to ownership of the land. (2) The evidence of ownership of land such as a deed for the property.

title company A company that ensures that the seller has the clear, legal right to sell a property and issues a title insurance policy to protect the buyer or lender against possible challenges to the buyer's new title.

title insurance A policy insuring the owner or mortgage against loss by reason of defects in the title to a parcel of real estate, other than encumbrances, defects, and matters specifically excluded by the policy.

title search The examination of public records relating to real estate to determine the current state of ownership.

town house An attached home that is not a condominium. The unit may share a common wall with another unit or stand alone, but the development does not require the minimum setbacks of single-family homes. Owners may share common areas, maintained by their homeowners association fees.

tract home A mass-produced home in a development built by a specific builder who owns the land. Also called a production home, tract homes can appear remarkably dissimilar when the builder varies elevations (exterior enhancements), color palettes, and unit placement.

VA loan A mortgage loan on approved property made to a qualified veteran by an authorized lender, and approved by the Department of Veteran Affairs to limit the lender's possible loss. A government loan that often requires discount points to be paid by the buyer or seller.

Further Resources

Trade Associations

American Homeowners Foundation (1724 S. Quincy Street, Arlington, VA 22204; 703-979-4663). Dedicated to helping homeowners maintain and upgrade their homes. Offers model home-improvement contracts. Offers free brochure about the foundation.

American Society of Home Inspectors (932 Lee Street, Des Plaines, IL 60016-6546; 847-290-1959; 800-743-2744, www.ashi.org). Publishes guidelines detailing what home inspectors are and are not expected to do. For example, they are expected to inspect a home's structural components, roofing, doorways, windows, plumbing, heating and electrical systems, and insulation; they are not expected to estimate the life expectancy of a component, offer warranties, perform engineering services, or inspect home appliances. Will send a free Standards of Practice publication giving details on dealing with a home inspector.

Appraisal Institute (875 N. Michigan Avenue, Suite 2400, Chicago, IL 60611-1980; 312-335-4100; www.appraisalinstitute.org). Represents real estate appraisers. Formed out of the unification of the American Institute of Real Estate Appraisers and the Society of Real Estate Appraisers. Sets minimum standards for real estate appraising and confers several professional designations. Publishes the *Appraiser News* and *Appraisal Journal* newsletters. Will refer you to a qualified appraiser near your home.

Mortgage Bankers Association of America (1919 Pennsylvania Avenue, NW, Washington, DC 20006-3438; 202-557-2700; www.mbaa.org). The trade group of mortgage bankers. Offers the following publications: *Applying for Your Mortgage; Closing on Your Mortgage and Your Home; Finding the Mortgage That Is Right for You; Get a Running Start on Good Credit; How to Manage Your Mortgage Obliga-*

tions; Make Shopping Easier: See Your Mortgage Lender First; Refinancing: Does It Make Sense for You; and *When Your Mortgage Loan Is Rejected.*

National Association of Master Appraisers (PO Box 12617, 303 W. Cypress Street, San Antonio, TX 78212-0617; 800-229-NAMA; www.masterappraisers.org). Represents those involved in real estate appraisal, including appraisers, assessors, brokers, salespeople, developers, and bankers. Publishes guidelines detailing appraisers' responsibilities and offers continuing education for appraisers. Will send free brochure titled "The Master Appraiser." The association is also home to the Real Estate Law Institute, which compiles an annual Registry of Real Estate Specialists, available free of charge when you call 800-486-3676 or write to PO Box 12528, San Antonio, TX 78212-0528.

National Association of Realtors® (430 N. Michigan Avenue, Chicago, IL 60611; 312-329-8200; 800-874-6500; www.realtor.com). The trade group for real estate agents. Has a real estate Q&A with hundreds of questions and answers on over 50 real estate subjects on its Web site. Also has a Learn About section with information under the following headings: Getting Started; Buying; Selling; Offer/Closing; Moving; and Owning. Affiliated with the following groups at the same address:

- *American Society of Real Estate Counselors,* which confers the Counselor of Real Estate (CRE) designation on those who give real estate investment advice
- *Institute of Real Estate Management,* which confers the Certified Property Manager (CPM) and Accredited Residential Manager (ARM) designations on those who manage real estate properties
- *Realtors® Land Institute,* which confers the Accredited Land Consultant (ALC) designation on those experts in all facets of buying and selling agricultural, urban, transitional, and recreational land
- *Realtors® National Marketing Institute,* which confers the Certified Real Estate Brokerage Manager (CRB) and Certified Residential Specialist (CRS) designations on brokers experienced in running brokerage offices and active in residential real estate
- *Society of Industrial and Office Realtors®,* which confers the Professional Real Estate Executive (PRE) designation on experts in industrial and office real estate transactions
- *Women's Council of Realtors®,* which confers the Leadership Training Graduate (LTG) designation on women who have exhibited leadership

Federal Government Regulators

Department of Housing and Urban Development (451 7th Street, SW, Washington, DC 20410; 202-708-1422; www.hud.gov). The main regulatory agency overseeing housing and real estate issues. HUD's Office of Fair Housing and Equal Opportunity (800-669-9777) can be contacted if you think you have been a victim of housing discrimination.

Fannie Mae (formerly Federal National Mortgage Corporation) (3900 Wisconsin Avenue, NW, Washington, DC 20016; 202-752-7000; www.fanniemae.com). Creates a secondary market in mortgage-backed securities. Offers several brochures about real estate, including "Fannie Mae National Housing Survey"; "Home Equity Conversion Mortgages: You've Worked Years to Own Your Home. Now It's Time Your Home Worked for You"; and "Housing America Corporation." Also offers a book titled *Foreclosure Prevention.*

Federal Reserve Board (20th Street and C Street, NW, Washington, DC 20551; 202-452-3946; www.federalreserve.gov). Oversees bank and savings and loan mortgage lending. Branches offer several free brochures about real estate, including "Consumer Handbook on Adjustable-Rate Mortgages"; "Consumer Handbook to Credit Protection Laws"; "Home Mortgages: Understanding the Process and Your Right to Fair Lending"; "Looking for the Best Mortgage: Shop, Compare, Negotiate"; and "When Your Home Is on the Line: What You Should Know about Home Equity Lines of Credit."

Federal Trade Commission (6th Street and Pennsylvania Avenue, NW, Washington, DC 20580; 202-326-2222; www.ftc.gov). Has jurisdiction over many real-estate-related practices. Will send a free copy of the following brochures: "Getting a Loan: Your Home as Security"; "Home Equity Credit Lines"; "Home Financing Primer"; "Home Equity Scams: Borrowers Beware!"; "Lawn Service Contracts"; "Looking for the Best Mortgage"; "Mortgage Servicing"; "Refinancing Your Home"; "Reverse Mortgages"; "Second Mortgage Financing"; "Timeshare Resales"; "Timeshare Tips"; and "Using Ads to Shop for Home Financing."

Office of Thrift Supervision (1700 G Street, NW, Washington, DC 20552; 202-906-6000; www.ots.treas.gov). Oversees the nation's savings and loan industry.

Frequent Flier Miles Mortgage Programs

Some airlines have started to link up with mortgage lenders, allowing you to accumulate thousands of frequent flier miles while you buy and pay for your house. The largest such program is run by American Airlines. Under their AAdvantage Program for Mortgages, you can earn 15,000 AAdvantage miles per $100,000 of purchase or sale price of your home, if you use a real estate broker enrolled in the program. If you sign up for a mortgage through a lender enrolled in the program, you qualify for one AAdvantage mile for each $10 of the mortgage loan amount. This applies whether you are refinancing your existing home or financing a new one. For more information on this program, call 800-852-9744 or visit their Web site at <www.aa.com>. United Airlines offers a similar program called Residential Rewards at 800-717-5330 or <www .ual.com>. Delta offers its Fly Home SkyMiles Program through North American Mortgage at 800-759-0306 or at <www.delta-air.com>.

Index

Bulk Pricing Information

For special discounts on
20 or more copies of
Everyone's Money Book on Real Estate,
call Dearborn Trade Special Sales
at 800-621-9621, extension 4455,
or e-mail bermel@dearborn.com.
You'll receive great service
and top discounts.

For added visibility, please
consider our custom cover service,
which highlights your firm's name
and logo on the cover.
We are also an excellent resource
for dynamic and
knowledgeable speakers.

Dearborn™
Trade Publishing
A **Kaplan Professional** Company